BECOMING
NICK & NORA

BECOMING NICK & NORA

THE THIN MAN
and the Films of
William Powell and
Myrna Loy

Rob Kozlowski

APPLAUSE
THEATRE & CINEMA BOOKS
Essex, Connecticut

APPLAUSE
THEATRE & CINEMA BOOKS
An imprint of Globe Pequot, the trade division of
The Rowman & Littlefield Publishing Group, Inc.
4501 Forbes Blvd., Ste. 200
Lanham, MD 20706
www.rowman.com

Distributed by NATIONAL BOOK NETWORK

British Library Cataloguing in Publication Information Available

Library of Congress Cataloging-in-Publication Data
Names: Kozlowski, Rob, author.
Title: Becoming Nick and Nora : William Powell, Myrna Loy, and the movies'
    perfect marriage / Rob Kozlowski.
Description: Essex, Connecticut : Applause, 2023. | Includes
    bibliographical references and index.
Identifiers: LCCN 2022058809 (print) | LCCN 2022058810 (ebook) | ISBN
    9781493062850 (cloth) | ISBN 9781493062867 (epub)
Subjects: LCSH: Powell, William, 1892-1984. | Loy, Myrna, 1905-1993. |
    Motion picture actors and actresses--United States--Biography. | Thin
    Man films--History and criticism. | Detective and mystery films--United
    States--History and criticism. | LCGFT: Film criticism.
Classification: LCC PN2287.P58 K69 2023 (print) | LCC PN2287.P58 (ebook)
    | DDC 791.4302/8092273--dc23/eng/20230223
LC record available at https://lccn.loc.gov/2022058809
LC ebook record available at https://lccn.loc.gov/2022058810

For Uncle Ron

CONTENTS

INTRODUCTION   1

1   MINNIE AND BILL   9

2   THE HEAVY   27

3   THE VAMP   49

4   THE GENTLEMAN AND THE BRAT   65

5   THE EVERYMAN AND THE SEDUCTRESS   89

6   BECOMING NICK AND NORA   117

7   THE MOVIE STARS   143

8   THE SCREWBALLS   161

9   THE INSTITUTIONS   185

10   THE END   207

ACKNOWLEDGMENTS   219

BIBLIOGRAPHY   221

INDEX   227

INTRODUCTION

In 1947, William Powell was filming his eighty-seventh picture, a political satire called *The Senator Was Indiscreet*. It would be the first and only film directed by George S. Kaufman, one of the great American playwrights of the twentieth century. Kaufman had won two Pulitzer Prizes for drama and had worked with everyone from the Marx Brothers to Moss Hart to Edna Ferber.

While many of his plays had been adapted for film, Kaufman's experience in the medium was extremely limited. In fact, it was so limited that the technical aspects intimidated the great man—enough that Associate Producer Gene Fowler Jr. became the de facto director of the film, yelling "action" and "cut" while Kaufman worked solely with the actors. In interviews later in life, Fowler claimed that Kaufman wouldn't even look at the actors while he worked with them, judging their performances only audibly.

The result was a technically inept film with the kind of static visual and editing style one would have expected in primitive silent films from the first decade of the century. Powell, however, was enjoying his role as buffoonish Senator Melvin G. Ashton, a departure for the actor. Powell had been in pictures for a quarter of a century, and his screen personas had evolved from swarthy silent-film villain to suave and sophisticated detective to screwball comedy superstar.

He had long been one of the country's most private movie stars, and even though he was still a working actor, he had long since retreated to a quiet life in Palm Springs with his third wife, Diana Lewis, and had not consented to interviews in years. He must have been particularly enthusiastic about his role as Senator Ashton, however, because he actually participated in its publicity.

Powell's comments in an interview echoed those he had made in the early 1930s during the brief period when he was interviewed frequently by fan magazines:

> If an actor works a long time at one studio, his bosses develop a tendency to see him only in the kind of part that he has been playing for them. They aren't likely to think of him for a role widely different from those they are accustomed to seeing him do successfully. That is why many stars begin to grow restless after staying with one employer a number of years. They can't convince their bosses they can do—and should do—other types of portrayals.
>
> Since I obtained permission from my home studio for loan outs, I have had the opportunity to play two fine parts, completely unlike those I have been enacting. . . . I obtained permission for the loan outs simply by pointing out that such pictures would do me, as well as my home studio, much good. (Friedman, n.d.)

It is telling that Powell did not mention home studio Metro-Goldwyn-Mayer by name. In fact, his career at MGM was all but over as leading roles quickly dried up for the fifty-five-year-old Powell, who would only appear in eight more

Myrna Loy and William Powell's final appearance together in *The Senator Was Indiscreet*. *Author's Collection*

pictures before retiring from the industry and blissfully retreating from public life entirely for nearly three decades.

For now, however, Powell was enjoying his role as the political buffoon. On one particular day in 1947, Powell, Kaufman, Fowler, and the crew were shooting on location at Baldwin Lake at Rancho Santa Anita in Arcadia, California. It was the scene at the very end of the picture, and security was tight. Producer Nunnally Johnson, an accomplished screenwriter whose credits included the adaptation of *The Grapes of Wrath* for John Ford, decided to keep the finish of the new comedy a secret for as long as possible. No photographers were allowed, Johnson teased to the trade papers, in the hope of keeping the ending as much a surprise as possible for fans.

At the same time, Myrna Loy's career as a leading lady in the movies was also beginning to wind down. In just over two decades, she had made over one hundred pictures. Like Powell, she had begun her career as a silent-film villain, and her screen persona would evolve from vamp to selfish party girl to the perfect wife. While she had been one of the industry's most successful and beloved movie stars for over a decade, the first seven years of her career consisted of a series of films she was forced to make as she clawed her way up the industry ladder, playing roles for which she was often spectacularly unsuited. She regretted making more than a few of those films.

By 1947, however, Myrna Loy saw no reason to make pictures she would later regret. Her priorities had completely changed from her days as a starstruck youth living in Culver City, in the shadow of the MGM studio lot. During World War II she had practically abandoned her film career to work for the American Red Cross on the East Coast, and in the years that followed she would emphasize public service.

Her most recent picture reflected that emphasis. *The Best Years of Our Lives*, William Wyler's Oscar-winning masterpiece about veterans returning to the home front after World War II, was the apogee of her career as Hollywood's perfect wife. After starring in a few more pictures over the next five years, however, her career as a leading lady would end. Between 1952 and 1980, she would appear in only eight more theatrical films, all in supporting roles.

As Loy recounted in her autobiography over forty years later, she received a call from George S. Kaufman when he was about to start production on *The Senator Was Indiscreet*. "Do you think it's possible for you to do a bit at the end of the picture as Bill's wife?" Kaufman asked. "We can't hire you. We couldn't afford your salary. It's just a gag."

"Great!" she said. "Of course I'll do it" (Loy, 1988).

The whole gag revolves around "Momma," the beloved unseen wife whom Senator Ashton speaks of constantly and reverently and whom he telephones throughout the picture. At the end of the film, after his presidential run is in tatters and he is exiled on a South Seas island to be the peoples' king, we see the back of Momma in a sarong as the senator apologizes for their new circumstance: "I'm sorry, Momma. They say it's quite an attractive little island, Momma, with plenty of grapefruit and coconuts and a lovely little white house for us."

Momma turns around, revealing Myrna Loy with her famous sparkling eyes and loving smirk known the world over. "A little white house isn't exactly what you promised me, darling," she says. "But still . . . " She embraces and kisses the man who millions of people mistakenly assumed was Myrna Loy's husband in real life, and with the final fade-out, one of the great screen partnerships of all time came to an end. It is a lovely and sentimental farewell and one of the great little "meta" moments in Hollywood history.

Few partnerships have ever captivated audiences quite like the one forged by William Powell and Myrna Loy, and even fewer have had their kind of remarkable staying power. *The Thin Man* was released in theaters nearly ninety years ago, and it still retains its appeal for audiences today on television, on streaming video, and in film festivals around the world. It is nearly impossible to conceive of any of today's screen couples still attracting a similar level of attention in the year 2113.

The two were, in fact, remarkably lucky to work in the film industry when they did. In the 1920s, the American film industry had blossomed in a few short years into the fourth-largest industry in the country, producing hundreds and hundreds of short subjects and features every year. Those short subjects and features needed actors—actors who flocked by the thousands to studios every year, hoping to become the next Mary Pickford, Douglas Fairbanks, Norma Talmadge, or Wallace Reid.

The movie actor had come a long way by the time William Horatio Powell first appeared on screen in 1922 and Myrna Loy appeared for the first time three years later. Just fifteen years earlier than Powell's debut, the very idea of even crediting the actors who appeared on screens in nickelodeons across the country was preposterous. Actors saw moving pictures as a last desperate stand if they could not make a living wage on the stage, and they happily accepted anonymity in exchange for a few extra dollars for gesticulating on the silent screen. In the new, rural communities of Southern California, moving picture actors were seen as second-class citizens at best, and hotels often denied entry to the bedraggled performers by displaying signs using the newly created derogatory term for the performers, which would quickly evolve into a term for the medium itself: "No movies allowed."

Actors certainly had reason not to be proud of appearing in American films of the first decade of the twentieth century. While there were some exceptions, the industry as a whole had not come very far since Edwin S. Porter's *The Great Train Robbery* had revolutionized the motion picture in 1903 with its use of parallel editing and crosscutting in an epic, eleven-minute tale. Actors on screen still utilized the declaratory technique of acting they had learned on stage, making grandiose physical gestures that were meant to convey emotion to audiences far back in the balcony who had no hope of clearly hearing the actors. Rarely adjusting their performances for the camera only a few feet away, the actors looked ridiculous. Even famous stage performers like the great Sarah Bernhardt looked a bit ridiculous on screen.

Remarkably, the craft of screen acting matured quickly as some producers, directors, and the actors themselves realized how absurd the declaratory technique was on camera and adjusted the performances appropriately. American Mutoscope and Biograph Company Director D. W. Griffith and his stock company of actors including Lillian Gish, Lionel Barrymore, Robert Harron, and Mary Pickford are among the best known of the innovators. Griffith and his cameraman Billy Bitzer moved the cameras closer to the actors, sometimes letting the actors move toward the cameras, and an intimacy began to develop between actor and audience. Even while the actors were anonymous, audiences began to recognize specific performers. Florence Lawrence was known as the "Biograph Girl" before anyone knew her name, and while companies like Biograph were perfectly happy to keep their actors anonymous in order to keep their pay low, a producer named Carl Laemmle and his company, Independent Motion Pictures (IMP), changed the young industry forever when it signed away Lawrence and gave her credit in his films. He would later do the same for the next Biograph Girl, Mary Pickford.

In 1911, Pickford would become one of the first legitimate credited movie stars, and it was only three years later that slapstick comic Charlie Chaplin made his debut at Keystone Studios. By 1915, it was no exaggeration to say that Chaplin and Mary Pickford were the most famous people who had ever lived. More people could watch Chaplin and Pickford perform on a movie screen in a single day than had seen Sarah Bernhardt on stage in the great lady's entire lifetime. The whole structure of the industry would quickly revolve around movie stars as studios did everything they could in order to replicate the success of Chaplin and Pickford. Young aspiring actors like William Powell and Myrna Loy and their contemporaries would idolize the new screen personalities.

Remarkably, although Powell was born a full thirteen years earlier than Loy, the two forged uncannily similar paths to stardom. Both began in silent films, and film executives decided they looked the part of villains. Powell was often cast as the swarthy, charismatic swashbuckling heavy who commanded as much respect as fear, and Loy was the vamp, often cast in racist roles that preyed upon white audiences' fears and suspicions regarding the sexuality of "others." Both almost immediately and in surprisingly public ways aired their displeasure with the typecasting. And both quickly acquired reputations for being very private people and preferring quiet living to the usual Hollywood hullabaloo.

Dorothy Spensley wrote in one of the first features on Powell in the August 1926 issue of *Photoplay* magazine:

> Bill Powell is really not the kind of man to be written about. He is rather to be chatted about, informally, over the small coffees, with gray wisps of cigarette smoke hazing a low ceiling. Chatted about, understand—not talked about or gossiped over like the latest bit of scandal. To write about Bill would dispel all the debonair charm which is his. He would appear like a ready-made Oppenheim clubman, and his wit, which is fast becoming recognized in Hollywood as it was in New York, would be as flat as seltzer uncorked all night. (Spensley, 1926)

It is not surprising, then, that Powell and Loy became great friends in real life. He called her "Minnie" and she called him "Bill," and they remained friends well after Powell had retired. A romance never developed because, as Loy put it, the two were far too alike, and their wisdom in not pursuing a relationship likely contributed to the ease and joy they felt in working together.

Audiences have shared that joy for over eighty-five years. The original *The Thin Man* was that rare beast, both a commercial and critical smash hit. Shot in just over two weeks in the spring of 1934 with a B-movie budget of $226,000, the film ended up grossing $1.4 million worldwide and was nominated for Academy Awards for Best Picture, Best Actor, Best Director, and Best Adapted Screenplay.

Powell and Loy had magnetic appeal together, and even though both actors were always delightful on screen, the magic of their on-screen combination creates something far more than the individual parts of two fine, charismatic actors. Even though *The Thin Man* by itself was a delightful picture, it was the chemistry of Powell and Loy that critics and audiences found so completely besotting.

"The most attractive feature of 'The Thin Man' to me is the charm of the husband and wife as played by William Powell and Myrna Loy," wrote Seton Margrave in his review of the picture in the *Daily Mail*. "These two people have a glorious time. They are completely in love with each other and with life. They share a marvellous sense of humour. They sharpen their wits mercilessly on each other. I cannot recall any film in which this happy understanding between husband and wife has been more joyously presented" (Margrave, 1934).

Nearly a century later, it is still hard to recall such a film. The characters of Nick and Nora Charles remain the standard for married couples in the movies. If a film features a married couple trading clever quips with each other, the comparisons inevitably pop up. As recently as 2005, when Angelina Jolie and Brad Pitt were teamed up in the action-comedy *Mr. and Mrs. Smith*, reviewers compared their repartee to Nick and Nora Charles.

Other couples, however, rarely match up to the extraordinary chemistry of William Powell and Myrna Loy. One could almost say it was magic, but it was far from it. Both were fine actors who had the benefit of extraordinarily long apprenticeships to stardom and were the beneficiaries of a system that, true, both of them hated at times—but without it, we never would have had Nick and Nora Charles to enjoy for the ages.

This is the story of their journeys to immortality.

1

MINNIE AND BILL

William Powell was born on July 29, 1892, nearly exactly thirteen years before Myrna Williams would enter the scene on August 2, 1905. While the difference in their birthdates may imply changes in social and cultural circumstances that different generations sometimes experience, little in show business had changed in the years between their arrivals.

Little, that is, except for the emergence of the motion picture, which would eventually revolutionize not only show business but the cultural perception of actors. When Powell was born in the last decade of the nineteenth century, actors were considered second-class citizens, and any notion of fortune and fame was patently ludicrous. Anyone who wanted to enter the acting profession could never state fortune or fame as a reason for their chosen profession.

The United States was still a new country and widely considered a cultural infant. Its first popular form of entertainment was the minstrel show. At this point, the United States displayed its long-standing institutional racism proudly on its sleeve, with the minstrel show essentially being the early form of the modern sketch comedy show. Stock characters performed by white people in blackface had become the national artform by the middle of the nineteenth century.

While minstrelsy was still popular by the time Powell and Loy were born, it had been supplanted by vaudeville as the primary form of popular entertainment. While the minstrel show was a tightly constructed long-form show in which all the main performers and characters would recur throughout the evening, vaudeville developed a more open-ended bill of ten to fifteen completely unrelated acts that could cover literally any genre of staged entertainment.

The "legitimate" theater also thrived at the end of the nineteenth century, with barnstorming troupes traveling the country performing American melodramas filled with outlandish adventurous plots, mustache-twirling villains, and damsels in distress.

A number of the most famous silent-film performers had been born into show business, including Charlie Chaplin, Mary Pickford, and Buster Keaton, whose families were already involved in entertainment in one way or another, so their training sometimes literally began from infancy. By the time these actors reached their teenage years, they were already well-seasoned performers who were ready to graduate to the next phases of their careers. Pickford would appear in her first Broadway play, *The Warrens of Virginia*, at age fifteen and would start her motion picture career at age seventeen (Whitfield, 1997).

In some ways, both Powell and Loy were among the first of the modern-day actors, who were initially raised in circumstances completely outside the realm of show business and who, as they were growing up, developed interests in their art forms and would eventually receive formal training to learn their crafts.

William Horatio Powell was born in July 1892 to Horatio Warren Powell and Nettie Manila in Pittsburgh. Little is known of his parents' lives before his birth, except that Horatio was an accountant and thus likely a very practical man, who apparently and rather impractically decided when young Bill was only six months old that his only son was going to be a lawyer. According to *Photoplay*, this was because of a "raucous yell and a few bellicose syllables given from his highchair. Undoubtedly accompanied by the beating of his pewter mug to emphasize the roar" (Spensley, 1926).

Why Horatio thought his infant son's performance made him a good fit for the courtroom and not the stage is lost to history, but it is certainly known that his son's eventual desire to act for the stage did not please him at all.

That desire was born after the family moved to Kansas City in 1907 and Powell was enrolled in Central High School. Young Bill Powell took a public speaking course in school and won the lead role of Captain Jack Absolute in the school's December 1909 production of *The Rivals*, Richard Brinsley Sheridan's eighteenth-century comedy of manners.

Playing the young aristocrat who poses as a penniless ensign to win the love of Lydia Languish, a part that also requires the athletic fighting of duels, must have been intoxicating to the young man.

Powell quickly became besotted with the legitimate theater, joining the Central Shakespeare Club and Glee Club and appearing as Malvolio in Shakespeare's *Twelfth Night* in the spring of 1910. It was quickly becoming apparent that young Bill had a far higher calling than law. After graduating from high school in the spring of 1911, Powell got a job at the Kansas City Telephone Company, with the prospect of a dreary education ahead in pre-law. It was then he made a fateful decision.

Powell decided he wanted to attend the American Academy of Dramatic Arts in New York. The school was founded in 1884 by Franklin Haven Sargent, a Harvard graduate who had become a professor of speech and elocution there and eventually came up with the radical idea of opening a school to turn the trade of acting into a respected craft. It was, in fact, the first acting school in the English-speaking world, and quickly created a revolution in its approach to creating a sense of personal authenticity in acting. The school is still operating today, and its starry litany of famous alumni including Cecil B. DeMille, Lauren Bacall, Spencer Tracy, Robert Redford, and Kirk Douglas, among others, helps justify annual tuition and expenses of over $60,000 for the 2022–2023 academic year (American Academy of Dramatic Arts, n.d.).

Fortunately, in 1912, the tuition was not nearly so lofty, but it was still well beyond young William H. Powell's means. His brainstorm was to ask for help from his wealthy great-aunt, Elizabeth "Lizzie" Heywood, in Sharon, Pennsylvania.

In an epic eighteen-page plea, written with a humility and formality belying his young age, Powell asked Heywood for a $1,400 loan to enable him to attend the American Academy of Dramatic Arts, and he even included a proposed payment plan including 6 percent interest.

"Dear Aunt Lizzie," he begins.

> In writing this letter to you, I am taking a step which I have for some time contemplated, but have hitherto refrained from taking because of its peculiar nature and of my uncertainty as to its propriety. That I am little more than a stranger to you, I am well aware, and I realize further that a letter such as this must necessarily imply some presumption on my part. However, my object in writing is of much importance to me, and even though I may incur your disapproval, I am going to take that risk. (Powell, 2018)

He goes on to dissociate himself from his father, who never paid back a loan Aunt Lizzie had made to him, and summarizes his high school career performing with theatrical clubs and choirs.

In requesting the loan, Powell writes, "I have been loath to make a request of this sort [but] at heart I feel that it is surely not wrong for me to seek whatever honorable means I can, to further my ambition" (Powell, 2018).

Aunt Lizzie was moved enough by the letter to acquiesce to Powell's request, although she would loan him only $700 and provide him with $50 a week living expenses. Remarkably, considering the struggles he inevitably experienced in his attempt to make a living as an actor over the next ten years, he kept up with the payments and wrote the final check in 1922.

When he made it to the American Academy of Dramatic Arts, Powell was overwhelmed by all that New York had to offer.

"That was real education," Powell would recall in 1931.

In some ways maybe it was better education than I could have obtained in four years at college. I came to know people, their expressions, their ways of moving and dressing, their reactions. I used to stand around staring and listening until it's a wonder I didn't get shot. I never thought about that. To me, it was a panorama being staged especially for my benefit. (E. Gray, 1931)

It was a romantic notion with the benefit of hindsight, but Powell struggled mightily in his first years in New York. After leaving the academy early in 1913 because he thought he had learned enough to try his hand as a professional actor, he learned quickly how difficult that could be. Now out of school, he would no longer receive his weekly stipend from Aunt Lizzie.

After securing a part in a play called *The Ne'er-Do-Well*, in which Powell played four or five roles (depending on the source), he spent six months in vaudeville and then spent six months completely jobless.

Dorothy Spensley would later describe Powell's hard times:

He met Ralph Barton, now a nationally known illustrator. They pooled their funds and sauntered forth with twenty-five cents between then for the evening meal. But the quarter was bum. Their only hope was a near-sighted delicatessen proprietor. They found one and purchased a nickel's worth of candles to light their little room, ten cents' worth of lemon wafers and ten of apricots. After they ate them they drank water. Plenty of it. It's surprising how apricots and wafers expand. (Spensley, 1926)

Like most actors, Powell was always broke. But in late 1913, Margaret Illington with her American Play Company cast him in a national touring production of *Within the Law*. It was his first real steady professional work as an actor.

Written by Bayard Veiller, *Within the Law* is long forgotten today but was popular enough to be adapted for film in 1917 and again in 1923. It is the melodramatic tale of Mary Turner, an employee of Gilder's Department Store, who is put on trial, convicted, and sent to jail for three years after stolen goods are discovered in her work locker. Innocent of the charges and fully aware that the rich are protected by the law, she vows revenge once she is released, but only "within the law."

In prison, Mary makes one friend, the fun-loving Aggie Lynch, and once they're both released, they work with con man Joe Garson on an ongoing scheme in which Aggie seduces old rich men and then fleeces them with breach-of-promise suits. Things go awry when Mary meets and falls in love with Richard Gilder, the department store heir, and Joe meets English Eddie, a crook who promises a quick windfall if the gang steals some smuggled tapestries from the Gilder mansion.

Trouble ensues when it turns out English Eddie is a stool pigeon for the police trying to set up Mary's gang, and Joe winds up shooting Eddie to death when he learns of the betrayal. The young Powell played English Eddie.

In 1923, screen icon Norma Talmadge would star in the second screen adaptation of *Within the Law*, produced by her husband Joseph Schenck and directed by Frank Lloyd. (The 1917 version is lost.) The role of English Eddie was played by Ward Crane, best known to silent-film fans today as the villain in Buster Keaton's *Sherlock Jr.*

Dressed in top hat and tails, Crane is not the kind of greasy caricature that silent-film viewers might associate with a stool pigeon, but carries himself more like a sophisticated thief. It isn't much of a stretch to imagine that a twenty-one-year-old William Powell would have equipped himself admirably in the role, given his future roles as sophisticated men in excellent clothes.

English Eddie is a small part, and Powell didn't get singled out for praise, but an actress named Eileen Wilson did get some notice in her role as Aggie Lynch. In the 1923 version, as portrayed by Eileen Percy, Aggie is the comic relief, pretending to be a poor, innocent and naïve girl for the wealthy stooges she seduces, comically repeating "I'm so fwightened!" to stroke their egos.

The young Ms. Wilson had a flair for comedy, it seems, and one anonymous reviewer reserved special praise for her: "Miss Wilson made a veritable hit in her comedy role and her work was the equal in its particular line to that of any member of the company" (*Daily Northwestern*, 1914).

She made a hit with William Powell, too. The two met and fell in love during the tour. Not much has been written about Wilson, or their marriage, but it is fair to guess based on existing evidence that it was not an easy one. While they were clearly in love, their marriage was a quick example of two acting careers butting heads with each other. Both were young and ambitious and had to take parts as they got them. While they did the best they could to appear in plays together, they were often separated for significant lengths of time in the early years of their marriage.

Tensions also must have been high, because if Wilson was further ahead in her career than Powell, with a bigger part and critical raves in *Within the Law*, that may not have sat well with the traditional, conservative Powell.

Over the years leading up to his debut in motion pictures in 1922, Powell experienced a slow, gradual, and sometimes discouraging crawl up the ranks in the American theater, playing stock in multiple cities. After he finished his tour with *Within the Law* in May 1914, that September he began his first stint in stock with the Baker Stock Company in Portland, Oregon. Founded by businessman George L. Baker, the company had been active since 1901 and would include future stars Edward Everett Horton and John Gilbert in its ranks until it shut down in 1923.

Powell received a brief mention in the *Oregon Daily Journal* (September 7, 1914) for his work in the company's debut production of the season, Channing Pollock's four-act comedy, *Such a Little Queen*, that he made a "decided impression with his work as the juvenile." It is rather a vague mention, but it must have thrilled the young struggling actor

It was only two weeks after the debut of *Such a Little Queen* that the players would open *Stop Thief*, a three-act farce by Carlyle Moore. The *Oregon Daily Journal* (September 20, 1914) said the play about an absent-minded former kleptomaniac dealing with his daughter's wedding day "presents a mixture of misunderstandings that is one long laugh." Powell played the doctor chum of the bridegroom.

The amount of experience a stock company could provide a young actor like Powell was invaluable, although it was low-paying work and Portland was not likely to be a desired destination for an ambitious young actor. There was, however, the benefit of being exposed to an abundance of character parts in a tremendous variety of productions. The Baker Players would debut a new production every single week. Fortunately for posterity, Powell dutifully listed on paper every single professional production in which he appeared on stage and on film from 1914 to 1955, complete with his character's name and sometimes his salary. The eleven-page handwritten and typed list was sold at auction in 2018 for $1,875.

The list of parts he played with the Baker Players from November 1914 to March 1915 was visible on the Bonham's auction website and is a remarkable recording of how relentless the schedule could be for a young actor in a theatrical company in early-twentieth-century America.

November 22, *Merely Mary Ann*—Peter
November 29, *Ready Money*—Stephen Baird
December 6, *At Bay*—Judson Flagg
December 13, *The Rosary*—Bruce Walton
December 20, *Leah Klessna*—Raoul Berton
December 27, *The Rejuvenation of Aunt Mary*—Herbert Kendrick Mitchell
January 3, *The Blindness of Virtue*—Archibald Graham
January 10, *Officer 666*—Alfred Wilson
January 17, *The Virginian*—Steve
January 24, *Big Jim Harrity*—Dr. Hugh Malone
January 31, *The Dawn of a To-morrow*, Olives Holt
February 7, *The Parish Priest*—Dr. Edmund Welsh
February 14, *Sherlock Holmes*—Dr. Watson
February 21, *Secret Service*—Lewis Dumont (Capt. Thorne)
February 28, (OUTSIDE ATTRACTION)
March 7, *The Awakening of Helena Richie*—Lloyd Pryor
March 14, *Tess of the Storm Country*—Ben Letts
March 21, *Genesee of the Hills*—Charles Stewart

Most of these plays are long, long forgotten today, but they were hits at the time. For example, the comedy *Ready Money* by James Montgomery had just been adapted as a silent film by the Jesse L. Lasky Feature Play Company and distributed by the new Paramount Pictures. For the Bakers Players production, Powell played Steven Baird, the affable owner of the seemingly worthless Sky Rocket Mine who has only a quarter in his pocket. Approached by a counterfeiter to pass his phony money, the honest Stephen refuses, but when the counterfeiter suggests Stephen just "flash" the money to pretend the mine is bringing in excellent returns, his friends automatically start investing in the mine, bringing Stephen a fortune. And, of course, in a happy ending, the mine winds up panning out.

Powell's performance did not make the papers, but in his next production, *At Bay*, a melodrama by George Scarborough about a lawyer who makes blackmail his profession, the *Oregon Daily Journal* (December 7, 1914) said, "William H. Powell does some splendid work in the second act." He also received a positive notice in the *Journal* on January 4, 1915, for *The Blindness of Virtue* by Cosmo Hamilton, about a completely naïve girl who in her ignorance finds herself in a compromising position, and the innocent boy who is blamed. As the innocent boy Archibald Graham, Powell was "very well cast" and "played the part with discretion." In a February production of *Sherlock Holmes*, Powell even got to play Dr. Watson.

Also in the cast of *Sherlock Holmes* was Powell's paramour Eileen Wilson, who had joined the Baker Players late in the season to play ingenue parts. It must have been a relief for the couple to be reunited after Powell's time away in Portland. One of Powell's final productions of the season was rural melodrama *Tess of the Storm Country*, in which he played a villain named Ben Letts. His performance received a positive notice from the *Journal*: "William Powell carries conviction with his portrayal of a slinking scoundrel" (*Oregon Daily Journal*, March 15, 1915).

At the end of the season Wilson left Portland for New York, and Powell followed her. They would be wed there on April 15, 1915.

The *Oregon Daily Journal* trumpeted the wedding between the Baker Players alumni on May 2, 1915: "Word has been received from New York of the marriage in that city of two of the popular former Baker players, William Powell, who was frequently the villain in the play and sometimes played hero parts, and Miss Eileen Wilson, who, prior to the close of the stock company's season about nine weeks ago, took ingenue parts."

After their wedding, Powell and Wilson traveled to Buffalo to join the Bonstelle Players at the Star Theatre, one of two stock companies managed by pioneering actress, director, and manager Jessie Bonstelle. Powell would appear in May and June in a succession of plays familiar to contemporary audiences such as *Too Many Cooks* and *Seven Keys to Baldpate*, and then he and Wilson would continue the cycle, traveling the country to appear in months-long stints with various stock companies.

It was a familiar cycle for young twentysomething actors in the early twentieth century, and Powell—sometimes with and sometimes without his new bride—would struggle mightily in his attempt to find stage work. Stints with other stock companies in Boston, Detroit, Northampton, and Pittsburgh would follow, along with first, second, and third road companies, with Powell sometimes even getting the opportunity to play small character parts in New York.

It was in 1917 that a significant turning point came for the young William H. Powell as the result of a chance meeting with Leo Ditrichstein, a well-known and respected New York actor-manager who led his own company and took the lead roles in his productions. He took a great interest in Powell.

"The interest manifested in bawling the dickens out of me," Powell would remember (E. Gray, 1931).

Never, before or since, has anyone had such beautiful, all-embracing tongue lashings as Dietrichstein [*sic*] gave me. He would call me into his dressing room and sit looking at me, as though I were some strange animal out of a zoo. Then he would begin, delicately, with polished sarcasm and a nice choice of invective, to tell me just how rotten I was. He would explain in the most minute detail how bad my performance was, how I missed every good point, destroyed every possibility.

Fully expecting on a daily basis to be fired, Powell soon realized he was the only actor in the company to whom Ditrichstein paid any attention:

When he had finished combing me over, he'd invite me out to supper and over our beer and boloney he'd give me inspired lectures on the art of acting. "Acting," he would say, "is both an interpretative and a creative art. It must have depth, sincerity and technique. . . . First, there is the depth, the understanding of life, people, character. Then, sincerity—to believe in your work. Next, technique. The knowledge of how to convey to your audience what is in your mind and heart."

He taught me more about acting than I have ever learned in all the rest of my experience put together. If I've ever given a good performance, I owe more of it to Leo Dietrichstein [*sic*] than anything else. I know he believed I had possibilities, or he wouldn't have bothered to correct me. So I began to hope and not get discouraged, realizing all the time I was laying up capital which would some day bring me returns. (E. Gray, 1931)

In the fall of 1917, Powell joined Ditrichstein and his company in Chicago to appear in an old Spanish play titled *The Judge of Zalamea*, appearing as the villainous Captain Don Alvaro, a womanizer and rapist who is eventually hanged (Powell seemed to die a lot on stage). He didn't get many notices in the run in Chicago, and the production itself was seen as a flop, but Ditrichstein was undaunted and took his company to New York and the George M. Cohan Theatre on Broadway, where Ditrichstein starred in a satirical farce called *The King* (*Le Roi*) by Gaston Arman de Caillavet, Robert de Flers, and Emmanuel Arène. Powell in his Broadway debut was ninth-billed, playing a character named Rivolet.

The *New York Times* (November 21, 1917) pronounced the production a hit: "The wit of the play sparkles incessantly, and the laughable detail with which it is embroidered seems marvelously fresh and spontaneous." The play would run until March 1918, and Powell and Wilson would resume the routine of traveling the country in road shows and regional stock companies.

It would take just over two years before Powell would return to Broadway, and it would turn out to be his breakthrough.

Produced by Lincoln A. Wagenhals and Collin Kemper, *Spanish Love*, written by Avery Hopwood and Mary Roberts Rinehart, opened at the Maxine Elliott Theatre in August 1920. Hopwood and Rinehart are names long forgotten today, but they were among the most successful playwrights of the era. So much so, in fact, that they opened a second play on Broadway that very month, a mystery melodrama called *The Bat*, which would have a spectacular run of 867 performances before closing in September 1922 (Internet Broadway Database, n.d.).

The huge success of *The Bat* would overshadow *Spanish Love*, the script of which is completely unavailable today. What is known is that it was the tale of hot-blooded Spaniards Javier (Powell) and Pancho (James Rennie) battling for the love of Maria del Carmen (Maria Ascarre). While Javier burns with passion for Maria, *her* love is reserved for Pancho. But after Pancho injures Javier in a savage knife fight, Pancho is arrested and Maria then agrees to marry Javier in order to stop his persecution of Pancho. However, Javier dies of his injuries before the wedding.

Alexander Woollcott, in his review of the play for the *New York Times*, said that despite its uninspired title, *Spanish Love* "proved to be a sumptuously mounted, colorful and almost continuously interesting play."

> As it happens, *Spanish Love* is pretty well acted . . . very well acted indeed by one William H. Powell, a young newcomer who was graduated from the John Craig stock company in Boston, where so much that is serviceable on Broadway has been licked into shape.
>
> The Spanish atmosphere, created by lavish use of Spanish music, sweet-voiced chimes, mellow sunlight, castanets, gorgeous shawls and all, is altogether seductive and persuades you to accept as true and natural the hissing hate, the lachrymal love and the panting passion of all that follows in this story of wild courtship and still wilder revenge. It bids the players cut loose from all the restraints that modern plays have taught them and some of them break free as if they had longed for just such freedom all their days in the theatre. This is true in marked degree of Mr. Powell, who has probably been on the stage so short a time that he has never been thoroughly repressed.

Woollcott reserved some special and amusing ire for Maria Ascarre: "Apparently it (the role) was assigned to her because of her Spanish blood and appearance. It would have been better to have tried for a first-rate actress, even if she was born in Chicago and named Mame Gilhooley" (Woollcott, 1920).

In a later review of the touring production, *Washington Times* critic Louis Ashley echoed Woollcott's rave:

William H. Powell as Xavier, dying from a knife wound inflicted in a fair fight with Pancho, carries the brunt of the action, and he does it well. There is not a weakness in his portrayal of the young man burning with love for Maria and consuming with hate for Pancho. . . . *Spanish Love* is one of those dramas that keep one on edge, causing fair women to weep with pity for the poor heroine and the dying Xavier and to exult in the strength of Pancho. (Ashley, 1921)

While Powell doubtlessly enjoyed his first great professional success, his personal life was proving more difficult. His wife Eileen was also on Broadway at the time, having opened in Earl Carroll's *The Lady of the Lamp* at the Theatre Republic in August. That play closed in November, and the following January, Eileen filed for divorce in New York Supreme Court, alleging she was forced to support Powell for three-quarters of their married life and that "he had beaten and choked her some months ago" (*New York Daily News*, 1921). Whatever had happened between the two has been lost in the century since, but they reconciled after *Spanish Love* closed on Broadway in May 1921 after 308 performances. In September, Wilson was added to the cast, with Powell still playing Javier.

Powell would later acknowledge that the play was his big break. "Before that I had put in four years with stock companies, then more years in plays which were tried out in dog towns, but never got to New York. We'd rehearse, then flop. But finally my luck turned at Maxine Elliott's Theater. In *Spanish Love* I died of love and a stab wound, a magnificent death—the actor's delight" (Darnton, 1935).

Despite the success of the production, Powell was growing weary of the grind of the stage. "There is practically no road any more," he said in an interview in 1925.

Whether it's the movies, or the radio, that has killed it, is hard to say. But the stage actor to-day can depend really only upon the New York runs, and there are so many miserable plays that open only to flop that even that is becoming more hazardous all the time. Why, I know any number of clever, responsible actors who are hanging around the Lambs Club and other places, without jobs, pretty nearly broke. (Fergus, 1925)

Most accounts have Powell himself hanging around the Lambs Club one day when movie director Albert Parker spotted him there and struck up a conversation, let him know how much he enjoyed Powell's performance in *Spanish Love*, and offered him a role as one of Moriarty's henchmen in his upcoming film adaptation of *Sherlock Holmes*, which was going to star John Barrymore as the great detective. While most sources say it was Parker who spotted Powell, Powell himself said in his 1925 interview that it was Barrymore who invited him.

Whoever invited Powell to join the production, he saw it as an opportunity to "do something to insure a livable income" (Fergus, 1925). The tour of *Spanish Love* had ended and he was looking for work yet again. At the time, Powell did not think of abandoning the stage for film, because there were still plenty of films produced by the major studios in the New York area, so he could conceivably appear both in films and on stage for the foreseeable future. Things were finally looking up for William Powell.

While Powell was getting cast in his first motion picture, young Myrna Williams was sixteen years old and dreaming of stardom herself. Born in Helena, Montana, on August 2, 1905, she was the daughter of Della Mae Johnson and David Franklin Williams. David, the descendant of pioneer Montana ranchers, at age twenty-three became the youngest man ever to serve a term in the Montana Legislature, and met Della while serving in the capital city, Helena. After marrying, David and Della relocated to his family's ranch in Crow Creek Valley, where young Myrna spent her first five years. David decided the ranch life wasn't for him, and they moved back to Helena. David never returned to politics, but instead moved on to real estate and banking. The family lived in a middle-class neighborhood just down the street from Judge Cooper, whose son Gary was four years older than Myrna and would become equally famous as a movie star.

When Myrna was six, her grandmother took her to a stage production of Maurice Maeterlinck's *The Blue Bird*, and the fairy tale so enchanted Myrna that she began producing her own plays in the cellar. Despite her interest, however, Myrna's father disapproved.

It was in 1911 that Della gave birth to Myrna's younger brother, David, and soon afterward nearly died of pneumonia. Myrna would recall oxygen tanks scattered throughout her home for months that year, and as the winter approached, her father decided to ship Della, Myrna, and young David to La Jolla, California, so that Della could avoid the harsh Montana winter.

The three wound up staying in a rental home by the beach throughout the winter, then the spring, and then the summer of 1912. When David visited that August to celebrate Myrna's seventh birthday, he and Della quarreled. Della had fallen in love with Southern California and implored her husband to buy property there. David, however, declared himself a "Montanan, by God," and brought his family back to Helena with him.

Southern California had made a permanent impression on Della, however, and when she needed a hysterectomy in the summer of 1916, she insisted it could be performed better by doctors in Los Angeles. The elder David acquiesced by sending her, Myrna, and young David back to Southern California, where Della rented a house in Ocean Park, near Santa Monica.

There, Della would undergo her surgery and convalesce in the "healing climate." Most significantly, the three would stay long enough for Myrna to attend school for several months, which included dancing lessons for the first time.

After Della fully recovered, David summoned her and the children back to Helena yet again, and Della reluctantly returned. Of course, the marriage suffered from the growing disagreement of where they should live, with David continuing to refuse to allow the family to leave Montana permanently. It appeared that Della would never see her dream of living in California come true, but fate intervened in November 1918 when David became one of the millions worldwide to die in the Spanish flu epidemic.

Della, Myrna, and young David were not left with much. In a sign of how much the marriage must have been faltering, David Williams in his last will and testament had made his sister Nettie the executrix of his estate and guardian of his children, only leaving a provision that Nettie should give Della twenty-five dollars a month provided she remain "single and chaste." However, it wasn't as if David had denied them very much. At his death, he only had a little over a hundred dollars in savings.

Now free to do as she wished, Della packed up Myrna and young David and finally made the permanent move to Southern California she had desired for years. Culver City, home to Goldwyn Studios, was their final destination.

There, the thirteen-year-old Myrna found new life, now that Della had the full authority to allow her to indulge her love of performing. Della immediately took both of her children to as many concert and live theater performances as she could possibly afford, and enrolled Myrna in dance classes with the famous Denishawn Company and ballet classes at Mme. Matildita's Ecole de Choreographie Classicet. When Myrna was eventually enrolled at Venice High School, she even studied sculpting, and while Loy claimed she wasn't very good, her experience with art teacher Harry Fielding Winebreiner led to a new career: modeling. Loy recalled:

> The administration decided to decorate the fountain in a large lily pond in front of the school. Mr. Winebreiner commissioned to create an appropriate sculpture group, chose a typically symbolic motif of that period: a girl reading a book, a young male athlete, and, towering above them, a figure symbolizing youthful aspiration. He chose me as the model for "Aspiration." (Loy, 1988)

CULVER CITY GIRL FIGURE FOR NEW VENICE FOUNTAIN

Myrna Williams, Culver City Girl, Who Posed for Venice Statue. Photo by Anderson

Myrna Williams in the *Venice Vanguard Evening Herald,* August 1, 1922. *Author's Collection*

When the statue was finished, a local promoter named Bert Lennon worked it into the city's Memorial Day pageant, hauling both a plaster cast of the statue and Myrna Williams onto the deck of the USS *Nevada*, where there was a staging of Myrna coming to life by Thomas H. Ince, the pioneering filmmaker based in Culver City.

Myrna's modeling assignment landed her on the front page of the *Venice Vanguard Evening Herald* the day before her seventeenth birthday on August 1, 1922. "Miss Williams has features so nearly classic that she has been highly praised by art critics," the article read. By the time the statue was installed in May 1923, Myrna had dropped out of high school to earn money for her family. "I had to," she wrote years later. "Not being able to graduate was a big tragedy at the time, but money was running low and I had to work, that's all. I suppose it was that sense of responsibility instilled by my father. I don't mean to play the martyr—the chance to get on with my dancing probably delighted me" (Loy, 1988).

After dropping out, Myrna got a job working for a brother-and-sister dance team called Fanchon and Marco, who were hired to create a prologue at Sid Grauman's Egyptian Theatre for Cecil B. DeMille's *The Ten Commandments*. Silent movie prologues were elaborately staged theater productions that would either provide a literal preview of the action in the movie that was to follow or provide a sense of the atmosphere to give audience members an impression of the movie's time, place, and characters. "The dance was supposed to be Egyptian to complement the picture's Biblical sequences so we rehearsed all those square movements associated with ancient Egypt," Loy wrote. "We wore little pants and sort of Egyptian halters with headdresses. It was very interesting and apparently quite beautiful, we were told" (Loy, 1988).

While it is certain young Myrna Williams was not the focal point of the prologue, she could not have had a better place to experience her professional debut at age eighteen. Sid Grauman's massive and ostentatious Egyptian Theatre had opened in 1922 and quickly became one of the most famous movie theaters in the world. Located at the center of the film industry, there were film industry professionals scattered among the 1,771 seats every evening, watching young Myrna Williams dance in the prologue to DeMille's original silent biblical epic.

And it was her dancing at Grauman's Egyptian Theatre that indeed opened the door to her film career. Myrna's second prologue at the Egyptian in 1924 was for Douglas Fairbanks's epic *The Thief of Bagdad*. According to Myrna, after a few months when the crowds for the Fairbanks picture began to thin out, her stage manager decided to put pictures of the dancers in the courtyard. Eventually, portrait photographer Henry Waxman saw the pictures and chose Myrna and several other Grauman's dancers for shoots. It was in Waxman's studio that legendary screen lover Rudolph Valentino spotted a photo of Myrna and asked Waxman to send her to his wife, Natacha Rambova, who also served as his professional adviser. They gave Myrna the opportunity to do a screen test for Valentino's upcoming picture, *Cobra*.

"Natacha even bought me a dress to wear," Loy said in a 1937 interview. "When I went to see the test, there was something the matter with the projection machine and the test was horrible. I was skipping about so fast on the screen I couldn't follow myself. I rushed out of the projection room, ran home and cried for hours. I was really ashamed of myself. It was so awful I couldn't bear to face Natacha" (Mook, 1937).

Myrna also tried to take advantage of living right in the center of Culver City, next to Goldwyn Pictures. By 1924, the studio was faltering and merged with Metro Pictures and Louis B. Mayer Productions to become a powerhouse called Metro-Goldwyn-Mayer Studios.

In the spring and summer of 1925, "I used to sit for days in the casting office at MGM, waiting for someone to notice me," Loy said. "Finally the casting director called me one day and told me they wanted me to make a test. I thought, 'Here it comes.' But a minute later my hopes were dashed to the ground. He added, 'You don't need to put on any make-up. We only want to make a color test of a dress Kathleen Keyes is wearing in *Ben-Hur*'" (Mook, 1937).

Briefly dispirited, Myrna still decided to do her best and put on makeup anyway. She felt much better about the screen test, and that feeling was justified when it turned out that unit director Christie Cabanne saw the test and decided Myrna should play the small role of the Madonna in the biblical epic.

Cabanne assured Myrna she was going to get the part, provided they didn't get Betty Bronson, who had appeared in *Peter Pan* for Paramount Pictures the year before. Unfortunately for Myrna, they did get Bronson. Myrna received a consolation prize of a tiny part as a dancer in MGM's *Pretty Ladies*. In one scene, anticipating the choreography of Busby Berkeley, she is one of the dancers making up a living chandelier alongside another ambitious young performer named Lucille Le Sueur, who would soon change her name to Joan Crawford.

Despite the opportunity, nothing much came of that role and Myrna was still discouraged. "I was so broken-hearted I went back to Natacha," Loy said in the 1937 interview. "It was the first time I'd phone her or seen her since my first test. She'd seen the test in the meantime and told me it wasn't bad—that it must have been the projection machine that made it seem so. She gave me the lead in a picture she was producing herself" (Mook, 1937).

Filmed in May 1925, the picture was Rambova's first attempt at producing. Rambova herself had been ostracized in Hollywood for her outsized and unwelcome involvement in Valentino's career as his artistic adviser, to such an extent that when Valentino signed a contract with United Artists, he was forced to agree to a clause prohibiting Rambova's involvement, which even included her visiting him on set.

Despite the seemingly universal rejection, Rambova took one last shot at making it in Hollywood by producing a picture financed with a $50,000 loan from Valentino. The film was called *What Price Beauty?* Myrna Williams was cast in a role as "Vamp." *Motion Picture Magazine* (September 1925) trumpeted the arrival of the newcomer with a full-page Henry Waxman photo and the kind of absurdly exaggerated hyperbole you can only find in 1920s movie fan magazines:

> There's a great buzzing and roaring in our ears: It's the thousands upon thousands of readers asking "Who . . . is she? Who Is She? Whoisshe?" Well, she's what Mrs. Rudolph Valentino says is going to be the 1926 flapper model. You'll see her first in "What Price Beauty," Natacha Rambova Valentino's much-talked-about picture. Perhaps the word that best describes her type is "piquant"—or maybe "elfin." She's boyish—but bashfully boyish. She's lithe, and vivacious—but not muscular or "full of pep." She's the essence of grace; she is aloof; elusive; mysterious; sensitive. You don't know whether she's innocent or sophisticated; whether she's a low-brow or a high-brow; whether she's pretty or plain. But you do know that she is very, very young; and very, very fascinating. All you obvious, breezy tom-boyish 1925 flapper models had better practice changing your type or on New Year's Day you'll find yourselves frightfully out of date.

Sadly, Rambova could not find a distributor for *What Price Beauty?* There was one screening, and then it sat on a shelf for almost three years, during which time Valentino and Rambova were divorced, Rambova left for Europe, and Valentino's untimely death made him Hollywood's first movie star martyr. Independent pictures were extraordinarily difficult to distribute in the middle of the studio era, and Hollywood's distaste for Rambova must not have helped. By the time Pathé picked up the film that young Myrna Williams hoped would be her big breakout, it was 1928 and she had already appeared in over twenty films.

2

THE HEAVY

The film industry that welcomed William H. Powell to its ranks in late 1921 was only a scant few years old but had grown to unimaginable heights since the extraordinary box office and critical success of D. W. Griffith's *The Birth of a Nation* in 1915. Over a century later, it's difficult to imagine how the notoriously racist Civil War and Reconstruction epic from the bitter perspective of a defeated South essentially created an entire industry, but that's exactly what it did. Its enormous critical and box office success made rich men of distributors and exhibitors, and it was not long before the motion picture industry became the fourth-largest overall industry in the country.

The Sherlock Holmes we see in Albert Parker's 1922 film distributed by Goldwyn Pictures bears practically no resemblance to the Holmes with whom movie and television audiences have become accustomed over the past century. Arthur Conan Doyle's legendary detective has long been authentically portrayed by everyone from Basil Rathbone to Benedict Cumberbatch as a cold, calculating machine of deduction wholly uninterested in domestic matters such as marriage, but a hundred years ago, audiences were most familiar with an 1899 theatrical adaptation by William Gillette, in which Holmes is a romantic idol (horrors!) who falls deeply, immediately, and irretrievably in love.

Gillette himself played Holmes over 1,300 times on stage and revived his interpretation in a 1916 motion picture adaptation of his play. Here, in the second film adaptation of Gillette's work, the great stage actor John Barrymore, then revolutionizing the art of stage acting with his naturalistic portrayal of Shakespeare's *Hamlet*, would put his own spin on Sherlock Holmes.

Barrymore, alas, does not have a whole lot to work with here. The film is somewhat interesting in allowing audiences to view Barrymore and the film debuts of Powell and Roland Young (as Dr. Watson), but on the whole it's a dud. Critics of the time—often anonymous—agreed, and what praise they could muster was generally reserved for Barrymore.

Does William H. Powell make a notable film debut here? Not particularly. Absent his familiar mustache, with little to distinguish him from other characters, he plays Forman Wells, a toady of Holmes's nemesis, Professor Moriarty. Wells then switches his allegiance to Holmes when he is randomly wracked with guilt for the crimes he commits. If not for his future stardom, Powell here would not only be an insignificant footnote but an invisible one. Not one contemporary review mentions him.

It was hardly a life-changing cinematic debut and, with no immediate guarantee for future roles, it is no surprise that Powell returned to the stage. In February and March 1922 he appeared in the Russian Revolution drama *Bavu* at the Earl Carroll Theatre, and in April he appeared for two weeks in a Sam H. Harris–produced tryout of Edward Locke's comedy, *My Lady's Lips*.

Right after completing the two-week run of the tryout, Powell returned to a film set for a second time, and this time he would begin his evolution into one of the premiere villains of the American silent film era. Produced by newspaper magnate William Randolph Hearst's Cosmopolitan Pictures, *When Knighthood Was in Flower* was an elaborate costume showcase for Marion Davies, longtime paramour of the notorious publisher. Davies was a delightful comedienne best suited for light farce, but here Hearst eschewed those talents and pulled out all the stops in showcasing her in a blockbuster period production.

Publicity surrounding bloated movie budgets is nothing new. The trade papers, in promoting the picture a century ago, spent little space focusing on the story of the film, preferring instead to focus on all the time and money spent on its production, no doubt spurred on by Hearst. Boasting a total budget of $1.5 million, the mammoth production featured thousands of extras, a principal cast of fifty-five actors, thirty-three cavalry horses, and the largest movie set yet constructed, which cost exactly $41,726.26. Hearst spared no expense in showcasing his leading lady and made sure everyone knew just what that expense entailed.

Davies plays Mary Tudor, sister of Henry VIII, who falls immediately and deeply in love with soldier Charles Brandon (Forrest Stanley) just in time for her brother to announce that she is to marry Louis XII of France in an effort to forge an alliance. Mary, of course, rejects the idea because Louis XII of France is "withered and old." Mary goes through a great many attempts to escape her fate, eventually deciding she is going to run away with Charles to New Spain.

Inevitable complications and swordfights ensue during the first ninety minutes of the film's running time until Mary is brought back to the castle and finally accedes to the marriage with Louis XII to save Charles from execution, but not before securing a promise from her brother the king that if she is married a second time, that husband must be her choice and her choice alone.

Powell is mostly absent from the film's first ninety minutes except for one brief scene in which Louis XII is given a portrait of Mary. Powell, as the king's fiendish nephew and heir, Duke Francis, grabs it from Louis's hands and leers at it, followed by a nice bit of comic business in which Louis tries in vain to pry it from Francis's fingers. When we finally see Duke Francis again, he then dominates the proceedings for the final half hour of the picture. When Mary finally makes the journey to France and marries Louis XII, she finds he's a sweet, harmless old coot who has about five minutes to live. Powell wastes no time in leering at Mary and deciding that she will now be HIS queen! Here, Powell has plenty to do and makes an immediate impact as the sole actor in the film who can truly hold his own with the charismatic, talented Davies. The pace of the film immediately quickens as the true stakes are revealed.

Marion Davies spurns William H. Powell in *When Knighthood Was in Flower.* *Author's Collection*

Louis almost immediately dies, and the fiendish Duke Francis posts guards at Mary's bedroom doors before the king's body is cold. After quickly bolting her doors in fear of Francis's imminent arrival, a large portrait in her bedroom slides open, revealing a secret entrance and William H. Powell standing in the middle of its black void, like an unholy apparition. It's a hell of an entrance, and Powell takes full advantage of his first real opportunity to shine in pictures. After Brandon arrives and he and Mary quickly tie up Francis and escape, Francis is able to free himself and screams for his troops to give chase. There is a visible ferocity in Powell's delivery that might have seemed over the top in a talking picture, but in a silent film it fits. Calling his men to action as a thunderstorm brewing above echoes his royal fury, Powell has an undeniable presence as he bellows in silence from the balcony of Mary's boudoir, cast in shadows.

When Knighthood Was in Flower was trumpeted by Hearst in publicity materials as "The Most Beautiful Picture Ever Made," and reviewers were appropriately impressed by the Tudor-era pageantry. The *New York Times* (September 15, 1922) said the film was "dazzling to the eye, splendidly impressive and apparently true to the time and places of its setting."

Powell completed filming in late May 1922, and then spent the summer rehearsing for what would be his final appearance on stage, the Broadway production of *My Lady's Lips*, which after its spring tryout was retitled *The Woman Who Laughed*. It was a drama about a wife (Martha Hedman) who learns her sister (Gilda Leary) and her husband (Powell) are having an affair; she ties them to a bedpost, emotionally tortures them, drugs them, and pretends to poison them and subsequently pretends to shoot herself. The play opened on August 16, 1922, and only managed to eke out thirteen performances before closing the same month.

Alexander Woollcott in his dismissive review in the *New York Times*, noted that the new play "valiantly attacked" the audience at the Longacre Theatre and went on to say:

> Mr. Locke appears to have thought it would sort of add a fine Scandinavian note of irony to the proceedings if, instead of weeping all through this home-brew melodrama, Mrs. Neilson should laugh—a hollow, puzzling, chilling laugh. So, in order to live up to the title, the blonde and adorning Martha Hedman laughs away for dear life, a dismal, monotonous laugh that proves before the first act is half spent a fearful affliction to the innocent bystander. (Woollcott, 1922)

Woollcott went on to say Powell "deserves better plays than *Bavu* and *The Woman Who Laughed*." After the flop closed, the very next month *When Knighthood Was in Flower* opened to a rapturous response from both audiences and critics. Powell's thoughts at the time on fully abandoning the stage for the movies were unrecorded, but it is easy to imagine the actor—having just turned thirty years old—realized that the choice between building on the momentum of his outstanding supporting turn in a hugely successful motion picture or attempting to pick up the pieces after appearing in a Broadway flop was simple.

Powell's third picture, *Outcast*, is a lost film. Released in December 1922, the film was an adaptation of a 1914 play by Hubert Henry Davies and was notable for featuring the play's original star, Elsie Ferguson, in the lead role as a prostitute eventually redeemed by true love. By all accounts, Powell's role was a small one as a man named De Valle with whom Ferguson has a dalliance. The extent of that role is lost to the ages, but one review did mention that Powell had a "minor part which he handles capably" (*Film Daily*, December 10, 1922) and another noted, "William Powell is a fairly good bet as a South American" (*Variety*, December 8, 1922).

Outcast was directed by long-forgotten director Chet Withey, who took over after veteran director John S. Robertson dropped out (*Film Daily*, August 15, 1922). However, Robertson would helm Powell's next picture, which would be the young actor's real breakthrough as a reliable silent-film heavy. *The Bright Shawl* would give Powell his first really positive notices, a lifelong best friend in the picture's leading man, Richard Barthelmess, and a travel bug he would retain for the rest of his movie career.

Produced by Inspiration Pictures, *The Bright Shawl* was filmed on location in Cuba and at Tilford Studios in New York over ten weeks from December 1922 to February 1923, and features Powell in his most showy role yet as a charismatic and charming villain opposite Barthelmess, who had become one of the biggest stars in pictures in the past several years. Barthelmess had come to prominence in the D. W. Griffith films *Broken Blossoms* and *Way Down East* and had developed a screen persona of the innocent, guileless, and honest juvenile seeking danger and adventure. After breaking off from Griffith, as all of his underpaid stars eventually did, Barthelmess joined the newly formed Inspiration Pictures in 1921. The company's first film, *Tol'able David*, an Appalachian David-and-Goliath story directed by Henry King, exploited Barthelmess's gifts as a marvelously subtle pantomimic actor.

The Bright Shawl is of particular interest today not only for the presence of Powell, but future talking picture stars Edward G. Robinson and Mary Astor. Adapted from a novel by Joseph Hergesheimer, the film takes place in 1850s Spanish Cuba and opens with a somber dedication to "our martyred president William McKinley, whose true American statesmanship brought freedom to the people of Cuba." Barthelmess plays Charles Abbott, a young American who has come to Cuba with his friend Andres Escobar (Andre Beranger), a Cuban patriot returning to his family's home where his older brother Vincente (Luis Alberni) lies dying from wounds received in battle against their Spanish conquerors. The Escobar family, which includes patriarch Domingo (Robinson) and daughter Narcissa (Astor), are targeted by the Spanish authorities for colluding in a potential insurrection.

The Bright Shawl (1923). Directed by John S. Robertson. From left: Richard Barthelmess, William Powell. *Associated First National Pictures/Photofest © Associated First National Pictures*

The villain of the piece is Captain Santacilla (Anders Randolf), a loyal and fiendish Spanish spy who is accompanied by Captain de Vaca (Powell). We first see Powell lying languidly on three chairs lined in a row, smoking a cigarette as the title describes de Vaca as "a dandy from Madrid who lacked the vicious energy of his brother officer." A brief close-up of Powell shows him as a man so lazy it takes all his effort just to hold his cigar. Randolf as Santacilla, on the other hand, is the stereotype of a silent-film heavy that modern audiences might expect. His mustache is enormous, he is portly and leering, and prone to histrionics. Powell as de Vaca, however, shows admirable restraint: a raised eyebrow here, a smirk there. Powell with his mustache, soul patch, and aggressive sideburns certainly looks the part, but his stillness provides a fine counterpoint to Randolf's loud, villainous buffoonery and, paradoxically, we notice him more.

Dorothy Gish plays dancer La Clavel, the "brilliant flower of Spain," a seeming ally of Captain Santacilla but having a heart that eventually leads her to the Cuban cause. When Santacilla begins to suspect La Clavel of sending the rebels messages about Santacilla's plans that she overhears, he plants a false military plan with her to confirm her duplicity and to snare the rebels in a trap. When Charles Abbott learns of Santacilla's plans, a vicious fight ensues that ends with the deaths of both La Clavel and Santacilla.

It is a bit of surprise twist that the big star Dorothy Gish and the main villain Santacilla both die halfway through the film. Abbott still has to inform the rebels that Santacilla has laid a trap for them, and he rushes to warn them. What occurs then is William Powell's emergence as an outstanding heavy. Now that Santacilla has been killed, de Vaca is in charge. With calm efficiency, de Vaca has his soldiers kill Andres Escobar and takes Narcissa and her mother prisoner.

When Charles Abbott arrives at the Escobars' home to confront de Vaca, he's still exhausted from his battle with Santacilla. What makes Barthelmess effective as a pantomimic actor is his relatively subdued manner that belies an explosive nature, something Barthelmess and director Henry King successfully exploited in *Tol'able David* in a spectacular fistfight between him and Ernest Torrance. In the battle with Santacilla, Barthelmess really lets loose, and he does a fine job portraying utter exhaustion and hysteria at the same time when he later faces Powell, who turns out to be a master with the sword.

The fascinating transformation of Powell's character de Vaca—portrayed as a seemingly lazy gadabout at the beginning of the film—shows why Powell immediately captured the attention of audiences and critics. While he *seemed* lazy, what he was really conveying was a cool, steely confidence. You see it in the way he holds his cigar, his eyelids half-shut. De Vaca says to Abbott via intertitles:

"Would you care to be shot with your back against a prison wall Mr. Abbott? Or would you rather take a chance with me?"

Exhausted—surrounded by enemies—faced by the deadly swordsmanship of de Vaca, Charles resolves to die fighting, and the more hysterical Charles becomes, the calmer de Vaca becomes. Our hero seems far more unhinged than our villain, raging and held back by soldiers while Powell just stands there in quiet confidence, creating a fascinating contrast between the two performers.

As they begin the duel with swords, de Vaca bends his sword mockingly and begins his fight with Charles, with his left arm curled behind his back. When he manages to nick Charles's wrist, he simply nods slightly with his eyebrows raised. Again, not the demonstrative silent-film villain we might expect. He's cool. Way cool.

When a soldier knocks down Charles in order assist de Vaca, de Vaca slaps the soldier to the ground for interfering. Here is a villain who plays a fair game, shaking his head to see the exhausted Barthelmess, crumpled on the ground, exhausted, defeated. Charles says, "Kill me." De Vaca reluctantly, almost with an expression of pity, gives Charles a chance to stand up again. Charles attempts to begin the fight again but passes out. De Vaca simply looks down at him and places his sword in his scabbard, with that slight expression of pity tempered by a measure of respect.

After the blackout, the film then fades in to Charles tied to a pole in the underbelly of a ship headed back to America. He is given a note from de Vaca informing him that he admired Charles's courage, so he let him live and sent him and his belongings on a ship bound for home. The film ends with a door opening and Narcissa and her mother standing there. The villain had even allowed them safe travel because of his respect for Charles's courage. And re-markably, that's the end of film: a Hollywood film produced in 1923 in which the hero is defeated in disgrace and the villain lives on to continue to suppress the brave rebels. It's a starkly realistic ending, to be sure, and runs counter to everything we expect from Old Hollywood.

What the villain's victory accomplishes in the long run is cementing William Powell as a considerable force to be reckoned with in only his fourth film. Al-though *When Knighthood Was in Flower* somewhat showcased him as a heavy, here he has a real opportunity to shine. He establishes himself as a heroic villain: quiet, sure and confident. He's handsome, with a dash of swarthiness to make him seem "exotic" and "mysterious." He's not a Rudolph Valentino playing the Sheik, the dangerous seducer who women can't resist. No, he's a straight-ahead heavy, but an honorable one. Not the cartoon of his predecessor Anders Randolf, who seemed like your typical sexually aggressive buffoon, but a dignified villain. And William Powell *wins*. The climactic swordfight, popularized in the 1920s by cinema's first swashbuckler Douglas Fairbanks as Zorro, d'Artagnan, and Robin Hood, ends in disgrace and misery for the hero. Powell could not have asked for a better role. He smirks, smokes, buckles swashes, and defeats the hero.

In the July 1923 issue of *Photoplay*, William Powell's performance as de Vaca was listed as one of the industry's Six Best Performances of the Month. Powell began to earn a reputation as a "picture stealer." In a March 1929 *Photoplay* article devoted to Powell's status as a "picture stealer," Barthelmess had nothing but kind words for the man who bested him on celluloid.

"I remember the first picture we made together. It was *The Bright Shawl*. We went to Cuba to make it and Bill and I formed a friendship that we enjoy to this day," Barthelmess said.

> I was the hero, a rather dub part, and Bill was the bold, bad villain who showed me up for fair. It was a great part and he played it splendidly. It was then, I believe, that critics first called him a picture stealer. Bill took no thought of it, I know, except in the lightest manner. The morning after the picture opened on Broadway, I called him from the 125th Street Ferry House—I was on my way to the studio. "Hello, Bill?" I asked. "Yes." "This is Dick. Bill, you blankity-blank! You stole my picture, do you know it?"
>
> The reply came instantly back: "Certainly I expected to. Good-bye." And he hung up. But that was spoken in the greatest levity. Picture stealer or not I like to work with Bill. It's like playing a fast game of tennis with an expert, or playing bridge with a person who knows cards. It is stimulating. It keeps you on your toes. It makes you do your best. When Bill was a free-lance I tried to get him for each of my pictures. We did play together again in "The Beautiful City" and again I enjoyed that vigorous contact. (Spensley, 1929)

Now a full-fledged successful silent-film heavy, Powell took a turn in another film produced by William Randolph Hearst's Cosmopolitan Pictures. Like *When Knighthood Was in Flower*, it was another epic of old France. In *Under the Red Robe*, Powell played the Duke d'Orleans, this time graduating from the era of Louis XII to the era of Louis XIII. *Under the Red Robe* made little impression, likely because this was a Cosmopolitan production that lacked the strong star presence of Marion Davies, and it wasn't until his next film that Powell fully established himself as a full-time screen villain in another epic period piece.

After leaving D. W. Griffith's stock company following the production of *Orphans of the Storm*, Lilliam Gish—the great tragedienne of the screen—was invited by her old co-star Richard Barthelmess to join Inspiration Pictures, and Gish scored a great success with the company in Henry King's 1923 production of *The White Sister* co-starring a young Ronald Colman in his first significant movie role.

That film had been the first major Hollywood production to film in Italy, and Gish wanted to remain there to film *Romeo and Juliet*, but in her autobiography she said exhibitors back in the United States claimed that "Shakespeare's name kept people out of the theaters" (Pinchot, 1969). Instead, she said, a friend of the producers suggested adapting George Eliot's novel *Romola*. Returning to the director's chair was Henry King, and joining Gish along with her sister Dorothy and Ronald Colman was the young stage actor, William H. Powell.

According to Powell, it was Inspiration Pictures president Charles Duell who insisted on filming *Romola*, and both Lillian Gish and Henry King were both dead set against the project because the title character (whom Lillian would portray) was simply too weak and passive. Powell explained that Gish and King struggled mightily with the scenario so that the character would have a more active role in the story but ultimately gave up; "it became a case of trying to save what story there was, let the interest fall where it would" (Fergus, 1925).

Ultimately, to the benefit of Powell, that interest fell on him, and while he was billed fourth behind Lillian and Dorothy Gish and Colman, he was the true star of the picture. Set in fifteenth-century Florence, Italy, *Romola* revolves around the fiendish Tito (Powell), a Greek who arrives in the city following a mysterious shipwreck and proceeds to insinuate himself into a society torn apart by the recent death of its leader, Lorenzo de Medici. After Tito accidentally "rescues" blind scholar Bardo Bardi from an angry mob, Bardi invites Tito to his home, where daughter Romola (Lillian Gish) lives a cloistered life, exposed only to her father and painter Carlo (Colman), who adores her to no avail.

When Romola notices Tito is wearing a ring from the lofty Society of Pythagoras, she assumes he is a scholar. After her father drops dead, Romola then naïvely invites Tito to take on his work. After Tito is invited by Adolpho Spini to join the city's Council of Eight solely because he is wearing the ring, Tito begins a political climb, marrying Romola and also "mock" marrying peasant girl Tessa (Dorothy Gish).

Complicating matters for Tito is the reappearance of his foster father, Baldassarre Calvo. Baldassarre gave Tito the ring before their ship was attacked and sunk by pirates, and Tito abandoned him to his fate. Eventually, Tito's machinations come back to haunt him after he rises to the top of the Florentine government and orders the execution of beloved rebel Savonarola (Herbert Grimwood). The mob turns on Tito, who runs and is eventually discovered along the river by the suffering and homeless Baldassarre, who pushes Tito's head under the surface of the water and strangles him as he drowns.

Critics enthused over Powell's performance. In *Moving Picture World*, C. S. Sewell wrote, "Powell as Tito has the lion's share of the action and is not only a remarkably good type for the role but makes a distinctly fine impression and gives a wonderful performance." However, Sewell noted, "while we felt its pictorial charm, the story did not get a strong hold on our emotions and the interest was weakened by the maze of detail and incident, and we doubt whether the magnificence, splendor and beauty of this picture, plus the excellent work of the cast, will outweigh these other considerations in the minds of the average patron" (Sewell, 1924). And in the *New York Times*, Mordaunt Hall wrote, "William H. Powell, who gained no little fame by a part he played in *The Bright Shawl* . . . gives a splendid performance" (M. Hall, December 2, 1924).

It was a mammoth shoot. Powell was on location in Italy from August 1923 until May 1924, and even in the awful-looking video presentation most seen today—blown up from a Super 8 mm print—it's clear the film must have been visually spectacular when first seen in theaters. And it must have been an extraordinary experience for Powell, who quickly developed a deeper thirst for travel and would form another lifelong friendship during production, this time with Ronald Colman; he, Colman, and Barthelmess would be known over the next few years in Hollywood as "The Three Musketeers."

Unfortunately, *Romola* itself was no *Three Musketeers*. It is spectacularly dull, despite the impressive locations. Both Gish sisters, in their final joint appearance on film, are given thankless passive roles, and Colman in particular is criminally underused, with merely a few shots of him gazing helplessly at Romola with unrequited love. Every single narrative beat is driven by Tito. In just his sixth picture, Powell is unquestionably the lead character. As the dominating heavy, Powell is as charismatic as ever, even when forced to don a ridiculous period wig within an overstuffed plot, but he never has a chance to form a believable character. The film goes from beat to beat with rapid speed, without giving the audience an opportunity to understand *why* certain things are happening. What results is an almost laughably illogical string of events, all due to Tito having this seemingly magic ring that makes nearly everyone genuflect in front of him for no valid reason.

Worse yet, the demands of showing every detail of the location likely led the usually reliable Henry King to shoot almost everything in a long shot, so the film often seems as technically sophisticated as an early Edison one-reeler. King had proven himself a superior director before and would do so time and again in the coming decades, but *Romola* as seen today seems like a significant misstep.

Nevertheless, Powell came out of it shining. After completing filming in May 1924, Powell enjoyed some well-earned leisure time before returning in August to New York, where he would head to Paramount Pictures' Astoria Studios to film *Dangerous Money* opposite Bebe Daniels. Daniels was a child of the movies who had starred as Dorothy in the first film adaptation of *The Wonderful Wizard of Oz* at age ten and would go on to become Harold Lloyd's screen partner over the course of more than a hundred short films from 1915 to 1919. She left Lloyd to star in pictures for Cecil B. DeMille alongside big stars like Gloria Swanson and eventually graduated to star in pictures on her own.

Dangerous Money would represent Daniels's first official film as a Paramount star, as well as Paramount scenario writer Frank Tuttle's first film as a director. In the picture, Daniels plays a boardinghouse "slavey" in New York named Adele Clark, who is awarded the ownership of property called Clark's Field and suddenly finds herself transported to a finishing school, where her head-mistress suggests she should travel to Europe. So, off to Italy goes Adele and her sweetheart, Tim Sullivan (Tom Moore). Adele quickly gets caught up in the jet-set life, Tim leaves for America, and Adele winds up marrying an Italian count named Prince Arnolfo da Pescia (Powell), who quickly turns out to be a fortune hunter. After it turns out that Tim may be the rightful heir to Clark's Field, Adele and Arnolfo return to New York. Naturally, Arnolfo tries to steal the will and then winds up dying in a hotel fire.

It had not taken long for Powell to be typecast as an evil Mediterranean for-tune hunter. Unfortunately, *Dangerous Money* is a lost film, but by all accounts, he was marvelous once again. Mordaunt Hall in the *New York Times* said that "William Powell, scamp though he is as the Prince, is an actor whom it is a real joy to behold" (M. Hall, October 14, 1924). *Photoplay* (December 1924) dismissed the film, but not Powell: "Just another flabby fil-em story with one William Powell, the scoundrel who tries to get Bebe's money, running away with the opus."

Dangerous Money not only further established Powell as a heavy whom studios could depend on "running away" with their pictures. It also introduced Powell to Daniels, his first significant recurring female co-star, with whom he would appear in three more films.

It is particularly disappointing not to have *Dangerous Money* available to view today, because Powell's performance won him a long-term contract with Paramount Pictures. His first official picture under contract to the studio, *Too Many Kisses*, began filming in December 1924 just as *Romola* was opening around the country. It began a long string of pictures in which Powell would be a reliable heavy opposite some of Paramount's biggest contract stars.

Released in March 1925, *Too Many Kisses* is best known today for the presence of Harpo Marx in a small role as the "Village Peter Pan" (featuring the only dialogue he spoke in his career, albeit via intertitles) and is typical of the kind of ubiquitous, tightly constructed six-reel feature in which Powell would thrive over the next several years as Paramount's premier heavy. In *Too Many Kisses*, Richard Dix plays Richard Gaylord Jr., son of a millionaire who is forced time and time again to pay off women with whom Junior gets involved in order to avoid scandal. Dad sends Junior off to the Basque Country with lackey Mr. Simmons (Joseph Burke), when the latter informs him that women there only associate with their own kind and would never look twice at an American.

Dad strikes a bargain with his lothario son: Stay away from women for six months and I'll give you half the business and make you junior partner. While Richard behaves himself briefly on his trip, of course he immediately falls for the beautiful Yvonne (Frances Howard). The conflict arises when it is quickly apparent that Don Julio, Captain of the Guard (Powell), also believes that Yvonne is his property. Yvonne certainly doesn't think she belongs to Don Julio, but this is Hollywood's Spain in the 1920s, so it doesn't really matter. Here, Powell comfortably sneers his way through the role of the swarthy military creep, demonstrating his knife-throwing skills in an effort to intimidate the newly arrived American rival.

Richard Dix would later be known primarily as a tough, manly Western star, but he possesses a light touch here that belies his pugilistic appearance, and he and Powell have some nice comic moments, particularly in a scene in which Richard decides to woo Yvonne on her balcony while Julio cluelessly serenades her from below. Richard drops a flower onto the ground, which Julio misinterprets as an invitation from Yvonne to ascend. When he does so, in a rather peculiar compositional gag, Julio can only see Yvonne because her profile blocks Richard, whose arm is around her. Julio sees a hand on the ledge and kisses it, only to learn quickly it is the hidden Richard's hand.

Julio is appropriately dumbfounded and outraged all at once. It is a fine comic moment from an actor who didn't get much opportunity in his silent-film career to flex his comic muscles, and provides the tiniest hint of what Powell was capable of. It certainly wasn't enough at the time to change the trajectory of his career as a heavy, but it did show he was certainly capable of more than grimaces and mustache-twirling. Mordaunt Hall of the *New York Times* once again had nothing but praise for Powell, noting he "is excellent as Julio. It is a part which fits him like the proverbial glove. He is jealous, cowardly, vengeful, affectionate in a perfectly natural way" (M. Hall, March 3, 1925).

Too Many Kisses would begin a cycle for Powell over the next several years—of pictures filmed in four to six weeks, all running about sixty to seventy-five minutes, and covering a bevy of genres, most if not all featuring Powell as a dastardly villain. Unfortunately, among the ten pictures released by Paramount between February 1925 and February 1927, only one survives.

Powell did get to play a hero twice, in loan-outs to independent producers, a move that often allowed contract supporting players at the major studios to flex their muscles in leading roles. For his first leading role as a hero, Powell returned to Cuba in January 1925 to film *White Mice* for Pinellas Films, a production company founded by Harry P. Carver, a former general manager for Hearst's Cosmopolitan Pictures. The company would not last long. In trade advertisements for the film, Pinellas seems almost defensive in its justification for producing future films at Studio Park in St. Petersburg, Florida. Answering critics who decried the climate in Florida as not equal to that of Southern California, the ad claims, "From an exterior standpoint, it has hills, lakes and trees. For jungle, tropical and South Seas atmosphere, the conditions are perfect" (*Exhibitors Herald*, 1925).

It could not have been very perfect. Pinellas Films would die a quick death, but not before it managed to get a distribution deal with Associated Exhibitors, which released the film in January 1926, nearly a full year after filming was completed. Based on the novel by Richard Harding Davis, the film was the story of the White Mice Club, an organization dedicated to helping people in distress. Powell played Roddy Forrester, a charter member of the club, who is sent by his father to a Latin American country in order to free General Rojas, a former president of the island's overthrown republic, from prison. Of course, Roddy falls in love with the general's daughter Inez (Jacqueline Logan) and wins her love in return when he frees the general.

Unfortunately, the film did not make any kind of impression, and apparently only one 16 mm reel exists in a private collection. What is known is that Powell appears without a mustache in the film, possibly a nod to the popular conception in the 1920s that only villains donned them. Powell would have to shave again for his second heroic turn in 1925 for *My Lady's Lips*. Produced by B. P. Schulberg for his Preferred Pictures company, the film featured Schulberg's protégé, Clara Bow, in a small role.

The picture, which survives in the UCLA Film and Television Archive, is the rather tepid story of newspaper reporter Scott Seddon (Powell), who is dispatched by his editor, Forbes Lombard (Frank Keenan), to go undercover to investigate a criminal gang with which Forbes's daughter Lola (Bow) is consorting. Powell equips himself just fine in a mediocre film that does not feature him and Bow interacting nearly as much as one might hope. Ironically, he wears the mustache in his normal, everyday life as a reporter, and it is when he goes undercover as a heavy that he shaves it off. Of course Scott gets in too deep when he falls in love with gang leader Dora Blake (Alyce Mills), and the two are arrested and tortured by the police into signing confessions. When released from prison, Scott finds out that Dora has returned to crime, proposes to her, and they run off into the sunset together.

Released in July 1925, *My Lady's Lips* received mixed reviews although, as always, Powell received some praise. *Exhibitors Trade Review* (August 1925), for example, said "William Powell is well cast as the reporter, and almost succeeds in making the incredible portions of the film seem colored by realism." Unfortunately, the picture did not perform nearly well enough for Powell to have any hope of escaping his typecasting.

At his home at Paramount over the next several years, Powell oftentimes had little to do but grimace briefly, if *New York Times* critic Mordaunt Hall's reviews of his lost films are to be believed. He is often mentioned just as a footnote. In Hall's review of the lost *Aloma of the South Seas*, his lone mention of Powell comes at the end of the review: "William Powell is effective playing the scoundrel Van Templeton" (May 17, 1926). Then there was *Tin Gods*: "William Powell's characterization of Tony leaves nothing wanting" (September 20, 1926); *Love's Greatest Mistake*: "William Powell is effective as Don Kendall" (February 21, 1927); *The Beautiful City*: "William Powell makes the villainy as impressive as possible" (November 23, 1925); and *The Drag Net*: "William Powell does what he can to vitalize the character of Trent" (June 4, 1926).

Of the surviving features from this period, perhaps an apt example of Powell's typical roles comes in *Special Delivery*. It was the second (and final) of Ziegfeld Follies' comic Eddie Cantor's silent pictures. Here, Cantor plays Eddie Beagle, a mailman who is in love with Madge (Jobyna Ralston), who happens to be secretary to slimy Harold Jones (Powell), who proposes marriage to her literally every day. It turns out that Harold is secretly the infamous criminal known as Blackie Morgan, and now that the cops are closing in, he decides to take a boat to South America. Harold invites Madge to go with him, and she accepts the invitation because Eddie doesn't have the nerve to reveal his feelings. Of course Eddie learns that Harold is really Blackie, helps capture the villain, and finally reveals his feelings for Madge, which she happily reciprocates.

The picture is about an hour long, and Powell has about a minute of screen time in the first forty-five minutes in three brief scenes that establish very quickly his villainy, his lust for Madge, and his intent to sail for South America. Powell has some time to shine in the final act as he faces Cantor in a rollicking fistfight, finally getting arrested before he can sail to South America. Harold is a thankless, tiny part that could have been played sufficiently by anyone on the lot with a mustache, but Powell by this point was enough of an established heavy that exposition regarding any of his characters was moot. All he had to do was appear on screen for a few shots, and the audience immediately knew he was the heavy.

For a long-term contract player like Powell, this level of typecasting was not unusual. He just preferred not to think of it as typecasting. "You know, that's the important thing about screen acting," he said in 1925. "You have to be careful not to grow type-conscious, and to have a certain set of tricks for a heavy role and another set for a hero. No matter what kind of a part I play, I just try to act like that particular human being and let the story explain whether I'm good or bad" (Fergus, 1925).

What resulted was a naturalism in his acting that was absent in other screen villains. And while he was often stuck in films in which he was given little to do, Powell sometimes had the opportunity to do some outstanding work in supporting roles. One example was *Beau Geste*, a big-budget adaptation of P. C. Wren's novel of brothers joining the French Foreign Legion to hide the theft of a famous sapphire and fighting a hopeless battle against marauding Arabs.

Not only did the film give Powell the chance to work with his friend Ronald Colman again, here playing the title character, but allowed him to stretch his screen persona as a heavy with the character of Boldini. A craven opportunist who keeps rejoining the Legion, Boldini brings to mind the kind of character Peter Lorre would play in 1940s Warner Bros. movies. Boldini is a sniveling little man who, when he learns the Geste brothers have the sapphire in their possession, tells the brutish commandant (Noah Beery), who then plots to get his hands on the jewel by staging a counter-response to a planned mutiny that he hopes will leave no survivors to witness his theft. When Boldini loses his nerve and confesses the plot to Beau, the commandant essentially sentences Boldini to death by forcing him to stand at the top of a flag tower in plain sight of Arab marksmen.

By the time *Beau Geste* was released in August 1926, Powell's screen persona of a sophisticated, dashing, well-dressed villain was established. Here, he is the opposite. Boldini is vulgar, dirty, and desperate. Powell has Boldini crouching as low to ground level as possible, never standing upright, always slinking around like some kind of reptile, a creature driven entirely by fear as he tries desperately to ingratiate himself with whomever will listen.

Powell would be loaned to Fox Film a year later to appear in *Paid to Love*, directed by Howard Hawks. Released in August 1927, the picture is set in the fictional kingdom of San Savona, where King Leopold III (Thomas Jefferson) negotiates with American banker Peter Roberts (J. Farrell McDonald) for a badly needed loan. When Roberts learns Crown Prince Michael (George O'Brien) is only interested in automobiles and not marriage, he informs the king that his son's perpetual bachelorhood is a security risk for his loan. He and the king then head to Paris to find a beautiful woman to pique the prince's interest, and settle on bohemian performer Gaby (Virginia Valli). Through a series of convoluted events, Gaby ends up mistaking Michael's cousin Prince Eric (Powell) for the crown prince.

Powell is marvelous as the aristocratic, lecherous prince, dressed to the nines and even donning a monocle in a marvelous parody of Erich von Stroheim in *Foolish Wives*. The highlight of the film is Powell gleefully peeling a banana while leering at an oblivious Gaby undressing. Even viewing an awful print of the film, one can spot the joyful glint in Powell's eyes as Hawks cuts back and forth between shots of Gaby undressing and Powell peeling and peeling and then finally consuming the banana with a nearly obscene level of satisfaction.

Paid to Love is a delightful little picture and a bit of an outlier in Hawks's filmography because it feels more reminiscent of Ernst Lubitsch's European-set comedies than his own later penchant for purely American-set comedy. It is a pity that this would be the only time Powell would get to work with Hawks, who would later become a master of the screwball comedy with films like *Twentieth Century*, *Bringing Up Baby*, and *His Girl Friday*.

Perhaps the finest of all the silent films in which Powell appeared was Josef von Sternberg's *The Last Command*. Released in January 1928, the film featured the great German actor Emil Jannings as Grand Duke Sergius Alexander, a former general in the Russian Imperial Army, who now lives as a broken man with a noticeable tremor, offering his services as an extra in Hollywood. Powell is the director Leo Andreyev, who is making a Russian-themed war movie and casts the Grand Duke immediately upon seeing his headshot. We flash back to the Russian Revolution, where the Grand Duke leads the army and vainly tolerates the absurd whims of his cousin the Czar. Leo Andreyev, meanwhile, is the director of the Kief Imperial Theatre, who alongside his star actress Natalie Dobrova harbors the dreams of revolutionary revenge against the Czar and his imperialist stooges.

Through a series of unlikely events, Natalie falls in love with the Grand Duke, a man who stands against everything she believes, and she eventually sacrifices herself so he can escape the revolutionaries. Leo, meanwhile, has gone to prison and dreams of revenge, which we finally see on a film set where the frail Grand Duke is forced to re-create his own past. The emotional tables are turned, however, when the Grand Duke's impassioned and hysterical hallucinatory performance of enraged grief stuns Leo and the crew into admiration, until the great old general collapses and dies under the strain.

The reception to Powell's performance would be dwarfed by the rapturous response to Emil Jannings, who essentially plays a dual role as the Grand Duke in the midst of his glory days and then as the broken man in Hollywood. His performance, along with his role in his first American picture, *The Way of All Flesh* (now lost), would earn Jannings the first Best Actor Academy Award. It's easy to understand why; he is a towering presence in absolutely every way. But Powell more than holds his own. He is more than just a heavy here, and aptly personifies the frustration of a Russian people oppressed by the Imperial government. Much of the credit goes to von Sternberg, by far the best director at Paramount with whom Powell was fortunate to work. One moment in particular is electric: The Grand Duke slaps Leo, and von Sternberg cuts back and forth between the two men glaring at each other with supreme hatred. Powell is more than just a heavy here—he must stand as the representative for a people that cannot take any more, and he's excellent in the role.

When Powell completed filming *Forgotten Faces* in May 1928, he could not have known it would be his penultimate silent-film appearance. But the film industry in the spring of 1928 was in an unshakeable panic following the enormous success of Warner Bros.' *The Jazz Singer*, which had its world premiere the previous October. While the Al Jolson feature was mostly a silent film, the brief interludes of Jolson's singing and improvised patter created an unforeseen sensation that threatened the very existence of the film industry. Some studios were slower to embrace the sea change—MGM would be the final major studio to fully convert to all-talking pictures in 1930—but Paramount worked quickly to embrace the new realism, even if that meant ditching an entire movie and starting it from scratch.

That is exactly what happened with *Interference*, which began filming as a silent picture directed by Lothar Mendes in July 1928. Based on a play by Roland Pertwee and Harold Dearden, the picture was a melodrama about Deborah Kane (Evelyn Brent), who discovers her supposedly late ex-husband Phillip Voaze (Powell) happens to be alive and living under an assumed name. Kane then proceeds to blackmail Voaze's widow (Doris Kenyon), who has since remarried, threatening to reveal her inadvertent bigamy.

Filming was completed after twenty-six days in August 1928, and almost suddenly, in the midst of the talking picture panic, Paramount had a change of heart. The studio decided to start it over again as the studio's first all-talking picture. A special effects specialist who had never directed a film before, Roy J. Pomeroy (best known for engineering the parting of the Red Sea in DeMille's first version of *The Ten Commandments*), started filming over again just three weeks after production on the silent film ended, and a full talking picture was completed in ten days.

Released in December, *Interference* was greeted with raves. Judging by Mordaunt Hall's review in the *New York Times*, it would seem the mark of a great film at the beginning of the talking era was simply that the sounds were clear: "The ringing of a telephone bell was natural and so was the knock on a door," he marveled. "One even heard a pen scratching its way over the paper as Evelyn Brent wrote a missive with her left hand." Hall also noted that Powell was creditable in his role, even though he had to fill the shoes of "that brilliant actor, A. E. Matthews," who had created the role on stage (M. Hall, 1928).

Reading the enthusiastic reviews over ninety years later can be confusing to most contemporary readers, because the film is unquestionably dreadful. *Interference* was shot at the very dawn of the talking picture, when the newly motorized camera was confined to a soundproof booth and microphones were scattered throughout the set, necessitating blocking for the sole purpose of bringing the actors' mouths nearby. Shot almost entirely in medium shot on a single set with no camera movement and inevitably stiff performances by terri-fied actors, the film is nearly unwatchable, even when the context of its creation is understood.

For audiences who heard him talk for the first time at the end of 1928, however, William Powell was a glorious revelation. For modern audiences most familiar with his marvelous comic performances of the mid-1930s, it can hardly seem like he's the same man. His articulation is overly formal and he carries himself far too stiffly. Compared to co-star Clive Brook, however, who was such a staggeringly dull parody of a stuffy Englishman it seemed his head would explode if he smiled, Powell is practically Jerry Lewis. Most importantly, however, in 1928, his role in *Interference* quickly established Powell as an important commodity at Paramount Pictures. The level of terror and panic in Hollywood in 1928 could never be overstated, and the fact that Powell made such a considerable impression on critics, audiences, and the executives at Paramount meant he would at least stand a fighting chance at surviving the transition.

It was never a guarantee, however. Paramount, like the other studios, was quickly importing talent from the stage such as the Marx Brothers, Maurice Chevalier, Fredric March, and Ruth Chatterton, trying desperately to acquire talent to replace the silent stars who were suddenly unknown commodities. While the popular cliché is that many of the silent stars had terrible voices, the truth was often more economic. One of the first stars that Paramount dropped was Bebe Daniels, Powell's frequent co-star. Daniels could certainly talk and had a wonderful singing voice, but her contract was expensive, and the arrival of talking pictures provided the studio an ample excuse to save money by releasing her from her contract.

In many ways, Powell was the perfect new star. Interestingly, the real turning point in his career came before audiences ever heard his voice, with the April 1928 announcement that he would be cast as Philo Vance in Paramount's silent production of S. S. Van Dine's *The Canary Murder Case*, to be directed by Malcolm St. Clair (*Film Daily*, April 29, 1928). Not only did his casting represent his first leading role at his home studio, but it provided him with a high-profile part as one of the most famous literary characters of the late 1920s.

The character of Philo Vance is not well remembered today, certainly not as well as *The Thin Man*'s Nick Charles, but in 1928 he was America's most popular literary detective. After suffering a nervous breakdown in 1925, an American art critic named Willard Huntington Wright casually decided during his recovery period to try his hand at writing detective stories. Taking on the pseudonym of S. S. Van Dine, he created the character of Vance and wrote his first novel, *The Benson Murder Case*, which was an enormous success when published in 1926. Other Vance novels—*The Canary Murder Case*, *The Greene Murder Case*, and *The Bishop Murder Case*—quickly followed and were also smash hits, immediately making Wright the most financially successful detective fiction author of all time.

The novels featured Wright (as Van Dine) as narrator and companion to Vance. Van Dine was a completely passive character who never interacted with any of the other characters in the story except for Vance, so the narrator was an easy character to cut in the movie versions. For those familiar with Powell's muted portrayal of Vance, the novels can be a bit of a surprise. Vance is an aesthete, an obsessive art collector, an aristocrat, and one of the most insufferable characters in detective fiction history, with a level of antisocial arrogance that makes Sherlock Holmes seem like a social butterfly.

Modern editions of the novels label Vance as "the sleuth you love to hate," and it's hard not to hate him. He delights in playing mind games with the people he's purporting to help solve crimes. Throughout the first novel, *The Benson Murder Case*, Vance relentlessly mocks New York District Attorney Markham, taking him on wild goose chases to find the guilty party while teasing the baffled DA that he knows exactly who the murderer is. He never explains something in a sentence when he can explain it in a paragraph littered with Latin quotes, and Van Dine makes his faux British mannerisms even more insufferable by littering apostrophes throughout his dialogue.

It is not hard to imagine why Paramount softened the Philo Vance character. It would be difficult to get audiences behind such a completely unlikable hero. And at least at first, Paramount didn't have to deal with Vance's smug babbling, because *The Canary Murder Case* was first announced as a silent film.

With a cast including Eugene Pallette as Sergeant Heath (the cop who is constantly outwitted by Vance) and Louise Brooks as the murder victim, *The Canary Murder Case* had a quick, incident-free twenty-seven-day shoot that completed filming on October 11, 1928. However, like the studio had done with *Interference*, Paramount decided to transform the film into an all-talking picture. But instead of starting all over again this time, the studio instead decided to overdub existing silent footage with dialogue as well as shoot some new scenes (Canary Murder Case Production Files, 1928).

Brooks, who had already caused much consternation at the studio with her refusal to conform to strict studio dictates, had left for Germany in the interim to star as Lulu in G. W. Pabst's *Pandora's Box*. When called by Paramount to return to the states for retakes, Brooks refused, and the studio ultimately hired Margaret Livingston to act as Brooks's voice and stand in for some new sequences awkwardly shot from behind. Today, the film is better known as the one that ended Louise Brooks's Hollywood career than the one that started Powell's career as a leading man, although ironically the two films she shot with Pabst in Germany have secured her immortality far more than *The Canary Murder Case* ever could have done (Paris, 2000).

Released in February 1929, *The Canary Murder Case* was the first of three Vance films that Powell would make at Paramount. While the silent sequences in the first film were directed by Malcolm St. Clair, the talking portions of the film were directed by Frank Tuttle, who would go on to direct the second and third pictures, *The Greene Murder Case* (released in August 1929) and *The Bishop Murder Case* (released in April 1930). While Tuttle had equipped himself adequately as a craftsman, directing over a dozen silent films for Paramount since 1924, he showed absolutely none of the skill at making talking pictures demonstrated by his contemporaries at Paramount, including Dorothy Arzner, Josef con Sternberg, Rouben Mamoulian, and Ernst Lubitsch.

Perhaps the greatest tragedy for Powell in his early talking pictures at Paramount is that he never got to work with the studio's best directors. His frequent co-star Clara Bow was also saddled with Tuttle as a director in many of her early films, and the career of the fragile star—who was terrified of the microphone—did not survive (Stenn, 2000). Powell, however, did survive.

As Vance, Powell is a tuxedoed, dignified, restrained gentleman who is unfailingly polite and patient with the blowhard Sergeant Heath. Heath was played by Eugene Pallette, an accomplished silent character actor whose appeal reached new heights once audiences heard his extraordinary froggy voice. Powell is charming, the opposite of the Philo Vance portrayed in the books. Powell's Vance retains the literary character's belief in the importance of investigating the psychology of the criminal in detective work instead of simply relying on physical evidence (one could say he is American literature's first criminal profiler), but dispenses with the unpleasant personality.

One reason for jettisoning Vance's unpleasantness is simply utilitarian from an adaptation perspective. The literary Vance tended to babble endlessly in order to make a single point he could have easily summed up in a simple sentence or two. While his insufferable rantings can be amusing at times in the novels, they would undoubtedly bring the films to a grinding halt. And of course, especially in the classic film era, it simply wouldn't do to have a main character the audience is supposed to despise.

All of this helped Powell immeasurably in the transformation of his screen persona from silent-film heavy and gave his career new life. Not only was he a fresh new star who could demonstrate his ability to speak and be a charming gentleman, the Vance films also essentially created an entirely new cinematic genre: the detective story. Dialogue was an absolute necessity in order to get the audience fully involved in the detective's interrogation of suspects, demonstration of his methodology, and eventual solving of the crime.

Even though the Vance films are undeniably wooden early talkies, they did feature something new beyond just the novelty of people talking. Powell had finally emerged from years of typecasting as the heavy and could finally be the hero of pictures going forward.

While other supporting appearances were still coming in forgettable early talkies such as *Charming Sinners* and *Behind the Make-Up*, Powell's appearance as Philo Vance in *The Canary Murder Case* was successful enough that Paramount announced in June 1929 that Powell would be a star in the studio's 1929–1930 season. It took nearly twenty years, but a star was finally born.

3

THE VAMP

While William Powell was emerging as a heavy, Myrna Williams's life would change forever thanks to four immigrant Eastern European Jews named Albert, Harry, Sam, and Jack Warner. After years as successful exhibitors, in 1918 the brothers began producing films and formally incorporated Warner Bros. in 1923. The company launched immediately into an aggressive production schedule, producing thirty features over the next two years, signing actor John Barrymore and director Ernst Lubitsch to multipicture contracts, and buying the Vitagraph studio in Brooklyn and its thirty-four distribution exchanges.

Two early hires were key in the success of the new studio. In 1924, Darryl F. Zanuck was signed to write pictures for Rin Tin Tin, a charismatic German shepherd and the studio's first star. The twenty-two-year-old writer was extraordinarily fast and efficient and a nonstop workaholic who would eventually graduate to head of production. Also signed was Hal B. Wallis, who took over the brothers' publicity department in 1922 after managing their Garrick Theater in Wilmington, Delaware. Wallis developed keen marketing skills and eventually became a top executive at the studio, served as executive assistant and an extraordinarily successful producer for decades, and was responsible for everything from *Little Caesar* (1930) to *Casablanca* (1942) to the original version of *True Grit* (1969). It was Hal Wallis's sister Minna that Loy credited for ultimately getting her first movie contract with Warner Bros. (Leider, 2011).

Minna Wallis's place in film history is often unappreciated. She was Jack Warner's secretary when she recommended her brother Hal as a theater manager, and would eventually become a respected talent agent who was credited for discovering Clark Gable, among others.

Quoted in Loy's autobiography before her death in August 1986 at age ninety-three, Minna said she furtively inserted Myrna Williams in a movie (likely *The Love Toy*) as an extra standing next to star Lowell Sherman after being blown away by a series of photographs of the young beauty. "A couple of days later, when the rushes were ready, I went down to the projection room with Jack Warner and my brother," Minna said. "When the close-up of Lowell came on, they both noticed the girl."

"'Who's that next to Sherman?' Jack said. 'It's a girl I'd like to put under contract,' I told him. 'Sign her,' he said. 'Fast!'" (Loy, 1988).

Alma Young, a script supervisor at Warners, would credit investment banker Motley Flint, one of Warners' biggest financial backers and an alleged admirer of Myrna, for convincing Jack Warner to sign her, but Loy's biographer Emily W. Leider said that even if Flint had convinced Warner to sign Myrna due to his almost certainly unrequited affection for her, it was still Minna Wallis who was ultimately responsible for getting the contract done (Leider, 2011).

Either way, Myrna Williams, who by now had adopted a new surname of "Loy" because it sounded more exotic than "Williams," was in the perfect place at the perfect time. Despite Warner Bros.' aggressive efforts to ramp up production, the studio lacked stars, along with a reliable stable of contract players who could fit within certain character types. Wallis and Warner Bros. decided that the young woman fulfilled their need for a vamp. Loy signed her seven-year contract in July 1925.

Appearing in the press in August 1925 was the breathless news that Warner Bros. has signed a "new" type of vamp, likely in reaction to the public losing its appetite for the "old" type of vamp, personified in Theda Bara. Bara had been the industry's first vamp ten years earlier, sweeping men off their feet and titillating audiences with skimpy costumes and a vaguely Eastern European appearance before her studio, Fox Film Co., burned out audiences by starring her in an unending succession of mediocre costume dramas in the 1910s. Myrna Loy's new studio was intent on emphasizing that this vamp was *not* the same old tired Theda Bara type.

"The 1926 model in vampires!! As others catering to the public put out yearly models to catch the eye, Warner Bros. of the motion picture industry, have advanced the styles in the way of vampires," the ads hyperventilated.

Warner Bros. in signing Myrna Loy believe that have a type that is entirely new. Motion picture vampires and their types have changed in public favor during the past five years as many times as the heroines and heros [*sic*]. It is tradition that she be of a tall svelt [*sic*] figure, olive complexion, blue black hair and black come-hither eyes. That was the model of 1920. Today in the bobbed hair era a more finished type of girl is holding sway. Miss Loy is of medium build but possessed of oriental features, with a very white complexion, high cheek bones and slightly slanting eyes but crowned with a Cleopatra touch—red hair—but of course cut in the ultra boyish bob revealing the ears. (*Marysville Appeal*, 1926)

Loy was immediately put to work. She would appear in twelve pictures in 1926 alone. Some of her appearances would be extremely fleeting. In Ernst Lubitsch's *So This Is Paris*, released in February, she appears for only a few seconds, playing a servant who opens a door for a guest, closes it, exits, and then is never seen again. The Lubitsch film is sadly one of only four of her pictures that year that survives. Films with fascinating titles like *Why Girls Go Back Home* and *The Gilded Highway* are seemingly lost forever. By all accounts, Loy did get to do more than just open a door in some of these films.

In *Why Girls Go Back Home*, released in May, Loy was fourth-billed as New York actress Sally Short. When small-town girl Marie (Patsy Ruth Miller) follows actor Clifford Dudley (Clive Brook) to New York, Sally helps Marie become a chorus girl, at which point Marie gets on the front page by falsely announcing she's engaged to Clifford. Laurence Reid in his review for *Motion Picture News* wrote that "a first-rate bit of acting is contributed by Myrna Loy, who has that 'It' or what Elinor Glyn calls personality" (L. Reid, October 16, 1926).

Among the four existing 1926 films in which Loy appeared, *Don Juan* is by far the best known, and while no one knew it at the time, it was the first step toward the end of silent films. The previous year, Warners had announced its commitment to talking pictures, and in April the studio formed a partnership with Western Electric to form the Vitaphone Corporation. Most of what had come from Vitaphone in its first months were one- and two-reel shorts featuring Broadway and vaudeville performers, singers, and a multitude of other acts, filmed in the Vitagraph studios in New York and overseen by Sam Warner.

Sam's ambitions for the product grew, and eventually the studio decided to release an entire feature film with a soundtrack consisting of some sound effects and a score performed by the New York Philharmonic Orchestra. Warner Bros. had not considered all-talking pictures by this point, believing it would be advantageous to be able to supply small theaters with the kinds of orchestral scores that were solely reserved for the big-city movie palaces. All the theaters needed was the absurdly bulky Vitaphone projector, which included a turntable for discs that would be synchronized to the projector. While the disc system would be supplanted by sound on film within a few years, Vitaphone would represent an enormous windfall for Warners and transform the film industry forever.

Released in August 1926, *Don Juan* starred John Barrymore as the great Spanish lover, coming up against the evil Lucretia Borgia (Estelle Taylor) in fifteenth-century Rome. Loy played Lucretia's lady-in-waiting Maia, a clever spy who knows all the intimate gossip in the city and passes it along to her mistress. When Maia alerts her that the infamous Don Juan is in the city, Lucrezia decides she must have the great lover to herself.

Loy slinks along in ornate costumes that cover absolutely everything head to toe except for her face, and while the makeup and lighting make Loy unrecognizable as the star she would become in the 1930s, she makes a striking and mysterious presence. Hovering in the background throughout the picture, always visible over one of Lucrezia's shoulders, sometimes in focus, usually not, her constant leering presence makes the viewer uneasy. With little to do but lean into Lucrezia and whisper secrets, the appeal of Loy as a young performer is clear. Better things would come, and soon.

Myrna Loy as Maia in *Don Juan* (1926). Directed by Alan Crosland. *Author's Collection*

Released a month after *Don Juan*, *Across the Pacific* featured Loy in her first substantial role, third-billed after Monte Blue and Jane Winton. It would be the first time she played a native girl, a half-caste Filipino spy named Roma who falls in love with American spy Monte during the Spanish-American War. The picture represented a significant turning point in Loy's career. Adorned in a two-piece sarong displaying plenty of skin, Loy received plenty of good notices. In *Motion Picture News*, a mixed review of the film by Laurence Reid noted that "on the credit side, however, are a series of melodramatic scenes and some romantic ones which should stir a sluggish pulse—particularly when Monte Blue and Myrna Loy have the spotlight" (Reid, October 16, 1926). *Photoplay*'s anonymous review (December 1926) exulted, "Watch Myrna Loy! Give the little girl a big hand! She's good."

Unfortunately, the success of the role resulted in Loy being immediately typecast as an "exotic" type. Loy would lament in later years that once Darryl F. Zanuck, the screenwriter for *Across the Pacific*, gained power at the studio later, he could only see her in that kind of role (Loy, 1988). However, because Loy was needed in so many pictures and not every picture had that kind of "exotic" character, it meant she was able to enjoy at least a little bit of variety in the more than two dozen films she would appear in over the next three years. Some appearances in films like *The Third Degree* and *When a Man Loves* would be bit roles, but others would give her more things to do.

In 1927, her second year on the Warners lot, Loy appeared in nine films. Unfortunately, five are completely lost, two exist in partial form, and only two exist in complete form. One of the lost films gave Loy the opportunity for her first leading role that called for her to be something other than an exotic vixen. In *The Girl from Chicago*, released in November, Loy played Mary Carlton, a sweet Southern belle who receives a letter from her brother Bob in New York: He is about to face the electric chair for a crime he didn't commit. When Mary heads to New York and learns her brother has been mixed up with the underworld, she tries to root out the truth by posing as a gangster's moll from Chicago and insinuating herself into the world of gangster Handsome Joe (Conrad Nagel). Eventually, Handsome turns out to be an undercover detective himself, and he and Mary beat the gangsters and clear Bob's name.

It was an opportunity for Loy to stretch herself and parody her own "vamp" image by playing a sweet young girl simply pretending to be a vamp. However, even this early in her career, some critics could only see her as the dark and mysterious type. An uncredited review in the *Chicago Daily Tribune* (November 8, 1927) claimed, "Myrna Loy, in the title role, is the only one miscast, and she is utterly out of frame. Her work is conscientious BUT—where Myrna shines is as an adventuress of the subtle and dangerous type, NOT as the sheltered southern beauty she endeavors to portray in this film. She knows her line—and when she has ventured outside it. You can sense the discomfort Mary Carlton gives her. (Stunning looking creature!)" Others were kinder. *Motion Picture World* (December 24, 1927) noted, "Myrna Loy has a certain fragile beauty that passes muster."

While being cast in a lead role would seem to portend some kind of progress in the roles Loy would receive, she was simply a cog in the studio machine who had to take every role the studio assigned to her. For example, in 1927 she also appeared in *Ham and Eggs at the Front,* a blackface parody of the popular World War I drama, *What Price Glory?*

"How could I ever have put on blackface?" Loy would recall sixty years later. "When I think of it now, it horrifies me. Well, our awareness broadens, thank God! It was a tasteless slapstick comedy that I mercifully recall very little about" (Loy, 1988). Just as mercifully, the film is now lost.

By the beginning of 1928 Loy was seeing the first glimmers of recognition in the press. *Picture Play* in January 1928 recommended movie fans to "turn to Myrna Loy. She is regarded in film circles as a treat for those picture-goers who are becoming jaded from beholding too much similarity among the dazzling screen stars. Myrna is truly different and exotic, for the suggestion of the Orient that lies in her name also seems to hover over her film personality."

The timing was fortuitous. Warner Bros. was committed to talking pictures, and by the beginning of 1928, most of the silent films they produced were at least partial talkies, featuring perhaps one or two scenes of dialogue. Because audiences did not have any long-lasting preconceived notions about Loy's screen personality, she did not have nearly as much at stake as the big silent movie stars like John Gilbert or Greta Garbo. The studios and audiences waited with bated breath to hear whether their beloved stars had the voices to match their screen personas. Gilbert, a swashbuckling romantic lover on screen, did not possess the manly baritone that audiences expected, while Garbo, the tragic heroine, had an alto in a Swedish accent that perfectly matched her screen persona's world weariness. Gilbert crashed and burned, and Garbo became a bigger star than ever.

Loy's obscurity meant she had just as much opportunity to succeed as any of the throng of stage performers that Hollywood was recruiting for the new talkies. Still, she was terrified. Making pictures had suddenly become a technical nightmare, with microphones hidden throughout the set and the camera operator stuck in a soundproof booth that prevented any camera movement.

"We had a terrible time making those half-talkies," Loy would later say. "We were terribly conscious of the microphones hidden all over the set—in the flowers, under the furniture, everywhere." Loy noted with regret that the studio never gave stars like Patsy Ruth Miller and Marie Prevost a chance, not even employing a voice coach, something that Loy felt very fortunate to have had while still in school (Loy, 1988).

One of those half-talkies was *State Street Sadie,* released by Warner Bros. in August 1928. Sadly another one of Loy's lost features, the film paired her once again with Conrad Nagel, her co-star from *The Girl from Chicago.* In addition to that film's co-stars, the new film plucked much of its plot from *The Girl from Chicago.* While in the former film, Loy's character posed as a gangster's moll to clear her brother of a murder charge, this time her character posed as a gangster's moll to try to avenge the murder of her police officer father.

Critics were unimpressed with the picture, and they were beginning to tire of the novelty of sound as well. Herbert Cruikshank in *Motion Picture Magazine* said in a 1928 review that "folk familiar with 'Vitaphone' productions are already becoming blasé and bored with a production so utterly mediocre as *State Street Sadie.* Of course, any sound film is interesting in these days of the lightning-like development of the new medium. But the day is almost here when there will have to be pictures as well as sound to provide the entertainment for which the patrons of picture theaters are constantly shopping."

Noting also that "the dialogue is scarce worthy of mention" and "it is a moronic product decidedly devoid of merit," Cruikshank mentions that while Loy is attractive as always, "she speaks in but one sequence, and her voice in this is scarcely even audible" (Cruikshank, 1928). He then suggests the construction of theaters with better acoustics.

Not all of Loy's films in 1928 were partial talkies. Also in that year, she was loaned out to Samuel Sax's Poverty Row studio, Gotham Productions, for an adaptation of Edward E. Rose's play *Turn Back the Hours.* It is one of Loy's few surviving silent features in which she has a lead role, albeit in a badly damaged print in the UCLA Film and Television Archive. While she is again typecast as an exotic creature, here she is undeniably the heroine. In the film, Walter Pidgeon plays Ensign Phillip Drake, a sailor who is facing court-martial for cowardice, and the film opens with him standing humiliated as his buttons and badges are torn off his uniform. He shortly thereafter escapes and stows away on a ship bound for Las Cruces Island. Waiting there is the beautiful Tiza Torreon (Loy), an exotic tropical flower, eager for the sunshine of romance.

After a disaster hits the ship, Tiza spots Phillip in a life ring, rescues him, and is immediately besotted. She takes him to a party at the Torreon hacienda, where she lives with her father, formerly a prominent New Orleans gentleman.

Loy is perfectly charming in the role of Tiza, and while the role itself inhabits the unfortunate condescending racism of the era by making her so staggeringly naïve, what we see in the young Loy here is a refreshing change from the evil harpies for which she is best known in her formative years. In one lovely little scene, she notices Phillip needs a shave, and the intertitles show Tiza telling him, "I'll do it. I've always wanted to shave someone!" She's enthusiastic about everything! What results are some lovely comic moments as Tiza ineptly applies the cream, getting it all over Phillip's mouth and eyes. As a keepsake, she gives him a necklace adorned with a Badge of Courage.

A dark shadow, however, soon descends in the form of Ace Kearney (Sam Hardy), who the natives call "Diablo," an appropriately terrible fiend who wishes to conquer the island, crush the elder Torreon and, of course, take Tiza as his bride. When Ace shows up at the Torreon hacienda and threatens Tiza's father, Phillip does nothing, frozen by fear. Witnessing his cowardice firsthand, Tiza is outraged—"Why don't you do something??"—and in a nice dramatic moment, tears the necklace off his chest and confronts Ace herself.

Eventually, of course, Phillip finds his manly courage and saves the day, but rather than make Tiza the quivering weak female waiting for her man to save her, she is a surprisingly strong character given the assumptions about the silent era, and even once proclaims to her friends at the hacienda when Phillip abandons her: "I myself will lead you!!"

While the film itself—running less than an hour—is fairly straightforward, Loy is a revelation. Given the number of films from this period that are lost, it is impossible to give a declaration that it's the best of her silent film parts, but it is difficult to imagine a better one. Loy subverts whatever expectations there may have been at the time regarding her screen persona. Here she gets to be an action hero.

These kinds of opportunities were often confined to loan-outs to independent producers. Back at the major studios, Loy was mostly still relegated to offensive ethnic parts, usually exotic, oftentimes tragic. Loaned out to Fox for Howard Hawks's *A Girl in Every Port*, Loy played a Chinese woman for the first time, and would do so again in *The Crimson City*, in which she plays a love slave who commits suicide by jumping off a ship, a stunt that got Loy nearly drowned herself (Loy, 1988).

That kind of near-tragic accident reflected the working conditions a contract player like Loy faced in 1928, waking at 5:30 a.m. six days a week in order to have the excessive makeup she was forced to wear applied to her face, and then working through the night. While the conditions were severe, Loy was making $500 a week by this time, a salary that would be increased to $700 a week the next year, far above any amount of money she could have imagined as an aspiring dancer a few short years before (Leider, 2011).

Despite the money, and the house and the car she was able to buy, Loy was not necessarily happy. One of the earliest significant profiles of Loy appeared in the June 1929 issue of *Picture Play* by Margaret Reid, and it is striking to see how early in her career Loy publicly expressed unhappiness with the roles she was getting. In the article entitled "She Pays the Penalty," Reid writes that Loy was "beginning to feel uneasy. Her parts have increased in importance until she is a featured player. The roles are bigger, but in the main just as bad as ever."

She quotes Loy:

I've been a contract player for three years, and I still haven't done a picture to which I can point with pride. Two of three incidental parts have been good—the native girl in "Across the Pacific," an episode in Victor McLaglen's "A Girl in Every Port," which was a little gem of a tragedy and had to be cut out, because it killed the laughs, the lady-in-waiting in "Don Juan," which was fun to do. Outside of those I hide my head in shame.

But I'm not asking for the impossible. All I ask is that a part be consistent. No part can be completely dull if it is an accurate picture of a human being. The principal satisfaction in acting is taking a word picture of a person and making it live and breathe. Most of the roles I've had have been so appallingly inconsistent, so painfully fictitious, that nothing could be done with them. And I don't derive enough pleasure, otherwise, out of my profession to be content to just stand in front of a camera, and open my mouth and turn my head when the director tells me. (M. Reid, 1929)

Late in 1928, Loy fought for a role for the first time. The Warners bought the rights to the Sigmund Romberg–Oscar Hammerstein II operetta *The Desert Song* and decided to make it the first full all-talking, all-singing musical film with Technicolor sequences. The original Broadway production had just completed a very successful run of 465 performances, entrancing audiences and critics alike. It was the story of the Riffs, a band of Arab rebels fighting the French, and the "Red Shadow," the Frenchman who leads the Riffs. Loy wanted to play Azuri, the native dancing girl who knows the true identity of the Red Shadow. While the character fit well within the racist caricatures that the studio thought suitable for Loy, it would represent her showiest part yet, and she said in a September 1929 interview in *Photoplay* that the studio resisted the idea.

"It required a great deal of persuasion for me to get the role," she said. "They were afraid to give me my chance. The role of Azuri was difficult and dramatic. I lacked experience and I would be a member of a cast which knew all the tricks of the stage.

"I kept right on insisting," Loy continued, "and at last, with many misgivings, they told me I could have the role. I felt that they had given it to me against their better judgment, and that now I had to show them. It wasn't easy to work with that feeling" (Colman, 1929).

Loy did get the part, and despite its small size, she was billed third behind John Boles as the Red Shadow and Louise Fazenda in the comic role of Susan. Loy got the chance to wear skimpy costumes, speak in a vague accent, and even dance. It is a showy yet small part, and contemporary critics did not mention her at length.

In 1929, Loy would land a bigger, even more showy part than Azuri in *The Squall*, based on a 1926 play by Jean Bart. In the film adaptation, she plays an amoral gypsy named Nubi, who manages to pick her way through the hapless men of the Lajos family one by one, seducing them and tossing them aside like yesterday's trash.

Myrna Loy as Nubi in *The Squall* (1929). Directed by Alexander Korda. *Author's Collection*

"At first, I was not at all anxious to do Nubi. I had seen the play, and had not liked it, and such a person as Nubi, with every male in the cast falling into a faint when she looked at him, never existed," Loy said in *Picture Play*.

Then I decided that since nothing could make her human, I'd try to make her symbolic—a symbol of the various suppressed desires of the men about her, and a symbol of the conflict among them, of the storm, the squall. It was the only way of injecting any reason into her, but I don't know whether or not I got it across. Maybe when the picture comes out, I'll find it's just another dark-skinned wench with bad intentions. (M. Reid, 1929)

Released in May 1929, *The Squall* was directed by Hungarian émigré Alexander Korda. It is a fascinating, if aesthetically terrible, artifact of the kinds of absurd roles Myrna Loy was forced to play. In light of her expressed intention on how to play the role, *The Squall* presents a unique case study of Loy's performance style this early in her career.

Set in Hungary on the idyllic farm estate of Josef Lajos, the film is set on the wedding anniversary of Lajos and his idyllic wife Maria (Alice Joyce), the day they also grant their idyllic son Paul (Carroll Nye) his wish to marry his idyllic sweetheart Irma (a sixteen-year-old Loretta Young) after his studies are complete. As their happy-go-lucky workers finish the season's idyllic harvest, a band of gypsies arrive, which thrills Irma, who decides she wants her fortune told.

As the family sits for dinner, a literal and metaphorical squall arrives. As thunder crashes outside, Nubi the Gypsy (Loy) stumbles into the house, screaming in a vague accent, referring to herself in the third person, insisting that she is not a gypsy and that "El Moro" wants to kill her. The innocent and naïve family immediately buys her story and hides her in the cellar as El Moro enters looking for her. Despite the entreating and racist warnings of the suspicious Uncle Dani (Knute Erickson), Maria is sufficiently convinced of Nubi's honesty in about forty-five seconds that she agrees to take in the gypsy permanently as a servant.

Adorned in rags with a blouse seductively revealing one shoulder, her skin darkened, her hair an unruly mess, Loy goes whole hog, delivering a hysterically unhinged monologue out the front door as the gypsy wagons ride off into the distance. As she does so, Paul and family servant Peter can barely disguise their naked lust, and both succumb to her wiles immediately. Paul forgets all about Irma and his studies, and the servant Peter is driven insane by his passion for Nubi; Josef kicks him out when he catches Peter trying to rape her.

This being 1929, Josef blames Nubi for leading Peter on. Nubi replies, "I not want to take him. He want to take me! Always the man want Nubi and always she get the blame for the trouble. Can Nubi help if she be beautiful?" Loy delivers the line with feigned innocence, wriggling her body the whole time to make it perfectly clear to everyone in the audience (but no one in this extraordinarily idiotic family) that she doesn't mean a single thing she says.

Making things even more absurd is how much more at ease Loy is with talking pictures than her co-stars. Actors Alice Joyce and Carroll Nye are especially dreadful, delivering their silly dialogue at a sloth-like pace, and scenes between Maria and her son Paul seem to go on for hours. If Loy represents the tempest, the members of the family seemed to represent dead bodies in graves after the tempest has passed. Their performances certainly reinforce this idea.

The one thing that is readily apparent is that Loy is having a ball. Having made her choice not to take the character of Nubi at all seriously, she heightens her performance to the level of artful camp, not only because she delivers the ridiculous dialogue and broken English with glee, but because her performance—compared to the deeply uncomfortable actors around her—sticks out so completely.

While one may think the ludicrousness of the film is simply due to hindsight and nearly a hundred years of advancement in the art of cinema, reviewers at the time also thought the whole thing was ridiculous. "This film just doesn't click, that's all," said a review in *Photoplay* (June 1929). "And it's unconsciously funny."

And Loy did have a good time: "Interviewers often assume that I had a miserable time playing all those evil creatures, all those women with knives in their teeth. Not at all. I can't say that things came easily—it took a long, long time to find my real niche—but those roles were fun to play, despite their unreality" (Loy, 1988).

Most of Loy's early talking roles were equally unreal, and some of them remain fun, albeit guiltily so for modern audiences aware of the absurd inherent racism in them. Later in 1929, Loy was loaned out to Fox Film for John Ford's debut talking picture, *The Black Watch*, an epic tale of Captain Donald Gordon King (Victor McLaglen), a member of the British Army's Scottish Black Watch division, who is sent on a secret mission to the Khyber Pass to stave off a revolt by worming his way into the heart of Yasmani (Loy), the leader of the revolt who is seen by her followers as a goddess.

The film benefits from the professionalism of Ford, who with director of photography Joseph H. August produces one of the most gorgeous-looking early talkies. Unfortunately, McLaglen, Loy, and all the other actors enunciate their dialogue at such a glacial pace that the film gives the impression that the film would only be about fifteen minutes long if the actors were permitted to speak at a normal pace. There is also little of the camp appeal of films like *The*

Squall. Ford admitted later that he knew little of how to direct dialogue at the time, and while he would remedy that in no time at all, it is still a film that is difficult to watch even as it is a wonder to behold.

More along the lines of camp was *The Great Divide*. Released by First National in September 1929 and the third version of a novel by William Vaughn Moody, *The Great Divide* was directed by Reginald Barker, who had directed the most recent silent version for MGM in 1925. Loy plays Manuella, a Mexican girl who is madly and peculiarly in love with Stephen Ghent, a mine owner played by Ian Keith. She is one of the first characters we see on screen, waiting for Stephen in his house, eager to provide him with her love, while he dismisses her adoration as the rantings of a child.

"I am no child. I am woman. I am jour beautiful Senorita. And choo are my grand caballero!" It is a cringing line that Loy delivers with all the game enthusiasm she possessed in her portrayal of Nubi, and once again she wipes the screen with her co-star. Keith is undeniably wooden, and while he would prove to be a reliable supporting actor, particularly in Cecil B. DeMille films in later years, he was no leading man.

Even though Loy's Manuella disappears off-screen for long stretches of the film, it's hard to forget her. The nominal female lead of the film is Dorothy Mackaill, who plays spoiled party girl Ruth Gordon. Mackaill had a world-weary quality that was particularly suited for Warner Bros.–First National Pictures' pre-Code movies. Here, her performance is unpolished given her lack of experience with talkies, and she does the best she can with the material. Her character attends a party and sees Stephen, mistaking him for a Mexican, so Stephen plays along, eventually seducing her in a really bad fake accent until Manuella appears again, forcing Stephen to scold her in his real American voice.

Loy's other big moment takes place during the party scene, which includes a couple of pointless musical numbers that required both Loy and Ian Keith to poorly lip-sync to operatic voices. She does best during the dance sequence, where she clearly seems far more at home. Her final film of 1929, released in November, allowed audiences to witness her skill again in the variety revue *Show of Shows*, which was the Warners' version of the type of revue the major studios had popularized at the beginning of the talking era. Emceed by Frank Fay, *Show of Shows* was simply a series of sketches and musical numbers featuring studio contract players. Loy's main feature was "Chinese Fantasy," introduced by canine superstar Rin Tin Tin, showing her dancing accompanied by Nick Lucas singing "Li-Po-Li." It is an amusing enough showcase, but it highlights Loy's talent in the musical genre that audiences would quickly tire of. By the beginning of 1930, "musical" was a dirty word in Hollywood.

Loy would still be searching for her niche as an actor in 1930. That year, she would appear in an extraordinary eleven films, including *Under the Texas Moon*, a two-color Technicolor Western featuring Frank Fay inexplicably cast as a romantic lead and Loy as yet another jealous Mexican, and now-lost films with titles like *Isle of Escape*, *Cock o' the Walk*, *Bride of the Regiment*, and *The Jazz Cinderella*.

By October 1930, Loy had appeared in forty-eight films and reached a significant turning point in her career when Warner Bros. loaned her to Fox for the picture that would result in her eventually switching studios. Directed by Victor Fleming, *Renegades* was the latest of many retreads produced at the time of *Beau Geste*, featuring the then-ubiquitous trope of emotionally scarred men of multiple nationalities joining the French Foreign Legion and gathering in the desert to fight Arabs.

Warner Baxter, then one of the busiest leading men at Fox, portrays Deucalion, a Frenchman in the Legion who has been betrayed by evil spy Eleanor, yet another one of Loy's hot-headed mixed-race temptresses. After Deucalion flees the Legionnaires, he becomes the omnipotent military leader of a tribe led by Arab leader The Maribout (Bela Lugosi), kidnaps Eleanore, and treats her cruelly as a servant. Soon afterwards, Eleanor plots her own revenge by seducing The Marabout, the Arabs attack the Legionnaires, and a spontaneously reformed Deucalion sacrifices his life to save the Legionnaires from the Arabs.

No synopsis can really do the goofy thing justice. It makes for fascinating viewing, as it is another example of Loy throwing herself shamelessly into the role of the vengeful harpy with unlimited aplomb. She is delightfully trashy, and any viewer who knows her only as Nora Charles would likely be surprised by seeing an unhinged Loy at the end of the picture screaming "TEAR THEM TO PIECES," her eyes aflame with orgiastic pleasure as she directs her fellow villains to spray bullets everywhere with their oversized machine guns.

By the end, after a mortally wounded Eleanor crawls toward Deucalion and shoots him dead—point blank—before finally expiring herself, one gets the distinct impression that Loy can't possibly do anything more with the exotic vamp character. Indeed, the roles into which she was cast would begin to move away from the racist trope.

In her very next film, *The Truth About Youth*, released by Warner Bros. in November 1930, Loy plays a notorious nightclub singer named Kara, who is dubbed "The Firefly" and spoken of in hushed tones as if she's Mae West. Poor Loy is forced to dance in skimpy costumes and lip-sync poorly to a singer who sounds not dissimilar to Mae West. It is the first of two films in two months in which Loy would share the screen with seventeen-year-old Loretta Young, who played well above her years at this point in her career.

Here, Young plays Phyllis Ericson, engaged to Richard Dane (David Manners), known by everyone as "The Imp" for some unexplained reason. Unfortunately, The Imp is obsessed with The Firefly, who pursues him believing he is wealthy. It is only after they're married that The Firefly learns The Imp is not wealthy at all!

"You're not RICH? Surely you're joking!" Loy gives it her all in this scene, becoming rather hysterical with greed. She screams, "Get your hands off me, you dirty little rat!!" as he tries to convince her money doesn't matter, and then proceeds to give him a rather impressive double slap. While Loy is again able to chew the scenery, now the upper-class setting allows her to act at least slightly more human, and it turns out to be a milieu in which she fits rather naturally. While Loy was certainly not plausible as a Mae West–like nightclub singer, she was plausible as an ambitious young woman trying to climb the ladder to wealth among society.

Remarkably, *The Truth About Youth* was Myrna Loy's fiftieth film in just over five years, and she would appear in two more films in December 1930. One was a Poverty Row Western called *Rogue of the Rio Grande*, produced by Cliff Broughton Productions, in which Loy received top billing as yet another Mexican girl, which at least gave her the opportunity to dance on film again.

The other was a loan-out to Samuel Goldwyn called *The Devil to Pay*, featuring an original screenplay by British playwright Frederick Lonsdale. Perhaps most notably, when Minna Wallis sent her to the Goldwyn lot to inquire about a part in the film, Loy met with production supervisor Arthur Hornblow Jr. Loy recounted that Hornblow was surprised when she entered his office: "What is this? You're not a stuffed China doll. You don't look anything like those silly parts they've been giving you." Loy not only won the part, but would eventually win Hornblow, too.

In *The Devil to Pay*, Loy plays opposite Ronald Colman, who plays William Hale, an irresponsible gadabout whose thirst for adventure and lack of financial know-how has resulted in an auction of his possessions so he can make the trip back home to England from Africa. Following the auction, Willie returns to the arms of showgirl Mary, played by Loy.

Here, she makes one of her early appearances as a platinum blonde, embodying the kind of carefree party girl that audiences would soon begin to view as familiar rather than her exotic temptress roles. While she is not portrayed as exotic, she is still presented as a sex object. There is one amusing censorship-friendly shot of her talking on the phone to Willie while she's roasting in a sweatbox. She opens the doors and steps out, the steam bellowing forth furtively covers her nude body.

Notably, the film allows Loy to participate in a drawing room comedy populated by upper-class characters. And while Loy is once again "the other woman," she is not forced to resort to the histrionics of her earlier films that year. She even steps aside gracefully when Willie chooses Dorothy (Loretta Young). There is an overall sense of playful sophistication to Loy's character, and she makes the most of her chance with the part. While George Fitzmaurice's direction is painfully pedestrian (as it would remain throughout his undistinguished career), it's hard to go wrong with Frederick Lonsdale's dialogue.

The Devil to Pay was the last of the throng of films she appeared in during 1930, and while she did not set Hollywood ablaze in her fifty-two films in five years, her unflinching commitment to the roles she portrayed, no matter how absurd, no matter how patently offensive or loony, showed she had what it took to thrive in the ridiculous world of show business. There was much better yet to come. Fox was calling.

4

THE GENTLEMAN AND THE BRAT

A s 1930 opened, Hollywood studios were just starting to figure out talking pictures after an extraordinarily painful birth of the form. Worse yet, the enormous capital required to upgrade studio facilities had landed the studios in a serious financial bind just as the Great Depression was starting. Still, the true devastating effects of the depression were still two years from being felt by an industry that at this time felt practically immortal. Theater attendance was high, and the new fad of talking pictures was a giant, short-term success.

In April 1929, Paramount Pictures announced that William Powell had been elevated to stardom and would receive top billing in the 1929–1930 season (*Film Daily*, 1929). By February 1930, Powell's name appeared for the first time above the title in *Street of Chance*. Directed by John Cromwell, the picture provided Powell a scenery-chewing role as a notorious gambler, "Natural" Davis (based on real-life New York gambler Arnold Rothstein), who desperately tries to keep his younger brother out of the racket and suffers a cruel fate as a result.

The role perfectly positioned Powell for audiences to accept him as a hero. Despite his success as Philo Vance, most movie audiences still saw him as a heavy, and casting him as a hero with connections to the underworld was the perfect way to transition Powell in the minds of moviegoers. While Natural Davis is technically a bad fellow, and even orders the assassination of a two-bit hood who tries to swindle him at the beginning of the picture, he is a sympathetic figure thanks to his unflinching devotion to family.

When Davis's frustrated wife Alma (Kay Francis in her second of six films with Powell) proclaims their marriage is through, he vows to give up the racket even as his younger brother "Babe" (Regis Toomey) arrives in the big city with his new bride (Jean Arthur) and Natural is forced into one big, last game to try to break Babe of the gambling bug. Misunderstandings and complications ensue; Natural has to cheat in order to try to beat Babe, and he inevitably gets caught and then killed for his trouble. The tragic ending frightened the studio, according to producer David O. Selznick, who later wrote:

> Paramount was actually headed for trouble at this time. They were making strictly formula pictures and were way behind time in material and the treatment of it. All sorts of things were still taboo there. . . . I was told by the Paramount executives that the so-called "tragic ending," the death of the gambler, had cost them hundreds of thousands of dollars in gross.
>
> I asked them to believe that this was utterly ridiculous. The picture would have been nothing without this ending, and in fact, the entire story was built in terms of the gambler suffering for his own code: he had killed a man for violating this code and was himself killed when he violated it. Any other ending would have completely destroyed the picture. With [B. P.] Schulberg's increasingly antagonistic attitude toward me, and with his increasing use of his veto power over me, I encountered this sort of thing on everything I did. And it was this approach to pictures generally that within the space of a few years took Paramount disastrously downhill. (Selznick, 1972)

Street of Chance successfully framed Powell as an ongoing star and painted his heroic character with dark enough shades to make his new persona more palatable to those who were familiar with him as a heavy. However, it still suffered from the exceptionally dull shooting style of the early Paramount talkies. Powell himself, however, showed signs of significant improvement and depth as an actor.

A key sign of things to come is apparent in a scene in which Kay Francis says she's through with their marriage, and all of Powell's low-key suave and charm is unable to get through to her until he finally proclaims that he's going to quit gambling tonight. *Now*. Powell shows all the enthusiasm and passion he would show in his later MGM years, shedding the staid formality of his early talking roles. He also equips himself well in the final act in which he becomes desperate enough to cheat and gets caught. It's by far Powell's best speaking role thus far, and a relatively solid beginning to his new exalted status as star.

But as was often the case for Powell's tenure at Paramount, with every step forward came another step or two back. Next for Powell came *The Benson Murder Case*, another Philo Vance picture, and another directed by Frank Tuttle. Full of slowly delivered dialogue, endless medium shots, and a clearly bored Powell, it is viewable but a dreary bore, like the other Paramount Vance pictures.

Powell fared little better in *Paramount on Parade*, a latecomer among the major studios' talkie revues. Released in May 1930, the film featured twenty individual musical numbers and comedy sketches from eleven different directors that varied wildly in quality and entertainment value. The vignette in which Powell appeared, unfortunately, was one of the lesser ones.

William Powell and Kay Francis in *Street of Chance* (1930). Directed by John Cromwell. *Paramount Pictures/Photofest © Paramount Pictures*

The premise was meant to be funny: Powell as Philo Vance and Clive Brook as Sherlock Holmes up against Warner Oland as Dr. Fu Manchu, with Eugene Pallette reviving his role as the hapless Sergeant Heath from the three Vance pictures. Shot in long shot like the earliest talkies, the sketch falls flat thanks to the presence of a staggeringly unfunny Jack Oakie as the film's emcee. Still, Powell's presence in the all-star revue was further confirmation that Paramount did consider him, in fact, a star. His next two pictures further cemented the screen persona established in *Street of Chance*, that of a well-meaning, tragic hero mixed up in criminal activity who is willing to sacrifice himself for noble purposes as a final act of redemption.

First up was a remake of *The City of Silent Men*, a 1921 silent film that starred Thomas Meighan. The first two years of talking pictures were rife with remakes of silent films, an easy way for studios to recycle existing properties that had quickly been seen as antiquated and disposable. In the retitled *Shadow of the Law*, Powell plays Jim Montgomery, an engineer who kills a man in self-defense, but when the woman who witnesses the act and can exonerate him runs away, he is convicted of murder and sent to prison.

Once there, Powell has to suffer the terrifying indignity of having his mustache shaved off, but after several years he ingratiates himself with the warden enough to get the job as foreman of the prison's machine shop. The position gives him the resources to escape, and in a short two years, he takes on an alias and magically works his way up to become the manager of a mill in North Carolina, where he becomes the paramour of the owner's daughter. Despite his seeming escape from the law, however, Powell has spent all this time trying to track down the witness to the killing, and finally does so. The woman, however, refuses to testify on his behalf unless he hands over $50,000. Powell's willingness to go back to prison rather than capitulate to her demands convinces the detective who's been trailing him to help convince the woman to testify.

The film ends there. While the film lacks the tragic ending of *Street of Chance*, it is open-ended enough for us not to know whether the woman will actually testify, although it is lightly implied that the detective is willing to resort to violence to make her talk. While the film is no masterpiece, the opening sequences in which Powell is convicted of murder are surprisingly effective, especially a courtroom scene in which there is some bravura camerawork and editing that are oddly absent in the second half of the film. Powell is also especially effective as the tragic figure. A moment when he is sitting hunched and silent in his prison cell shortly after arriving there is a testament to his confidence—as well as that of director Louis Gasnier—in not having to wail and gnash his teeth in torment.

For the Defense, his next film, was a reunion with *Street of Chance* screenwriter Oliver H. P. Garrett, director John Cromwell, and co-star Kay Francis. Here, Powell is a notorious defense attorney whose heart is broken when he discovers that his lover (Francis) spent a night out with one of his clients, and when it's clear that Powell is going to lose the case defending that client, he drunkenly submits to the temptation of bribing a juror in the case and winds up on trial himself. When Francis offers to clear things up, Powell refuses to believe her and ends up pleading guilty. At the end, on his way to prison, Francis asks him: If she waits for him until he gets out, will he believe her? We're left with the possibility of reconciliation following his one- to ten-year prison term, but the last thing we see is Powell being driven through the prison gates. It is another tragic ending, but with the sense of hope in a redemptive spirit. If Paramount did indeed claim that these kinds of tragic endings made for poor box office, it was a weak argument, because *For the Defense* was especially successful.

Released in July 1930, the film was the last time Powell would be seen on screen until the following March, an eight-month absence that may seem brief by today's standards, but in the early 1930s, this lengthy absence for a star of Powell's caliber was almost an eternity. Consider, for example, that between December 1929 and July 1930, Powell had appeared in a staggering eight features! Then, for the next eight months, nothing.

By all accounts, Powell had been exhausted and demanded a vacation. After filming *For the Defense* completed on May 10, 1930, he left for a two-and-a-half-month trip to Europe, touring London, Paris, the Riviera, and Italy and spending much of his time with Ronald Colman as well as the character actor Ernest Torrence and his wife. After Powell returned to New York on the steamship *Conte Grande* on August 4, Paramount didn't seem to know what to do with him (*Exhibitors Daily Review and Motion Pictures Today*, August 5, 1930). Trade papers announced he would film scenes for a picture called *Ladies' Man*, but the studio changed its mind and gave the lead role to Paul Lukas, the Hungarian actor that the studio seemed to perceive as a second-string Powell. *Motion Picture News* (August 23, 1930) claimed that "the role is on the 'gigolo' order and Paramount thought it best not to risk Powell in such a spot."

Then it was announced Powell would stop in Chicago on the way back to the West Coast to film a regatta sequence for *New Morals*, based on the play *Spring Cleaning* by English playwright Frederick Lonsdale (*Exhibitors Daily Review and Motion Pictures Today*, August 25, 1930). Originally slated to star Clive Brook and Ruth Chatterton, *New Morals* was set to be directed by Ludwig Berger, then John Cromwell, then Victor Schertzinger, and then John Cromwell again. On September 2, Paramount announced that Juliette Compton would play opposite Powell, who had filmed his scenes in Chicago; William Boyd then joined the cast, and then references to the film mostly disappear (*Film Daily*, September 2, 1930).

While trade papers continued to trumpet *New Morals* as Powell's next picture, the project appears to have migrated to Paramount's British studio as *Women Who Play*, which would be released in 1932. Considering Lonsdale's original play is about a husband who hires a prostitute to live in his house to shock the wife whom he believes is on the verge of committing adultery, it's hard to imagine even in the pre-Code era how that plot could have been faithfully adapted into a Hollywood film.

Several months would pass before Powell would get back on a set. His five-year contract with Paramount was close to expiring, and while he was never on the record regarding his feelings about the matter, he could not have been pleased with Paramount's inability to make a project stick for him. In early November, Powell was attached to a picture with the tentative title of *Buy Your Woman*, and that project seems to have dissolved; later that month, he wound up filming *Ladies' Man*, back in the lead role that Paramount had given to Paul Lukas. Maybe they were fine now with Powell as a gigolo? After he completed filming *Ladies' Man* in December, he went on to film *Man of the World*, which turned out to be his final picture at Paramount.

After nearly a decade in the movies, Powell was at a turning point. In an interview with Gladys Hall, Powell said he attended conference after conference with executives at Paramount, pleading with them to give him a different type of part because he was tired of critics noting how "suave and polished" he was and felt that level of typecasting would quickly end his career. After getting a part that pleased him, however, the critics were still stuck on his persona, noting "Bill Powell gave his usual suave and polished performance" (G. Hall, 1931).

However, Powell was fortunate to have Myron Selznick as his agent. While his brother David was rising in the ranks as a studio executive, Myron was rising in the ranks as a studio executive's worst nightmare: an agent who was ruthless in protecting the interests of his movie-star clients.

On January 16, 1931, the *New York Times* reported Warner Bros. had declared war on Paramount by signing Powell and his fellow Selznick client, Ruth Chatterton, to new contracts before their then-current deals had expired. While Powell's deal was set to finish following the filming of *Man of the World*, Chatterton's contract did not expire until October 1. The report implied that Warner Bros. was signing Paramount stars as retribution over a conflict involving theater chains.

Two days later, Harry M. Warner said the signings of Powell and Chatterton, as well as Constance Bennett, were not a declaration of war. "Such transactions are a daily part of our business procedure," he said. "We bear no hostility toward any other company" (*Film Daily*, January 18, 1931). Paramount didn't believe him. When Warners also signed Kay Francis to a long-term deal, Paramount sued, and the suit was settled only when Warners agreed to loan Francis back to her original studio for a single film at no charge. That turned out to be Ernst Lubitsch's masterpiece *Trouble in Paradise*, featuring one of Francis's finest performances.

After signing with Warner Bros., Powell announced he would take a two-month vacation to celebrate the new deal. And celebrate he could. Myron Selznick negotiated a $6,000-a-week deal ($150,000 annually) for his client, taking full advantage of Paramount simply being unable to match the offer given its precarious financial position. Before Powell would begin his tenure at Warners, audiences would still have to see him in his final two films with Paramount. *Man of the World* would be released first despite being his last picture produced, followed by *Ladies' Man*. The films are most notable today for starring Powell alongside his future wife, Carole Lombard.

Born to a wealthy family in Fort Wayne, Indiana, on October 6, 1908, Carole Lombard spent her childhood as a spirited tomboy and enthusiastic athlete, and it was her appearance in a baseball game that landed her in a small role as the younger sister of Monte Blue in *A Perfect Crime* (1921). While her two days on the film set didn't bring any notice to the young beauty, the experience motivated Carole and her mother to seek future opportunities. After a contract with Fox in 1924 only resulted in bit parts, it was her signing by Mack Sennett to appear as one of his "Bathing Beauties" in his slapstick comedy shorts that got her noticed by the larger studios. After a brief sojourn with Pathé, Sennett's distributor, Paramount Pictures signed her to a $350-a-week contract (Gehring, 2003).

If there was one thing Lombard had in common with William Powell in her early films, it's that often the studio didn't know what on earth to do with her. Appearances in early talkies like *Fast and Loose* and *Safety in Numbers* show absolutely no sign of the comic genius that would seemingly emerge from nowhere a few years later. In these early films, all she seems required to do is be beautiful, and she appears to make little effort to be anything more than that. She is unbearably bland, and it can only be the fault of the studio given the litany of brilliant performances to come in films like *Twentieth Century* and *My Man Godfrey*.

Man of the World features Powell as Michael Trevor, an American ex-newspaperman living in Paris who runs a weekly scandal sheet. He spends his days befriending tourists and getting enough dirt on them to blackmail them to prevent him from printing their peccadilloes. Playing befuddled tourist Harry Taylor is Guy Kibbee, the unquestioned king of befuddlement among character actors of the early 1930s. Lombard plays Harry's niece Mary, who's engaged to Frank (Lawrence Gray), an idiot who leaves for London and encourages Mary to hang out with the handsome Trevor while he's gone. Of course, Mary and Trevor fall in love. When Trevor confesses his nefarious past to Mary, he's astonished to find she accepts him for who he is, but when his partner in crime Irene convinces him there's no way he can escape those he hurt, he buckles, blackmails Harry over his relationship with Mary, and goes off to South Africa, seemingly to resume his sleazy criminal career.

The ending of the picture reflects the great standard of old melodrama: The great noble sacrifice in which the leading man (or woman) decides he's not good enough for the one he loves, so he pretends not to care about her in order to release her from the burden of an undeserved love. Powell pulls off the sacrifice well enough, although it's hard to buy that Irene's speech would convince him to sacrifice his future love for Mary.

And the best thing to say about Lombard is that she appears to have adequately memorized her lines. There is one lovely scene on a bridge in the late evening in which the two hesitantly talk around the love they've developed for each other. But ultimately, despite a screenplay by the accomplished Herman J. Mankiewicz, it is a curiously flat and cheap-looking production from the struggling Paramount.

Released in April 1931, *Ladies' Man*—featuring another screenplay by Mankiewicz—stars Powell as Jamie Darricott, a gigolo who makes a living pawning the expensive gifts from society ladies with whom he carries on affairs. His latest paramour, Helene Fendley (Olive Tell), is the lonely wife of a wealthy banker whose chief virtue is her generous disposition. Matters become complicated when Darricott starts seeing Helene's daughter Rachel (Carole Lombard), who falls in love with him and begs him to stop seeing her mother, even while he falls in love with lively society woman Norma Page (Kay Francis).

The film is yet another of Powell's that suffers from a static camera, dialogue littered with numerous unnecessary pauses, a lack of a music score, and artless compositions. Lombard is given the opportunity to show some comic life in a couple of drunk scenes, but she can't quite pull them off the way she could a few short years later. Powell, meanwhile, enunciates his words carefully, has excellent posture, and looks fine in a top hat and tails.

If the viewer didn't know the film wasn't released in 1931, one would have guessed it was released around the same time as *Interference* three years earlier.

It feels like a technically shoddy early talkie. While the actors were certainly appealing enough, Powell's final Paramount film is a dud, and it brought a quiet and sad end to his tenure there. One needs only look at a roster of some of the directors with whom he was saddled in his early talkie years: Roy J. Pomeroy, Lothar Mendes, Richard Wallace, and Malcom St. Clair, to name a few.

This was the studio that boasted the talents of extraordinarily accomplished directors Ernst Lubitsch, Josef von Sternberg, Rouben Mamoulian, William A. Wellman, Dorothy Arzner, Edmund Goulding, and Leo McCarey, and Powell did not work with any of them after the coming of sound. It was a testament to his natural charisma and charm that he was an attractive enough commodity for Warner Bros. to decide he was worth poaching.

After signing with Warner Bros., Powell's name began to appear in the fan magazines more often, and he even consented to interviews. Given his reticence about his fame, it is more likely he was obligated to participate in the interviews, as the exceptional size of his new contract was nowhere near proportional to the box office success of his Paramount films.

One of the more notable interviews appeared in the April 1931 issue of *Screenland*, the same month that *Ladies' Man* opened. "Not a Ladies' Man! Bill Powell Denies All!" screams the headline. It reads very much like a total repudiation of the screen image that Paramount had cultivated for him, not to mention his role in his final Paramount film.

When asked if the character of Jamie Darricott in *Ladies' Man* was a villain, Powell said, "Never! He was just weak. He hasn't any of the characteristics of the parts I like to play, that I feel I can play best. No mentality. None of those sparkling facets of character which make personality." The article goes on to mention Powell's reputation for being a recluse, his preference for the companionship of men, and his love for travel (House, 1931). It is another example of the press emphasizing how Powell just wants to be left alone. However, they would do just the opposite, because Powell was about to marry Carole Lombard.

Earlier in 1931, Powell had finally divorced Eileen Wilson after over fifteen years of a tumultuous marriage that included multiple separations and reconciliations. It was after one such reconciliation that Eileen would give birth to William Powell's only son, William Jr., in 1925. Not much is known of how the marriage proceeded, if at all, after that point. Both Powell and Wilson remained silent. Given the publicity surrounding his European vacations with Ronald Colman that do not mention Wilson at all, it is fair to guess they had been separated for years. Meanwhile, the existence of William Powell Jr. was generally ignored.

Powell's reticence about publicity served him well during his unhappy first marriage. There was little to no gossip. However, he could not avoid gossip when it came to Lombard. Their romance had gotten off to a fast start after they met while shooting *Ladies' Man* in November 1930, and he was so besotted with the young beauty he gave her a Cadillac a month later for Christmas. It was a peculiar match to some observers. Not only was Powell sixteen years older than Lombard, he was a quiet intellectual while she was an effervescent young woman whose propensity for peppering every other sentence with colorful profanities was quickly becoming Hollywood legend.

However, Powell was fascinated. Lombard was an accomplished intellectual herself in an era when a beautiful woman had to keep that sort of inclination buttoned up. On their first date, they talked for seven hours and would soon have dinner every night and talk for hours on the phone every day. While their differences would ultimately doom their relationship, they got married anyway thanks to the strong endorsement of the union by Lombard's mother. They were married on June 26, 1931, at the house Lombard shared with her (Gehring, 2003).

In a fan magazine interview allegedly conducted a couple of days before the wedding, Powell seemed to think he and his movie star bride would be able to have a quiet life together.

> After our honeymoon, we're going to settle down in the old-fashioned idea of a calm and very unexciting life—as exciting lives are judged in Hollywood. We have a few close friends who mean much to us. We're going to play tennis, and quietly attend theaters—other than opening nights, and take drives to the beaches, and get our own meals on the cook's day out, and go places and do things—always together. I've found a pal, a sweetheart, a friend, a wife—let those who will keep their freedom! (Standish, 1931)

The fan magazines, as they were wont to do, were all atwitter over the Powell-Lombard nuptials. Gary Gray, in the October 1931 edition of *Screenland*, hyperventilated: "Hollywood's prize-package bachelor, the catch of this season and a lot of other seasons, the man whose name headed the guest lists of more cinema colony hostesses than any other—and who avoided social crowding with an earnestness of effort that amounted to a phobia—has gone the way of all masculine flesh."

The marriage of the two stars was fodder for all kind of conjecture. The couple was featured in a column by Dorothy Manners in the December 1931 edition of *Movie Classic* called "Can the Newlyweds of Hollywood Stay Married?"

> Can William Powell and Carole Lombard stay married? It's up to Bill, the suavely elegant Powell, who is neither suave nor elegant where Carole is concerned. If

ever a man was madly in love, indulgent and proud of a woman, that man is William Powell. And it is up to Bill to stay that way, proud of Carole's beauty and youth—and understanding it.

The marriage would end amicably in August 1933, and the experience of such a public marriage almost certainly made William Powell more guarded then ever against unwanted publicity. The inevitable publicity surrounding his romance with Jean Harlow two years later, followed by her tragic death and his own battle with cancer, would only strengthen his resolve to remain out of the public eye.

The same month Powell signed with Warner Bros., Myrna Loy would appear in her final film at the studio for nearly half a century. Released in January 1931 under the First National banner, *The Naughty Flirt* stars Alice White in one of her final leading roles. White debuted in 1927 as a kind of blonde Clara Bow for First National and went on to moderate success in a series of now-lost silent films (including the first film version of *Gentlemen Prefer Blondes*), but her talkies had experienced diminishing returns.

In *The Naughty Flirt*, White plays Kay Elliott, a spoiled heiress whose partying has gotten her expelled from numerous colleges. After an evening of revelry, she and her friends are arrested and carted off to night court, where she meets and immediately falls in love with Alan Ward (Paul Page), a lawyer who just happens to work for her father, John. Kay's new romance foils the plans of snooty social climber Linda (Myrna Loy), who has been conniving for her brother Jack (Douglas Gilmore) to marry Kay so they can get at her money.

Her final film at Warners represents a continuation of Loy's evolution from vamp to brat. While most accounts of her career describe her trajectory as steering from exotic villainess to perfect wife, there was a distinct transitional phase, and that could be seen in the nine films she made in 1931. Her roles began to move away from the racist "exotic" portrayals into which she had been mired during the beginning of her career, and she would also change professional homes for the first time: She signed with Fox Film Co., which was in the midst of the death throes that would ultimately end in the studio's merger with Joe Schenck's and Darryl F. Zanuck's 20th Century Pictures four years later.

Fox Film had suffered from the outsized ambitions of its namesake and founder, William Fox, who had borrowed mercilessly to purchase and build movie palaces to showcase his studio's productions, and when his fortune fell apart following the stock market crash of 1929, he quickly lost control of the studio in a hostile takeover. By the time Myrna Loy signed with Fox, the studio was under the supervision of bankers. While movie studios decades down the road would suffer creatively from being overseen by executives who knew nothing about the movies, Fox Film during the 1930s was a kind of free-for-all, and many of the films—while often very difficult and sometimes impossible to view today—are among the most entertaining of the era because writers and directors simply ran rampant with their creativity, no longer hampered by any kind of strong oversight by producers.

What resulted was a studio defined by its directors. Directors like Raoul Walsh, Frank Borzage, John Ford, and William K. Howard had far more freedom than they would have had at any other studio. While directors had relatively free hands to make the films they wanted, the studio's biggest stars were Will Rogers, the world-famous folksy humorist, and Charles Farrell and Janet Gaynor, an adorable and sweet romantic team. As a result, the studio's reputation was one of folksy, homespun Americana, seemingly a tough fit for Myrna Loy, the vamp.

Loy's first film under her Fox contract was *Body and Soul*. Released in February 1931, this was a World War I film about flyers, mistaken identities, and German spies, and was notable for featuring Humphrey Bogart in one of his earliest screen roles. The picture starred Farrell alongside Elissa Landi in her first American screen role. Fox signed the Italian actress after she appeared in a successful stage run of *A Farewell to Arms*, hoping she would be the studio's Greta Garbo or Marlene Dietrich. Unfortunately, it was not to be, and Landi's career took a parallel and opposite trajectory to Loy's. Only five years later, she had a supporting role and Loy had the leading role in *After the Thin Man*.

In *Body and Soul*, Loy was still stuck as a "slinky siren," as *Modern Screen* magazine (June 1931) put it, this time as the German spy nicknamed "Pom Pom." While Farrell and Landi received some plaudits, reviews barely mentioned Loy. In the May 1931 issue of *Motion Picture Magazine*, the review simply states at the conclusion: "Myrna Loy plays the other woman." *Photoplay* (April 1931) ends its review with, "And is that Myrna Loy a mean one? You'll say so."

It was hardly an auspicious debut for an actress eager for a change in her circumstances. She fares a little better in her next film, *A Connecticut Yankee*, released in April, which gave Loy her only opportunity to work with Fox's biggest star, Will Rogers. The film was a smash hit, earning $1.3 million at the box office, and was named by numerous publications as a Top Ten film of the year. Despite having to play evil once again, the film represents a significant turning point for being the first genuine comedy in which Loy played a significant role.

Will Rogers at that time was already a legendary folksy social commentator, humorist, and entertainer who had appeared in dozens of films, essentially play-

Myrna Loy and Will Rogers in *A Connecticut Yankee* **(1931). Directed by David Butler.** *Fox Film Corporation/Photofest © Fox Film Corporation*

ing himself. In *A Connecticut Yankee*, very loosely based on the Mark Twain story, Rogers is Hank Martin, the fish out of water, and the humor is intended to play off the contrast between the folksy time traveler's "present day" and the medieval setting. Loy plays Queen Morgan le Fay, sister of King Arthur, who kidnaps Arthur's only daughter, Alisande (Maureen O'Sullivan). Rogers, who has been dubbed Sir Boss, wins a jousting tournament to win the right to save Alisande, and Loy is highly amusing as the queen whose heart is very dramatically stolen by the folksy star.

Loy's part is small, but she displays her full willingness to make a complete fool of herself in her over-the-top seduction of Rogers, who is appropriately embarrassed as we hear le Fay's victims wailing in the torture chamber while she spouts lines like "Could you but love me and thou shall have anything thou wishest." It's funny, and Loy had fond memories of Rogers, who she said was just as embarrassed in real life as he was on screen by the ridiculous love scene (Loy, 1988).

While it was all good fun, there was little evidence that Loy would be allowed to do anything but be the same vamp she had played for years at Warners. But after a small part in the gangster movie *Hush Money*, she finally had an opportunity to stretch. In her 1988 autobiography, Loy cited William K. Howard's

Transatlantic as her favorite during her time at Fox, and it's not hard to see why.

Released in August 1931, the film covers the lives of various passengers on the ocean liner the SS *Transatlantic*, and its sophisticated structure of lightly connected vignettes within a giant setting anticipates MGM's far more famous *Grand Hotel* by a full year. Featuring a beautiful Art Deco set by Gordon Wiles and extraordinary deep-focus work by the cinematographer James Wong Howe, the film is criminally underseen today, only widely available on the internet in bootleg copies that do no justice to Howe's beautiful camerawork.

Loy is fourth-billed and her part is relatively small, but it is notable because *Transatlantic* features her neither as an "other woman" nor a vamp. She plays Kay, the wife of cold, ruthless banker Henry Graham (John Halliday), who learns his Graham Investment Corporation is about to declare bankruptcy. His personal fortune seemingly safe thanks to securities he has with him, Henry is eventually murdered, and the film shifts to a murder mystery with a gambler, an aggrieved investor, and a gangster as suspects.

Loy treasured the experience, especially director Howard:

> He had respect for me and my work, which pleased me to no end. It was nice occasionally to meet someone you respected, who respected you for your craft. Fox greeted my departure from exotica with publicity handouts labeled "Revamped Vamp," then thrust me back into a series of bad-girl parts. Facing the same kind of typing that had limited me at Warners, I said, "I want out!" And Fox released me. (Loy, 1988)

It is a curious statement to make, because Loy as a freelance actor would still appear as the very same kind of "other woman" she claimed she was tired of playing. In fact, it may be more of a case of wishful thinking, with fifty years of hindsight. What actually occurred was that Fox dropped the option on her initial contract, which would have raised her salary above $750 a week, likely the result of a combination of the studio's dire financial condition, its lack of creative leadership in the front office, and an inability to figure out just what to do with Myrna Loy. Encouraged by Minna Wallis to go freelance, Loy would hop from studio to studio before landing at Metro-Goldwyn-Mayer (Leider, 2011).

Ironically, the film that seemed to inspire MGM to sign her was one of her freelance efforts at Fox, and it was yet another film in which she would play the other woman. The faltering studio took on another version of Felix Reisenberg's novel *East Side, West Side*, which Fox previously produced in a 1927 silent adaptation directed by Allen Dwan.

Sam Taylor directed the new version, titled *Skyline*. While Loy plays another brat in this melodrama released in October 1931, at least she's not outwardly evil. Wearing a platinum blonde wig again, Loy's character of Paula Lambert is, at first glance, yet another version of the vamps and the brats she had been playing early in her career, but Loy—clearly maturing as a screen actor—imbues her with more subtlety.

In the film, John Breen (Hardie Albright) has grown up on a barge on the East River in New York City, lamenting his life hauling bricks up the river with his abusive father, Captain Breen (Stanley Fields), and yearns to be an architect. When his mother reveals on her deathbed that Captain Breen is not really his father, he beats the old man into unconsciousness, escapes the barge, and collapses into the bed of a truck that unknowingly drives him to a large quarry.

When a kind construction foreman gives John food and boasts of his association with the great builder Gordon A. McClellan (Thomas Meighan), John decides to go to the top man for a job and cons his way into delivering blueprints to McClellan, who is hanging out on the top of his newest skyscraper under construction. Through a series of misadventures, Breen winds up becoming McClellan's protégé and romances Kathleen Kearny (Maureen O'Sullivan). We first see platinum blonde Paula Lambert (Loy) visiting McClellan at the construction site. She is adorned in furs, and when the friend accompanying her reminds her that a love affair with McClellan is over, Paula meows playfully.

The scene establishes Paula as glamorous and catty, probably a woman to inspire a little fear, but those rough edges are smoothed by Loy's developing ability to exude a casual, simple charm on screen. She's just a party girl out for a good time, not a vamp or a brat. In her autobiography, Loy dismissed *Skyline*, writing that "all that comes to mind is that I played Thomas Meighan's mistress in a blonde wig" (Loy, 1988). Even though Loy wasn't impressed with the role, she said that MGM disagreed and signed her based on the strength of her portrayal. For today's viewers more familiar with the perfect wife, it can be disconcerting to see a platinum blonde Myrna Loy as the "other woman," but these roles provided a solid transition for her as an actor. Studios could not possibly be interested in Myrna Loy's potential as a leading lady unless she moved past roles she openly admitted were not human beings.

Fortunately, Loy continued to have the opportunity to play actual human beings, even if the blonde wig was still a part of the equation. In her next film, *Consolation Marriage* at RKO, the blonde wig functions as an appropriate visual counterpoint to the angelic Irene Dunne. The film, released in November 1931, is the story of Steve Porter (Pat O'Brien), whose heart is broken when longtime paramour Elaine (Loy) breaks the news to him that she's marrying someone else. (Someone rich.) Meanwhile, Mary (Dunne) has her own heart broken when her man Aubrey (Lester Vail) tells her he's marrying a rich woman who can support his dream of becoming a great musician.

Both brokenhearted, Steve and Mary eventually meet cute, strike up a light friendship, and decide on a whim to get married, since they might as well just face the fact they will suffer unrequited loves for other people for the rest of their lives. Their marriage goes on for several years, Mary gives birth to a child, and the two both fall in love with each other without admitting it. Then, in a remarkable coincidence, both Mary's former lover Aubrey and Steve's former lover Elaine return on Steve and Mary's wedding anniversary. Mary decides to abandon husband and child and run off with Aubrey, but after she suddenly realizes Aubrey is a twit and she really loves Steve, she returns to her family just in time for Steve to realize also that he loves Mary.

As Elaine, Loy showcases how much she has matured as a performer in a short time. It had been just a year earlier in *The Truth about Youth* that she played the selfish gold-digging other woman, screeching when she learns her boyfriend isn't rich. Now, she is far more subdued as the other woman. There is a kind of resigned sadness to her. She doesn't actually have a lot of dialogue. All she really has to do is stand around in fabulous dresses looking pretty and vivacious compared to tired Irene Dunne, but Loy does far more than she should be able to do with a role that is solely a plot device. She manages to communicate a great deal more with silence than she ever could with the rather stilted dialogue presented here. She shows up at the end, not boldly confident that she's going to win Steve back, but rather just matter-of-factly, as if she's a kind of simple naïve girl instead of a backstabbing gold digger. When Elaine has Mary help her powder her back, Loy sits at the makeup table oblivious to the pain she is causing, Dunne is behind her in a defeated posture, the two pros clearly showing that they're going to be fantastic in the movies. It is a simple display of two actors deftly communicating their feelings without saying a word.

Myrna Loy was no longer a vamp, no longer a brat. Now she was a human being. Unfortunately, critics being as they are, they made little note of her now that her performances were no longer filled with histrionics. The most *Screenland* (February 1932) can say of Loy in *Consolation Marriage* is that she's "decorative," and *Photoplay* (November 1931) notes that she "scintillates briefly in a role that fits her as perfectly as her gown." Despite the lack of concentrated attention, Loy was pleased not to be stuck under contract to a single studio.

Released in December 1931, *Arrowsmith* reunited her with her *Black Watch* director, John Ford. The Samuel Goldwyn production also reunited her with Ronald Colman as well as Arthur Hornblow Jr., who was an uncredited executive producer. While filming, it was apparent to Loy that a mutual attraction was developing between herself and Hornblow, but he was still married to Juliette Crosby. He and Loy would not act on the attraction until he separated from his wife some time later (Loy, 1988).

While Loy did not become the "other woman" in Hornblow's faltering marriage, she once again played that role on screen in *Arrowsmith*. Based on Sinclair Lewis's novel, the film is the tale of Dr. Martin Arrowsmith (Colman) and his eventual journey to the West Indies, where he attempts to stave off an outbreak of bubonic plague. Rather than take the scientific approach by inoculating half the population with his experimental serum and half with a placebo, he's overcome by sympathy for the suffering population and inoculates everyone with the serum, outraging his mentor, Dr. Gottlieb, who immediately dies of a stroke.

While in the West Indies, Arrowsmith meets Mrs. Lanyan (Loy), a kind society woman with whom he carries on an affair before returning to the States to find his wife Leora (Helen Hayes) has died after being exposed to a cigarette contaminated with plague in a lab. While Loy is once again the "other woman," here she is once again a sympathetic character. Neither she nor Arrowsmith is portrayed as a seducer, and because the affair is only suggested rather than portrayed blatantly as it is in the novel (likely due to censorship concerns), it never feels like outright adultery.

There is a shot showing Mrs. Lanyan in bed looking at her door, then a shot of Arrowsmith in his bedroom. Back to Mrs. Lanyan, she's putting a nightgown on the bed; then back to Arrowsmith looking at his door. In the next scene, Lanyan enters the scene from a door and Arrowsmith enters the scene soon afterwards from the same door. Is it the door to his or her bedroom? It is hard to tell. Both Colman and Loy are excellent in their truncated scenes together, and there is a sense that their relationship has less to do with lust than with the fact of two lonely, scared people in a strange land finding some level of comfort with each other. It is another step in Loy's evolution from vamp to leading lady.

More freelance work followed in Fox's *The Woman in Room 13* and a Poverty Row production of *Vanity Fair* that featured Loy as Becky Sharp before Minna Wallis negotiated a five-year contract with Metro-Goldwyn-Mayer in the fall of 1931. Wallis had screened a clip from Fox's *Skyline* for production chief Irving Thalberg, and that impressed him enough to sign Loy to the contract. It had only been seven years since the merger of Metro Pictures, Goldwyn Pictures (which had deposed its namesake several years earlier), and Louis B.

Mayer Productions produced a powerhouse owned by theater chain Loews Inc. that immediately dominated the Hollywood landscape.

MGM's slogan was "More Stars Than There Are in Heaven," and while publicity departments have long been characterized by breathless hyperbole, it was hard to argue with the statement. By the beginning of 1932, MGM featured the biggest box office attractions in the industry. Along with Marie Dressler, Wallace Beery, Greta Garbo, Clark Gable, Norma Shearer, Joan Crawford, Jean Harlow, and John and Lionel Barrymore, there was a deep, deep bench of accomplished character actors and a production unit system developed by Thalberg that was unmatched in its efficiency.

It was the perfect home at the perfect time for Loy, whose show business career began in the shadows of MGM's massive studio complex in Culver City. She would not immediately become a star, though. MGM generally had the policy of throwing new contract players into every conceivable kind of role in their first year as a kind of intense audition to see where they will fit in. James Stewart was going through that kind of gauntlet when he appeared in *After the Thin Man* (1936). However, Loy was given very little to work with at the beginning.

Released in January 1932, her first film for MGM was *Emma*, starring Marie Dressler. Dressler, a beloved multifaceted talent who had won the Best Actress Oscar the previous season for *Min and Bill*, was Hollywood's number-one box office attraction. As a sixty-three-year-old overweight, bulldog-faced woman, she is certainly the most unusual person to hold that title in an industry that has only valued youth, beauty, and thinness. Loy adored her, just like everyone else.

In *Emma*, Dressler plays one of her patented working-class roles as the titular housekeeper for the Smith family, led by kindly inventor Frederick (Jean Hersholt). The film opens with the Smith mother dying giving birth to her fourth child, Ronnie, and then the film flash-forwards decades to show that Frederick's inventions have made him a wealthy man, and his three oldest children—Bill, Gypsy, and Isabelle—have become spoiled brats. Isabelle (Loy) is the eldest and most spoiled, having just married a French count. All take Emma for granted except for Ronnie (Richard Cromwell), who adores her as a mother. After Frederick marries Emma, he almost immediately dies of a heart condition and Emma is shocked to find out she's the sole heir. Ronnie is delighted, but the other three children eventually accuse Emma of manipulating their father into leaving her his fortune and then murdering him. She is found not guilty, but tragedy strikes when it turns out Ronnie has died in a plane crash while rushing to testify on her behalf.

Loy has little screen time in the picture, and with so few minutes available there is little depth to her character. She comes across far more as the kind of brat she played in her Warners pictures, but Loy does what she can. After the trial is over, the three spoiled children realize how much they've wronged Emma, a rather preposterous reversal considering they had been portrayed up to that point as one-dimensional fiends, but Loy is so earnest in her apology to Emma that is seems nearly plausible. Loy's natural appeal comes through. She seems less plausible as the vicious harpy, and that could have been because she was not at all happy about being given this part as her first MGM picture.

Sensing Loy's disappointment about the role, Dressler said to her, "Get your chin up, kid. You've got the whole world ahead of you" (Loy, 1988). If anyone understood the merits of perspective, it was Dressler, whose long career had hit bottom just a few years earlier. And Loy needed perspective. Her next two parts only gave her a scant few minutes of screen time. Released in March 1932, *The Wet Parade* was an overlong, star-studded spectacular of dull preachiness based on a novel by Upton Sinclair that somehow railed against both the evils of drinking alcohol and the evils of Prohibition. Once again adorned with a blonde wig, Loy plays Eileen, the actress girlfriend of Roger Chilcote Jr. (Neil Hamilton). When she opens a speakeasy called "Club Eileen," which rather foolishly has a huge neon sign, the club is raided. Later, in a scene in which Loy scolds Roger one morning after a bender, her scolding turns to concern when it turn out he drank bad liquor and has gone blind. Loy is as appealing as ever, but her character barely has enough time to make an impression, and most of it is near the end of the picture, when the audience is exhausted from all the moralizing.

Released in June, *New Morals for Old* was a melodrama about siblings Ralph (Robert Young), an aspiring artist who studies in Paris, and Phyl (Margaret Perry), who is devoted to her married lover Duff Wilson (David Newell). Loy has just a couple of minutes of screen time as Ralph's next-door neighbor and girlfriend, Myra. She has almost nothing to do, and it is a curious move by MGM to throw her into such an enormously inconsequential part.

Fortunately, something better came along quickly and, ironically, it took a loan-out to Paramount for her to get a decent part. Rouben Mamoulian, a well-respected Broadway director whose debut film, *Applause* (1929), was one of the finest of the early talkies, was an admirer of Loy and requested her to play the role of the conniving Countess Valentine in his new musical, *Love Me Tonight*.

Released in August 1932, the film starred Maurice Chevalier and Jeanette McDonald, and not only boasts a score by Richard Rodgers and Lorenz Hart but some of the most innovative uses of sound design yet seen in Hollywood. The opening sequence features a cacophony of unrelated sound effects one would hear on a typical Paris morning, all coming together into a percussive rhythm and eventually evolving into the score of the picture. The song "Isn't It Romantic?" was performed by crosscutting performers seen over multiple locations, creating a new kind of purely cinematic musical number audiences had never seen before.

In the tale of Parisian tailor Maurice (Chevalier) and his unlikely romance with Princess Jeanette (McDonald), Loy portrays the Countess Valentine, a royal who spends her days in the palace dreaming of nothing but men. Literally. Poor Valentine is so bored with her current circumstances, she sleeps almost all the time. In what is arguably her first genuinely comic performance, Loy shows glimmers of the star she was about to become. "Don't you ever think about anything but men?" Princess Jeanette asks. "Yes, schoolboys," responds Valentine. What is delightful is that Countess Valentine is just as hungry for men as the vamps of Loy's past, but now she was in the hands of a master filmmaker at the height of his powers, and she seems like an entirely different person on screen.

It's ironic that Loy was able to thrive in her one film at Paramount with a great director and spectacular cast, while William Powell had languished in mediocre pictures at the studio in the early years of talking pictures. And Loy, who had languished herself for years at Warners, gushed about the production in her autobiography over fifty years later:

Love Me Tonight (1932). Directed by Robert Mamoulian. From left: Myrna Loy (as Countess Valentine), Maurice Chevalier (as Maurice Coutelin), Jeanette MacDonald (as Princess Jeanette). *Paramount Pictures/Photofest © Paramount Pictures*

Oh, the riches in *Love Me Tonight*! Can you imagine what we had in that film? Charlie Ruggles and Charlie Butterworth punctuating that witty script, Maurice and Jeanette MacDonald singing those wonderful Rodgers and Hart songs: "Isn't It Romantic?," "Lover," and "Mimi," of which even I had a verse—the only time I've sung in the movies. (Loy, 1988)

Loy's role was relatively small, and most reviewers concentrated on Chevalier, McDonald, and the Rodgers and Hart songs, but Mordaunt Hall did note in his *New York Times* review (August 19, 1932) that "Myrna Loy is easy and graceful as Countess Valentine," and *Modern Screen* in November 1932 noted that Loy, along with Ruggles and Butterworth, was responsible for the laughs in the picture. It was still a significant turning point.

With that step forward, however, there were two steps back. Audiences (and executives at MGM) could not view *Love Me Tonight* until August 1932, and in the interim between the filming and release of that masterpiece, Loy was cast in two of the most absurd and offensive exotic roles of her career before she was finally able to hang up the awful makeup forever. To her credit, Loy threw herself into the terrible parts with unmatched zeal.

She is miles over the top in *Thirteen Women* and *The Mask of Fu Manchu*, but she has to be. Watching these films in comparison with something like *The Squall*, it's clear Loy had a greater command over her voice, her body, and her performance. The characters of Ursula and Fah Lo See in the two later films are just as absurd as the character of Nubi. They're both completely inhuman, but Loy is able to make them human. She's never hysterical, she never yells, and she has a far stronger sense of how to act in front of the camera.

Loy was loaned out to RKO for *Thirteen Women*, based on the bestselling 1930 novel by Tiffany Thayer. Released in September 1932, the film features Loy as Ursula, a half-Javanese Eurasian woman who vows revenge against the thirteen former sorority sisters (all white) who snubbed her at St. Alban's College by not allowing her to pass as a white woman. The women each receive letters of dire prognostication from the Swami Yogadachi (actually written by Ursula), and each is convinced they will meet tragedy somehow. June Raskob, trapeze artist, receives a letter predicting someone will die by her actions, so naturally when she's up in the air in the big top with her sister May, she recoils instead of catching her and falls to her death. As one woman after another is driven mad by the prediction and takes their own lives, we meet Laura, played by Irene Dunne, just as sweet and wholesome as she was in *Consolation Marriage*. Ursula squirms into the poor woman's brain by predicting the death of Laura's young son, Bobby.

When Bobby receives a mysterious piece of chocolate in the mail as a birthday present, Laura takes the chocolate to a scientist who informs her that Bobby would have choked to death in thirty seconds if he had eaten it. Frustrated in her efforts to kill the child, Ursula seduces the Swami's chauffeur and convinces him to give Bobby a big rubber ball with dynamite inside it. Fortunately, Laura and her paramour Barry learn that Bobby has been given a box with a dynamite-loaded rubber ball in it and manage to throw it out of a moving car, where it harmlessly explodes outside. At the end of the film, eventually defeated and driven mad, Ursula jumps off a train to her death.

It is the most ridiculous role Loy was forced to play yet. By the time the film was released, it had been nearly two years and seventeen feature film appearances since her last racist role in the 1930 Poverty Row production *Rogue of the Rio Grande*. It would have seemed at the time that she had successfully transitioned to a new screen type, but one potential explanation for her casting is the level of RKO's desperation in casting the role. Zita Johann, the original Ursula, was fired early in the production, and Loy, still with the reputation as a vamp on screen, was available at the right time.

Loy's fearless performance as the insane Ursula brought about some positive responses from critics. The *Modern Screen* critic said, "Myrna Loy deserves a big hand for making an unbelievable story a little more believable," while *Motion Picture Herald* noted, "She does a powerful job, with a difficult role, one that will win her no sympathy, but does show her as a villainess whom your audience will want to hiss." However, Mordaunt Hall of the *New York Times*, in a stark reversal of his plaudits for Loy the previous month in *Love Me Tonight*, said, "Myrna Loy creeps among her old sorority sisters like a young woman suffering from insomnia and a desire to become an actress" (M. Hall, October 15, 1932).

Today, the film is a very guilty, campy pleasure and easy to digest at just fifty-seven minutes long. Aside from the plot, one morbidly fascinating fact about the film is that it featured in her film debut an actress named Peg Entwistle, who would gain everlasting fame by jumping from the top of the Hollywood sign to her death two days after the release of the picture.

After filming *Thirteen Women*, Loy would return to home studio MGM to appear in *The Mask of Fu Manchu*. Dr. Fu Manchu was a Chinese supervillain featured in a series of novels written by English author Sax Rohmer and became the most notorious of the many negative stereotypes of the Chinese "yellow peril." The character proved popular enough to be adapted by Paramount for two films starring Warner Oland in the title role, and MGM snapped up the rights to Sax's latest *Fu Manchu* novel shortly after it was serialized in *Collier's* magazine from May to July 1932.

Fresh off his star-making turn as the monster in *Frankenstein*, Boris Karloff was borrowed from Universal to the play the titular fiend and Loy was cast as his daughter, Fah Lo See. The plot deals with Fu Manchu's insidious plot to steal the golden mask and sword of Genghis Khan from British explorers who find the objects in Khan's tomb. For some reason, possessing the mask and sword would enable Fu Manchu to become the new Genghis Khan and wipe out the white race.

The production was troubled. Original director Charles Vidor was fired days into filming and replaced by Charles Brabin, and original screenwriter Courtney Terrett was replaced by a rotating committee of three to five writers. Given the absurd plot, it's not hard to imagine that seasoned professionals like Karloff and Loy could not have taken it seriously, so they go whole hog into camp, and it all makes for another morbidly guilty pleasure. Both actors eschew the traditional pidgin English employed for Chinese characters in the movies of that era, and Loy relishes the portrayal of an unhinged, sexually ravenous madwoman screaming at her slaves in orgiastic pleasure to keep whipping a captured Englishman faster, faster, and faster.

The brief whipping scene is the highlight, and Loy usually remains silent throughout the picture, while Fu Manchu refers to her both as "ugly and insignificant" as well as "beautiful." Often shot in silent close-up, lit from below, her face cast in shadows, Loy is a model of old-time offensive Orientalism, and even when silent she revels in her character's deranged libido. As much as her performance is filled with lunacy, it's a far more legitimate and charismatic lunacy than she pulled off in her early Warners talkies. It helps that she follows Karloff's lead in not affecting an offensive accent.

The part, which Loy would later say was even toned down at her insistence because she was originally supposed to do all the whipping herself, would be her last "exotic" role, although she would recount that when she viewed a screening with Roddy MacDowell years later, "it astonished me how good Karloff and I were" (Loy, 1988). Their commitment to the absurdity of the comic book goings-on makes it a luridly fascinating viewing today.

Given that Loy had become more accustomed to playing actual human beings in films over the previous two years, it is not surprising that she finally put her foot down regarding her exotic vamp roles. After nearly seventy films, Myrna Loy's miscasting would finally and mercifully end. Given the heights of fame she would reach in the coming years, it would quickly become almost unbelievable to audiences that she had ever been a villain. The man Loy would have to thank for putting the final nail in her villainous coffin would be William Powell's staunchest defender, David O. Selznick.

5

THE EVERYMAN AND
THE SEDUCTRESS

Well, I'm a young girl with reddish hair and straight legs—
pretty straight—funny voice and a personality, so I'm told.

—Myrna Loy, *The Prizefighter and the Lady*

Now that Loy was determined not to play the vamp again, MGM loaned her out to RKO for its production of *The Animal Kingdom*. Based on a play by Phillip Barry, who is best known today for *Holiday* and *The Philadelphia Story*, later film versions of which would pair Katharine Hepburn and Cary Grant, *The Animal Kingdom* gave Loy a golden opportunity at long last to strut her stuff in a major studio release.

"Most casting successes are a matter of common sense," David O. Selznick, who by then had left Paramount for RKO, wrote later.

> Myrna Loy had been playing Oriental sirens for years, which was always a joke with people who knew her. She is a beautiful girl, but in real life she is no more a siren than I am. It was considered a revolutionary thing to put her into a polite comedy such as *The Animal Kingdom*, but when this casting was suggested to me by Ned [Edward H.] Griffith, the director, I leaped at the idea. Curiously, nobody objected very much, probably because they knew Myrna personally—but it's strange that she was so long in reaching her natural field. (Selznick, 1972)

While Selznick's claim that placing Loy into a polite comedy was revolutionary was slightly untrue—Loy had appeared in a number of them at RKO, Warner Bros., and Fox—what was revolutionary was the size of her role. While Loy was able to take second-lead status in independent pictures of the early talking era, her role in *The Animal Kingdom* was her highest profile yet at a major studio.

Director Ned Griffith was a workmanlike veteran of early talkies who had previously helmed an early version of Barry's *Holiday*, and *The Animal Kingdom* suffers like that film from a far-too-static, theatrical presentation. Not helping matters is the casting of Leslie Howard, who the audience is supposed to believe is a bohemian. In the film, Howard plays Tom Collier, a publisher of deluxe art books whose lover and mistress Daisy Sage (Ann Harding) returns from three months away to find that Tom has become engaged to Cecelia Henry (Myrna Loy). Daisy, who is devastated, is forced to watch Tom succumb to Cecelia's manipulative tactics as she draws him in with the temptations of society and easy money and further and further away from his circle of artsy-fartsy friends.

Ironically, someone like William Powell could probably have done wonders with the part of Tom Collier, as seen in his own portrayal of a carefree bohemian artist in the later *Double Wedding*. But Howard is woefully wrong for the part. It is nearly impossible to think of him as a bohemian. While Howard could do wonderful things with parts more suited to his buttoned-up screen persona (his Henry Higgins in the 1938 film version of *Pygmalion* is marvelous), he seems far better matched to Loy's Cecelia and her obsession with wealth and high society than Harding's Daisy. So when Collier chooses Daisy at the end, it doesn't really make very much sense. He shares a far more electric chemistry with Loy than he does Harding, perhaps a reflection of the real-life affection they had for each other.

If one's perception of Howard is as a stuffy Englishman, Loy certainly didn't think so. She had only recently moved out of her mother's house and had begun her relationship with Arthur Hornblow Jr. after he finally separated from his wife. Loy admitted years later she was besotted with Howard, and it was fully requited. She wrote that after she had resisted the temptation of an affair, "he stormed my house, imploring me to run away with him to the South Seas." While he was very persuasive, Loy wrote, her beau Hornblow arrived from an out-of-town trip "in the nick of time" (Loy, 1988).

On the surface, the role of Cecelia seems not too far removed in spirit from the vamps that Loy had portrayed in her earlier films, but she is in a far more winning position here. First, whatever the shortcomings of Griffith's direction, playwright Phillip Barry had a way with words, and Loy was clearly comfortable speaking his dialogue. She was also playing an adult and not a brat, and was finally given some time to really sink into a character's bones. One remarkable sequence is perhaps Loy's sexiest moment on screen, one that could have only taken place in the pre-Code era. Daisy is about to have her first great showing as a painter, and Cecelia seems willing enough to accompany Tom. She goes

Leslie Howard and Myrna Loy in *The Animal Kingdom* (1932). Directed by Edward H. Griffith. *Author's Collection*

upstairs to get dressed and comes down wearing a skimpy negligee and, just as she's about to successfully seduce her poor sop of a husband, she claims to come down with a headache, implores him to go to the showing alone, and slinks back up the stairs with a knowing smile, purring "You better take your heavy coat . . . and keep warm."

What else was poor Tom going to do? He went upstairs! What's particularly winning about Loy's characterization is that she is a three-dimensional human being who is definitely manipulative but never seems particularly evil. It's telling that after shooting was completed, retakes were ordered in December 1932 to beef up Loy's part just a couple of weeks before the New York opening.

Critics and audiences took notice. In *Variety*, Cecelia Ager wrote: "In 'Animal Kingdom,' Myrna Loy made her scoffers eat their words. From a ten-twent-thirt-slinking Oriental menace, suddenly she sprang forth full blown, a civilized intelligent young woman. It was a startling transformation." Most importantly, David O. Selznick took notice, borrowing her from MGM again almost immediately to play a "straight comedy role, the lead opposite John Barrymore in *Topaze*" (Ager, 1933).

Released in February 1933, just one month after *The Animal Kingdom* went into wide release, *Topaze* was based on the play by the great French writer Marcel Pagnol. It features Barrymore as Auguste Topaze, a hopelessly naïve chemist and professor at the Stegg Academy in Paris, who patiently lectures to the young boys in his charge that honesty and virtue are the best and only ways to achieve success in life. He begins his journey to the sad discovery of the truth about the world when he is dismissed by the school for giving poor marks to awful, bratty Charlemagne de La Tour-La Tour at the behest of his mother, the Baroness. Topaze is helplessly befuddled over being fired for giving bad grades to the son of influential, wealthy parents and, in his confusion, he stumbles into a scheme by the boy's father, the Baron Philippe de La Tour-La Tour, to market fake mineral water to the youth of France.

Topaze is hired to concoct a formula for this healthy water the Baron dubs "Sparkling Topaze," and assisting Topaze in the laboratory is the Baron's mistress, Coco, played by Loy. Once again she is the "other woman," but she is far from being a manipulative, conniving sort of other woman. Rather, she quickly develops some sympathy for the poor doctor, and it isn't long before she becomes his enthusiastic ally when Topaze learns to his horror that his formula is not being used, and the bottles of Sparkling Topaze on the market are no better than "ditch water."

On the surface, Loy doesn't have a great deal to do throughout much of the film, despite her second billing. This is very much Barrymore's film, but Loy does make a significant impact with her eyes and her Nora Charles–like smirk as the often-silent observer of the absurdity around her. She never outwardly displays any romantic interest or truly friendly affection for the Baron, or even any affinity for his wealth, but we can see through her eyes that she is intrigued by this foolish professor. There is a beguiling maturity in her performance as Coco that reaches new levels after Topaze accepts his new status as a patsy and gets his revenge on those who hurt him. She is impressed by the fool's newly cultivated moxie. When Topaze finally blackmails the Baron with the evidence of his affair with Coco, the Baron whines, "A divorce would ruin me! What can I do?"

"Softly and silently vanish away!" Coco coos.

It is a small line, but Loy delivers it with a quiet, sublime sense of satisfaction that she is finally in a position to tell this crooked old wealthy idiot to go stuff it. While Coco's backstory is negligible—we never learn how she became the Baron's mistress and have little sense she is with him for any other reason than access to wealth—Loy imbues the character with a real sense of inner life.

Cecelia Ager wrote of Loy in *Topaze*: "So she remains very quiet, listens carefully and observes the exquisite tricks of the star. It isn't long before people begin to notice her, conducting herself so unobtrusively. She must be a deep one, that well-behaved girl, they begin to think. That poise must well from some profound inner spring" (Ager, 1933).

While *The Animal* Kingdom and *Topaze* were real breakthroughs for the young actress, audiences and the fan magazines took a little longer to embrace the "new" Myrna Loy. A June 1933 article in the *New Movie Magazine*, for example, is entitled "Secrets of a Siren" and refers to Loy as a "sorceress" providing advice on how to "capture the male" (Cheatam, 1933).

While the back-to-back successes of *The Animal Kingdom* and *Topaze* in January and February of 1933 finally seemed to place Myrna Loy on the unalterable path to stardom, she was not a top-tier star yet. The main problem was that her best films in the past year had been on loan-outs to other studios, and MGM didn't seem to know what to with her. Loy herself found production chief Irving Thalberg's motivations murky at best, and one day decided to confront him. She related the encounter with the legendary producer, in which he kept her "waiting interminably in his outer office. When I finally got in, he turned his back on me, looked out the window and kept talking."

When Loy scolded Thalberg for not facing her, he turned around and was honest: Her shyness was putting a veil between her and her audience. "You've got to cut through the veil and take hold of that audience," Thalberg said. "Make it yours. It's there and they like you. They adore you. You're beautiful enough for the movies, you're making good progress here, so make it work for you." Loy said after that meeting with Thalberg, she felt for the first time that MGM had plans for her (Loy, 1988).

Those plans are apparent when viewing the five MGM films released between May and November 1933, which represented her true apprenticeship to stardom. While her screen persona did not yet reflect her future status as the world's "perfect wife," viewing the films provides some insight on how MGM was further developing Myrna Loy for stardom.

The first, *The Barbarian*, was released in May. Loy was cast as Diana, a respectable society daughter who is taken to Egypt by her fiancé, Gerald (Reginald Denny), who has some vague job there having to do with aqueducts. In Egypt, Gerald becomes wary of Jamil (Ramon Novarro), the passionate Egyptian dragoman who is clearly besotted with Diana.

Ramon Novarro was a Mexican actor who had hit it big in the silent era playing the lead in MGM's *Ben-Hur* and whose popularity in talking pictures was sadly waning. While Novarro was talented, with a light comedic touch and a fine singing voice, MGM did not handle his career particularly well, casting him in mediocre picture after mediocre picture playing every conceivable ethnicity except his

Myrna Loy in *The Barbarian* (1933). Directed by Sam Wood. *MGM/Photofest* © *MGM*

own. In *The Barbarian*, Novarro played an Arab with a distinctive Mexican accent in a throwback to the "Sheik" films that were the rage in silent pictures for a short time thanks to the hyperventilating sex appeal of Rudolph Valentino.

It is a ridiculous film, but morbidly fascinating as a pre-Code relic featuring Loy in various states of undress. It is also notable that the film takes great pains to remind us that Loy's character is half-Egyptian. While Loy fortunately doesn't have to wear makeup this time around to make her seem more "foreign," it feels like the verbal reminders of her "half-breed" state are just bones for audiences still inexplicably attached to the idea of Loy as exotic, as well as an antiquated, racist way to explain away her attraction to Jamil. In the early 1930s, miscegenation was seen as a far worse crime than adultery.

Every time Jamil sings to her, Diana half-closes her eyes not only to project a level of arousal but also as a kind of flashback to the old, vampish Myrna Loy. The part of Diana seems almost uncannily timed to act as a transition part for Loy, in which she plays a sophisticated, upper-class role while suppressing her darker nature, a nature that Jamil pries open with his Arabian sex appeal. At the end, despite being raped by Jamil in the desert, Diana abandons her fiancé Gerald for Jamil on her wedding day.

Perhaps more notable than the film itself was the growing willingness of the MGM publicity department to trumpet their new star. After Loy and Novarro became friends on the set, stories started to appear in the fan magazines about a romance between the co-stars. The headline in *Motion Picture Magazine* blared, "A SECRET WEDDING FOR MYRNA AND RAMON?"

> Is Myrna Loy going to marry Ramon Novarro? Has she married him already? She will not openly admit as much, but when the subject was broached, she colored rosily and she giggled. When a woman blushes and giggles, there is something on her mind. . . . Perhaps the secrecy is Myrna's own wish. She has always been mysterious about her private affairs. She is the one woman in Hollywood who has never been openly or publicly pronounced in love. (Fidler, 1933)

Whether the publicity department trumpeted up the fake romance to promote Loy or cover up Novarro's homosexuality can be up for debate, but Loy's star was on the rise and Novarro's already on the decline, so it seemed to behoove MGM's publicity department to try to pump up Loy. The article was the usual kind of poppycock with which many in the business had become familiar.

Even Loy's notorious shyness was highlighted, creating an article promoting a woman who didn't really want to be promoted. "It is a safe statement that Myrna Loy has been seen in public less than three dozen times during her eleven years in Hollywood," the article claimed (Fidler, 1933).

Loy remembered the shock of opening a newspaper and reading about her "torrid romance" with her co-star. "That particular thing hadn't happened to me before," she wrote. "It infuriated me and I raised hell. Whether or not that had anything to do with it, I don't know, but it never happened again" (Loy, 1988).

In June 1933, MGM released *When Ladies Meet*, which reunited Loy with her *Animal Kingdom* co-star Ann Harding, and once again they are rivals. Mary Howard (Loy) is an author having an affair with her publisher, Rogers Woodruff (Frank Morgan). Mary's frustrated suitor Jimmie (Robert Montgomery) introduces her to Woodruff's wife Clare (Ann Harding) without revealing the woman's identity.

We find out later that Mary has written a book about a love triangle uncannily similar to the one in which she finds herself and, still not knowing Clare is her lover's wife, asks her advice, as a woman, how believable she finds the ending, in which the husband chooses the lover over his wife. Clare knows full well her own husband's litany of adulterous conquests and tells Mary that any husband who has taken mistresses will never leave his wife. Mary—who is fully in love with Woodruff—disagrees. Then, suddenly (and of course) Woodruff stumbles into the room, and everyone's true identity is revealed. Clare tells Mary that she will allow her husband to leave with her, and then Woodruff tells Mary that he doesn't really love her and he will stay with his wife. Loy's devastation is tactile, and it results in one of her finest moments of acting in her early career.

Loy's next picture would introduce her to producer Hunt Stromberg, screenwriters Frances Goodrich and Albert Hackett, and director W. S. "Woody" Van Dyke, all of whom would be part of *The Thin Man* months later and change her life forever. Released in September 1933, *Penthouse* is one of the lesser-known films of Loy's career, but is perhaps the most important because of the outstanding working relationship she forged with Van Dyke, who would soon trumpet Loy as MGM's next big star.

Van Dyke at this time was known for his extraordinary efficiency, oftentimes getting a film in the can after only two or three weeks of shooting, which earned him the affectionate nickname of "One Take Woody." He was also known primarily for a series of ethnographic pictures featuring "exotic" locales, such as *White Shadows in the South Seas*, *The Pagan*, *Trader Horn*, and *Tarzan the Ape Man*. *Trader Horn* was notable for featuring location shooting in Africa, an exceptionally rare thing during the studio days, and despite the condescending and often baldly racist points of view of both that film and *Tarzan the Ape Man*, which featured primitive and clumsy back-projected footage from the former film, it is a fascinating artifact.

Penthouse, based on a *Cosmopolitan* magazine story by Arthur Somers Roche, is the complicated tale of shady defense attorney Jackson Durant (Warner Baxter), who is called to defend his ex-girlfriend's fiancé, Tom Siddall (Phillips Holmes), for the murder of call girl Mimi Montagne (Mae Clarke). Loy doesn't appear until thirty-four minutes into the picture as Gertie, a gangster's mistress and Mimi's best friend, who helps Jackson find the real killer. The whole plot is extraordinarily complicated, and it is a testament to accomplished screenwriters Goodrich and Hackett's skills that the viewer is even able to keep up, especially after Gertie appears out of nowhere and magically becomes the second lead.

Here, Myrna Loy was allowed to be Myrna Loy. As Jackson tells her sincerely near the closing of the picture, "You're fine. You're nice." While she doesn't play a literal wife, Loy still represents a kind of proxy "perfect wife." Here, Loy hints at things to come in her characterization of Gertie. She immediately adores Jackson, crinkles her nose, makes wisecracks, and even disobeys him when he pleads with her to stay inside his apartment to remain safe from murderous gangsters, just as she would disobey William Powell in the *Thin Man* movies.

Penthouse was too plot-heavy and didn't have the full charm and appeal of *The Thin Man* movies, but it was the most important film in Loy's career to that point. Loy showed that she could be an appealing lead actress, and Gertie embodied the most appealing traits of Nora Charles. It is the first film, for example, in which we see Loy crinkle her nose. Clearly, producer Hunt Stromberg and director W. S. Van Dyke saw something. Loy's transformation into a leading lady was nearly complete.

In her next film released in October 1933, *Night Flight*, Loy had a total of four minutes of screen time in two scenes, but the role—as an unnamed pilot's wife—was still a milestone because it was the first time Loy was truly portrayed as the "perfect wife." The film was an all-star effort featuring John and Lionel Barrymore, Clark Gable, Helen Hayes, and Robert Montgomery billed above Loy in a tale of South American aviators attempting the dangerous task of flying at night to deliver the mail. Produced by David O. Selznick, the film tried to be an all-star showcase of star personalities like the prior year's *Grand Hotel*, but wound up being a rather dull series of vignettes in which the stars barely ever appear together on screen.

Loy appears in a scene when her pilot husband (William Gargan) is called in the middle of the night to make a flight. She is appropriately concerned and devoted in a seemingly thankless part, but the significance of her role isn't in the character she played, but that she was the one who played it. It had been less than a year since Loy had appeared in *The Mask of Fu Manchu*, and now she had taken her rightful place in the position of a lady of high exalted status and ideal womanhood. When her pilot husband receives the call to danger, she is deeply concerned but unquestionably devoted to her husband.

"I know how sure, how STRONG you are, but be careful, darling!" she pleads. She puts on her brave face, but loses her nerve and finally collapses on the bed crying. While one can easily look at the scene as a dated cliché, it is an especially significant moment in Loy's career because this was David O. Selznick's second picture at MGM after he left RKO, and giving Loy this part—despite its brevity—reflected his and the studio's belief in her new screen persona. The man who had handed her *The Animal Kingdom* and *Topaze* continued to shape her career.

Loy's final film of 1933, *The Prizefighter and the Lady*, was another chance to work with director W. S. Van Dyke, now her biggest fan at MGM. She was given the challenging task of acting opposite Max Baer, a boxer with no acting experience. It was one of those projects that had gone through a multitude of lineup changes. The director Josef von Sternberg was originally attached and left early in preproduction and then Howard Hawks was assigned to the picture. While Hawks claimed he was only aboard for a short time to teach some acting pointers to the inexperienced Baer, co-screenwriter John Lee Mahin later said MGM fired him because Hawks was already six days behind schedule after two days of production (McCarthy, 1997).

The super-efficient Van Dyke was a natural choice to take over a production that had quickly gone behind schedule. While Van Dyke later claimed the part had originally been written for Loy, the original stars attached to the project were Clark Gable and Joan Crawford. It was only when Crawford left the project to make MGM's *Dancing Lady* with Gable and after Van Dyke came aboard that Loy was cast.

The casting made sense from Van Dyke's perspective. As in *Penthouse*, Loy plays a gangster's moll who transforms into a respectable lady and the "perfect wife." Here she plays Belle Mercer, girlfriend to notorious gangster Willie Ryan (Otto Kruger) and singer at his nightclub, who is rescued from a car wreck by genial meathead Steve Morgan (Baer). Morgan, who's on the rise as a boxer after being discovered by the Professor (Walter Huston), pursues Belle despite the danger of her mob ties; he eventually wins her and they marry.

Morgan's fame grows with every victory, thanks in part to his connection to the notorious Belle, who becomes a completely devoted wife, trading in her expensive gangster-moll clothes for an apron and duster. When his fame and his ego grow, Morgan blatantly accepts the attentions of adoring lady fans right in front of Belle. While she tries to put on a brave face, she eventually breaks when she catches her husband in a compromising position and gives him an ultimatum.

"If I mean anything to you, please don't let me hate you. It wouldn't be very nice," Loy says in the calmest, kindest possible way. When Morgan appears in an amusingly ridiculous vaudeville revue surrounded by chorus girls and Belle catches him in his dressing room with one of them later, she is finally fed up and leaves him, goes to Willie, and asks for a job. Morgan shows up, trying to take her home. Belle refuses and begs Willie not to kill him. Morgan leaves, but Willie believes Belle is still in love with the lug. He backs Willie's fight against World Champion Primo Carnera for $25,000 at Madison Square Garden so Primo will knock his head into the East River.

An out-of-control Morgan fires the Professor and approaches his fight with Primo as a total mess. When Belle attends the fight with Willie, she gamely pretends to hate Morgan, but Willie knows better. When a dispirited Morgan is getting the snot beaten out of him, Belle convinces the Professor to go up ringside, and inspired by the Professor and Belle's support, he is restored. A draw is called, Belle faints; she later goes back to Willie's nightclub, where Morgan shows up and declares, "I'm tired of being a big shot. I just want you."

The film itself is mostly of interest to boxing historians, with a full half hour at the end of the film devoted to Morgan's big fight against Primo Carnera, a real professional boxer playing himself. Ironically, the following year Max Baer would defeat Carnera in real life to become the heavyweight champion. Loy claimed later that it was Baer's studious observations of Carnera during filming that led to his victory.

The Prizefighter and the Lady completed a cycle of films that transformed Loy's screen persona forever from the cold, calculating, exotically attired villain into the "perfect wife." The speed with which this occurred is almost incomprehensible today, when films are far more infrequent and are often mired in preproduction for years. The studio system's extraordinary efficiency allowed it to take advantage of success and veer a star toward roles that the public and the critics embraced.

The characters Loy portrayed in *Penthouse* and *The Prizefighter and the Lady* paralleled her own career trajectory. Once a tarnished jewel associated with the criminal element, she emerges as a straight arrow, a wife (or wife figure) completely devoted to her mate's well-being, both personally and professionally. In *Penthouse*, she falls in love with Warner Baxter and insinuates her way into his legal investigation, and in *The Prizefighter and the Lady*, it's watching Max Baer fighting in the ring that makes her rediscover her love for him and forgive his many infidelities. It wasn't anything he said or did. It was watching him succeed at his chosen profession, beating another man to a pulp.

Meanwhile, William Powell was at Warner Bros. Like ships passing in the night, he had joined the studio just as Loy had left to sign with Fox Film Co., and while Loy's screen persona evolved into Nora Charles and the perfect wife rather quickly, Powell's path to Nick Charles was a bit more circuitous. At the beginning of the sound era, he was able to transition almost immediately from heavy to hero, but he was hampered by the mediocre pictures into which Paramount had cast him.

Fortunately for Powell, the Warners lot was starved at the time for marquee names, and someone of his stature was sorely needed. During its few years in the silent era, the studio was already short on stars, and few of those were making a successful transition to talkies. When Powell arrived on the lot in early 1931, newer contract players like Edward G. Robinson and James Cagney were not yet considered star material, with the impact of spectacular successes *Little Caesar* and *The Public Enemy* yet to come. With players like Cagney and Robinson, however, and other players like Barbara Stanwyck, Joan Blondell, and Douglas Fairbanks Jr. on the lot—and Darryl F. Zanuck still running things—Warners was quickly developing a hardboiled, working-class house style. In 1931, many Warners' films were muscular little melodramas that eschewed the glamour and sheen of the films of Paramount and MGM, and more than any other studio at the time, Warner Bros. had pictures that were steeped in the awareness that the Great Depression was really happening. It was still escapism, but Zanuck's gift was creating escapism that was rooted in realism.

Powell's contract provided for forty weeks of work at a salary of $300,000 per year, an extraordinary sum in the middle of the Depression and, notably, his contract contained some unprecedented clauses. Not only did he have script approval, he was to be the "sole star" of all his pictures, and the name of no other person was permitted to appear in the credits in type more than 50 percent the size of Powell's name. Also, the billing had to say "Warner Bros. Pictures Inc. Presents WILLIAM POWELL in 'Name of Photoplay.'" He even had full power to supersede any other actors' clauses. His power was seemingly limitless, as seen in interoffice memos in which the studio negotiates with him to get permission to include the names of the writers and director of his first film, *The Road to Singapore*, in the main titles (Walsh, 2013).

Now that Powell had a blockbuster salary, Warner Bros. actually had to produce films for him. While Powell was known primarily as a suave, debonair gentleman in his Paramount films, the Warners working-class milieu would give him the opportunity to stretch himself. The kind of sophisticated characters wearing top hats and tails that Paramount preferred were simply not part of the Warners style.

Powell's first picture for Warners, *The Road to Singapore*, was released in October 1931, nearly six months after his final film for Paramount was released. Powell plays notorious wife-stealer Hugh Dawltrey, who returns to tropical

Khota much to the horror of society and immediately falls in love with Philippa March (Doris Kenyon), the new bride of successful surgeon Dr. George March (Louis Calhern). Dawltrey also has to contend with the clumsy seduction techniques of Dr. March's very young sister, Rene (Marian Marsh).

On the surface it would seem that Powell picks up right where he left off. He's a sophisticated gentleman and cad who stumbles into real love for the first time and doesn't quite know what to do with himself. If not for the opening credits announcing this as a Warner Bros.–Vitaphone picture, one could easily mistake the screenplay for one of Powell's early Paramount films. The technique is better, however. Director Alfred E. Green will never be mistaken for one of the greats, but he was a capable craftsman for Warners during the pre-Code years and would direct one of the most notable films of that era, *Baby Face*, a couple of years later. There is one marvelous backwards tracking shot beginning with Philippa gazing through the window of her bungalow, the camera gliding through a miniature jungle setting before landing on Powell in his own bungalow, gazing at her from a distance, followed by quick cuts of the two in extreme close-ups. It's a rather bravura little moment.

Powell is perfectly fine in a role that requires him to transform from cad to noble lover, but the surprising highlight of the film is Louis Calhern as Philippa's ridiculous husband, who is so consumed with his work as a doctor that he blithely dismisses an inquiry about whether he and Philippa will have a honeymoon: "We're beyond such juvenile customs as that!" He is not only asexual; he seems never to have even heard of sex. There is certainly no suspense as to whether Philippa will choose William Powell over this very silly man, but Calhern—who was a fine character actor certainly not known for comic roles—is rather funny in the role. The dynamic between the two actors comes to a marvelous head at the end of the picture when Calhern points a gun at Powell, who's about to leave to run away with his wife. Powell, still dressing, responds: "Well, do you mind if I finish? I have a horror of an undertaker dressing me. I've never known one yet who could tie a bow correctly."

Powell calmly walks by Calhern and pauses in the doorway, daring the man to shoot him, and then walks out as Calhern stands there, frozen and impotent. It is a fascinating moment of comic sophistication that contains a hint of Powell's persona to come. Hugh is ultimately fearless because he knows George March is too much of a coward to shoot him, and while we don't necessarily think of Nick Charles as fearless, he does face death with a light sense of humor multiple times. Despite the marked differences between the characters of Hugh Dawltrey and Nick Charles, the seed is there.

Critics didn't spot the subtleties in his first Warners picture, which didn't change many minds about who William Powell was. As *Motion Picture Magazine* put it in the subhead of its November 1931 review, "Powell Still Playing the Charming Cad." It didn't help that Hugh is actually called a cad multiple times in the picture. Powell's second picture for Warners, however, displayed a bold move in his screen persona, and it was obvious to audiences and critics that he was capable of far more than simply being the suave and debonair cad.

As a heavy in silent pictures, Powell appeared in a number of comedies, yet all of the Paramount films in which he starred in talkies were deadly serious. While there was a wry smile from Powell now and then, there was rarely, if any, humor to be found in films like *Street of Chance*, *For the Defense*, or the Philo Vance films.

Released in January 1932 and directed by Mervyn LeRoy, *High Pressure* was the first opportunity for Powell to play comedy as a leading man. He still plays a charming cad but is no longer a romantic figure, and while he certainly dresses well, he's far from a gentleman. Powell plays Gar Evans, a fast-talking promoter who embraces a scheme to promote an invention that allegedly can create artificial rubber out of sewage. The opening scenes show his pal Mike Donahey (Frank McHugh) dragging a fellow named Ginsberg (George Sidney) around town to tell Gar about the marvelous opportunity. They find Gar passed out in a speakeasy after a multiday bender with a $108 bar tab, and what follows are comic scenes of Mike and Ginsberg trying to wake up the unconscious Gar.

In *High Pressure*, Powell is introduced off-screen, with supporting characters talking about him at length. This was a canny way to build some level of audience suspense regarding the star of the picture by withholding him from view, and it was also an efficient way to establish the character by simply having others talk about him. When the hyperactive Donahey spends the first few minutes rhapsodically describing Gar Evans's skill as a promoter and we finally see Powell passed out on a sofa, it provides a humorous counterpoint to the buildup of Gar Evans as this amazing professional.

More significantly, Powell is immediately established here as a comic character and as a funny drunk for the very first time. While modern viewers familiar with Powell's later work could hardly bat an eye at this display, it must have been a bit of a shock for Powell's fans at this time to see him so comically disheveled. The overall tone of the film has the rapid-fire pace of the best of the Warners pre-Code productions, and Powell has far more life in the picture than he ever did in his Paramount talkies. He delivers his dialogue at least twice as quickly as he did in those dull pictures, and there's a real energy to his performance that audiences had not seen since his days as a heavy in silent pictures.

High Pressure (1932). Directed by Mervyn LeRoy. Shown from left: Harry Beresford, Frank McHugh, William Powell. *Author's Collection*

Ironically, it is Powell's energy that cripples his chemistry with leading lady Evelyn Brent, who appears to be in a different picture altogether. She plays the role of the long-suffering girlfriend who has had to put up with Gar's promotional schemes, and she can't keep up with Powell and McHugh. It was a reunion for Powell and Brent, both Paramount emigrés who appeared together in Josef von Sternberg's *The Last Command* and *The Drag Net* and Paramount's first talkie, *Interference*. While Powell had thrived following that first talkie appearance, Brent's career had declined after a handful of appearances in Paramount talkies, reaching its nadir when she co-starred with blackface comedians Moran and Mack, billed as "The Two Black Crows," in *Why Bring That Up?*

Brent would go on to appear in B-movies until the late 1940s, but her days as a major studio leading lady were coming to an end. *High Pressure* was her lone appearance at Warners, and it's easy to see why. She is miscast opposite Powell in a role that would have been far better suited for someone like Joan Blondell. Still, like so many other Warners films, it moves at a fast enough clip that her scenes with Powell are over in a matter of moments.

For his second picture at the studio, Powell greatly benefited from working with director Mervyn LeRoy. LeRoy was the most important house director at Warners and its most efficient director of "A" pictures, having climbed the ladder since his cousin Jesse Lasky got him a job in the wardrobe department at Paramount. Despite the nepotism, LeRoy thrived when he eventually graduated to director. As Thomas Schatz put it, the key to LeRoy's success was his "feel for the contemporary and milieu—a sense of realism that he shared with Zanuck—along with his remarkable efficiency as a movie director" (Schatz, 1989).

LeRoy was the only contract director at Warners to get script approval and final cut. From 1930 to 1933, he directed a staggering twenty-three films for the studio. His productions would always come in on schedule and under budget, and while not all the films he directed during this time period were superlative, they all did a superlative job of representing Zanuck's preferred house style. His films, which often included some level of social commentary, included the gangster classic *Little Caesar* and prison drama *I Am a Fugitive from a Chain Gang*. While addressing social issues, the pictures never got bogged down in any kind of didacticism. These muscular little films rarely if ever exceeded eighty minutes in length and possessed a breathless pace that reflected the relentless quests of their driven male protagonists. It is one of the reasons that actors like James Cagney and Edward G. Robinson thrived at the studio. They had the necessary energy to drive these aggressive narratives.

William Powell fits extraordinarily well into the formula, as seen in *High Pressure*. He is masterful as a fast-talking con man in this social satire. If there was one problem with his continuing in that vein at Warner Bros., it's because James Cagney was not only just as masterful as a fast-talking con man, he could even talk faster. Almost exactly a year after *High Pressure* was released, in January 1933 Warners released *Hard to Handle*, featuring James Cagney in pretty much the exact same part that Powell played in *High Pressure*: a fast-talking con man coming up with grandiose promotion schemes. And the director? Mervyn LeRoy.

Darryl F. Zanuck eschewed the production unit structure that Irving Thalberg embraced at MGM, which designated specific teams of producers, directors, and crew members to specific stars (like Greta Garbo) or genres (like musicals). If anything, William Powell suffered from this lack of structure. Zanuck was all about story, and whichever star was available would be inserted into a picture. Cagney could easily have thrived as Gar Evans in *High Pressure*, but Powell played the role since he was able to choose his projects, and while he was wonderful in it, you couldn't have two stars play the same kinds of roles all the time. It was an inefficient system, and Cagney was too much of a supernatural, energetic presence in those roles to deny him the opportunity to be cast in them all the time. While Powell would make some fine pictures at Warners, he would never find the specific niche that would elevate him to the level of

Cagney or Robinson. For the rest of his run at the studio, Powell would switch from fast-talking con man to charming cad to romantic figure and back. While it was attractive for an actor seeking more variety, it didn't necessarily work for a studio trying to market him in a world where audiences had been trained to expect typecasting.

Powell's next picture for Warners was one of the better pictures that director Ernst Lubitsch never made. Directed by Lubitsch's fellow German émigré William Dieterle, *Jewel Robbery* is set up like the best of Lubitsch's European-set satires at Paramount Pictures. Set in the kind of Vienna that only existed in Hollywood, the sixty-eight-minute gem's plot is disarmingly simple. Powell plays a character known only as the Robber, who holds up a jewelry store and whose courtliness and adventurous spirit win the heart of the terminally bored Baroness Tina (Kay Francis).

Francis, also poached from Paramount, was appearing in her third picture at Warners, and it made sense to reteam her with her old co-star. Francis is charming as the idle wife of a Baron who is captivated by the Robber, and Powell is simply wonderful in his role as a gentleman thief. In many ways, the Robber is a combination of both Powell's silent-film villain and his distinguished gentleman

William Powell and Kay Francis in *Jewel Robbery* (1932). Directed by William Dieterle. *Warner Bros./Photofest © Warner Bros.*

from his Paramount talkies. He is impeccably dressed, he is polite even when brandishing a pistol, and he enunciates his dialogue to such an extent that it is hard not to think he is parodying his own performances in early talkies.

While *Jewel Robbery* does not quite measure up to Lubitsch in the end, the master's films are clearly an inspiration. The film opens with Baroness Tina's servants being alerted that she is waking up, and an absurdly large number of servants file into her bedroom, marching in time to the score. The blocking, the composition, and the wryly amusing commentary on the lives of the aristocracy are all Lubitsch, and Francis is wonderful as the Baroness Tina, talking on and on about the lack of adventure in her life as her endless stream of servants cater to her every need, even literally carrying her from one station of caretaking to the next.

The Baroness will take whatever pleasure in life she can get from her stuffy old husband the Baron (Henry Kolker), and the highlight of her day is a trip to Hollander Juwelier, the finest jeweler in Vienna, to purchase the $50,000 Excelsior Diamond. The Robber enters Hollander Juwelier just as the Baroness begins the purchase and softly requests: "Would you kindly put up your hands? With your permission, Mr. Hollander, we're robbing your shop." As he and his assistants purloin every piece of jewelry they can find on the shelves and on the persons in the shop, the Robber spends his time attempting to reassure Mr. Hollander that, since he's insured, the loss of all the jewelry will not adversely affect his business.

The Robber talks constantly throughout his robbery, explaining that conversation is calming. He unveils a portable phonograph and begins to play "The Blue Danube" as the robbery continues. He requests he be referred to as a "robber" and not as a "thief." The Baroness Tina is appropriately besotted, and even though his instincts tell him to resist her charms, the Robber is clearly intrigued by this strangely adventurous aristocrat. Some slapstick then ensues when the Robber provides everyone with cigarettes that are obviously marijuana to calm them down before he completes the robbery.

Afterwards, the Robber arrives in the Baroness's bedroom and invites her to join him in Nice, since he is now forced to flee Vienna before the authorities catch up with him. After his elegant exit through her bedroom window just as the authorities arrive, the Baroness pretends to have been kidnapped and says she must find some rest. Perhaps in Nice. She ends the picture by breaking the fourth wall, approaching the camera and bringing her finger to her lips, imploring the audience to shush up about it.

Bertram Bloch's English stage adaptation of Hungarian playwright Ladislas Fodor's *Ékszerrablás a Váci-utcában* premiered in January 1932, Warners snapped up the rights in February, and filming started in March, reflecting the rapid-fire competition between the major studios for literary and stage properties and the speed with which they could launch productions. Released in August 1932, *Jewel Robbery* received mixed reviews—critics were all too aware of the Lubitsch influence and may have judged it harshly as a result—although both Francis and Powell received fine notices in general.

Powell would get to work with Francis for the sixth and final time in his very next picture. Released in October 1932, *One Way Passage* would be the best received of all the Powell-Francis teamings at the time. It is radically different than *Jewel Robbery* and a testament to both Powell's and Francis's range. Written by Robert Lord, who would receive an Academy Award for Best Story (a now-defunct category), the film represents another 180-degree turn for Powell at Warners. A rather manipulative tearjerker of a melodrama, *One Way Passage* tells the story of Dan and Joan, who meet cute at a bar in Hong Kong, unaware of each other's secret: Dan is about to be escorted across the Pacific Ocean to meet his demise at San Quentin for murder, and Joan is gravely ill. Nothing is revealed about the nature of why Dan had to commit murder or which illness has beset Joan. Such details are swept aside in this sixty-seven-minute film.

Even with this brevity, however, the film often feels padded by a tiresome, comical B-story. Dan is accompanied by a cop named Steve (Warren Hymer), and the B-story involves two con-artist friends of Dan, played by Aline McMahon and Frank McHugh, who always distract the cop long enough to allow for Dan and Joan's assignations. While Powell and Francis make an engaging couple (again), there's little for them to do for much of the film except gaze lovingly at each other as we follow our two lovers on an ocean liner from Hong Kong to San Francisco with a stop in Honolulu. Of course, simply watching William Powell and Kay Francis gaze lovingly at each other is almost enough.

Powell here is a romantic figure in a role that requires him to become quiet and restrained. He is a tragic figure, and yet there is no melodrama. Powell had come a long way since the Paramount talkies, and by this point he had become a more fully cinematic actor, employing silent techniques in a chilling portrayal of a man who knows he going to die, even as we can see the wheels constantly turning as he tries to plot his escape from the inevitable execution, all while he's falling hopelessly in love.

Director Tay Garnett, one of the best of the early talkie filmmakers, keeps the action moving swiftly, even as the farcical B-story threatens to derail the main romance. The deftest touch of all comes following a recurring bit we see throughout the film: Dan and Joan take drinks together and smash their glasses on the bar. After the ship finally docks in San Francisco and the two lovers meet their fates, they vow to meet again on New Year's Eve at a nightclub called Agua Caliente. In the final shot, we travel to Agua Caliente on New Year's Eve, briefly see Frank McHugh drinking sadly at the bar, and the camera travels to two bartenders cleaning their glasses. They hear glasses smash, and we see two fragments of champagne glasses on the bar, but no lovers. The glasses slowly fade away. The shot, in which neither star appears, is arguably the finest moment in the film.

One would think that, having appeared in two so completely different types of films together in quick succession, Warners would have teamed the two actors again—especially since critics uniformly raved—but the studio didn't. Recall that, thanks to the powerhouse deal that Myron Selznick got Powell, the actor's $6,000-a-week salary came with script approval, and not every script he would approve would necessarily have the right role for Francis.

Also, Francis was becoming the unquestioned queen of the lot, a position she would hold for the next several years until Bette Davis snatched the crown from her, and Warners (along with the other major studios) generally did not team their A stars together. MGM would shatter that preconception in its huge, all-star production of Vicki Baum's *Grand Hotel* that same year, but they had stars to spare for such an effort. Warner Bros. did not.

Because of that, Powell was an invaluable creative resource for the studio. In his first four pictures for Warners, he had shown considerable range and demonstrated that he could fit nicely into any role. Sometimes he was a gentleman, sometimes a crook, sometimes a ladies' man, sometimes a venal con man, sometimes a noble hero making a tragic sacrifice for the greater good, and sometimes all of those characters in the same picture. *Lawyer Man*, his fifth picture at Warners, was one in which his various screen personas shared time in one film. Reteaming Powell with director William Dieterle, it is the prototypical Warner Bros. picture of the era, speeding through the plot with extraordinary speed as we see years pass by in just over an hour.

Powell plays Anton Adam, an East Side lawyer for the common people, and Joan Blondell plays Olga, his secretary, who secretly adores him while he chases other women. Years pass as Anton climbs the ladder of success, suffers disgrace, becomes a cynical tool for his city's political machine, then assistant district attorney, where he survives more disgrace and an assassination attempt, until he finally lands back on the East Side again, once again just a lawyer for the common people.

Warners bought the original story by Max Trell in April 1932 and intended it as a vehicle for either Powell or Edward G. Robinson (*Film Daily*, April 24, 1932). While Robinson was excellent in everything he did and was a contemporary of Powell's—just a year younger—Powell was far more plausible as a man with whom Joan Blondell would be romantically interested, which was unique for a star of his age. By the time Powell was shooting *Lawyer Man* in October 1932, he was forty years old, the second-oldest male star on the Warner Bros. lot after the ancient George Arliss. What made Powell unique was his ability to play a legitimate romantic lead for his age. While Robinson could play romance, his characters were often victims of hopelessly unrequited love, and he never really got to play love scenes.

Complicating matters for Powell at the time was Warners' growing financial difficulties as the grip of the Great Depression continued to tighten. It resulted in a feud between Warners and Myron Selznick and Selznick's partner Frank Coleman Joyce. After Selznick and Joyce declined to allow Warners to cut some stars' salaries, the studio barred their firm from its lot, citing the agency's price-raising tactics and releasing a statement that any of the agency's clients must transact business with the studio directly through Rufus Lemaire, Warners' casting director.

An article in *Variety* (May 10, 1932) mentioned Warners' campaign to cut high-priced star salaries, and the "latest to be approached to shrink their weekly pay check are Ruth Chatterton, Kay Francis and William Powell." As strange as it seems that Warners was regretting the deal with Chatterton, Francis, and Powell just a year after the actors joined the studio, Powell in particular was not paying dividends at the box office as much as Warners anticipated.

In August 1932, *Motion Picture Herald* published the ten biggest money-making Hollywood stars as ranked by a group of 12,000 exhibitors. The three top-ranked stars—Marie Dressler, Janet Gaynor, and Joan Crawford—were all women, and the highest-ranked male star, Fox Film's Charles Farrell, was thirty-two years old, impossibly handsome, and usually cast as the romantic lead opposite Gaynor. The other romantic lead in the top ten, Clark Gable, was thirty-one and also impossibly handsome. While the forty-seven-year-old Wallace Beery, the fifty-two-year-old Will Rogers, and the forty-one-year-old comedian Joe E. Brown were also ranked, they were certainly never cast as romantic leads.

Beyond the top ten, *Motion Picture Herald* also published a complete numerical ranking of stars, showing the percentage of times a star appeared in an exhibitor's list of top moneymaking stars. The top star, Marie Dressler, was mentioned in 71 percent of completed surveys, Janet Gaynor in 65 percent of surveys, and so on. At 30.5 percent, Joe E. Brown was the highest-ranked Warners star, followed by Constance Bennett at 27.5 percent, George Arliss at 26 percent, Barbara Stanwyck at 16 percent, Edward G. Robinson at 15.5 percent, and James Cagney at 13 percent. Powell came in at 1.3 percent alongside the likes of John Boles, Clara Bow, Nancy Carroll, Miriam Hopkins, and Jack Oakie. (Myrna Loy, of course, was not a star yet.)

It is almost inconceivable from today's perspective that Powell would have been less popular than actors like Joe E. Brown and George Arliss, but one likely possibility is that audiences knew exactly what they were getting from those two actors. Fans of Brown knew they were going to get broad comedy, and fans of the sixty-four-year-old, monocle-brandishing Arliss knew they were going to get some kind of sophisticated literary adaptation.

The question that begs to be asked, of course, is whether Warners really thought William Powell was worth $6,000 a week with script approval given his relatively low box office returns. The studio was keeping its eye on the bottom line. In the 1932–1933 movie season, Warners lost $14 million and owed more than $100 million to banks, and Harry Warner—the brother in charge of the business side—was determined not to see Warners go the way of Paramount Pictures and RKO (which also went bankrupt).

By the time *Lawyer Man* was released in January 1933, Warners decided not to exercise the option on Powell's contract after he once again declined a pay cut. A clause in the contract, however, required Warners to make a new offer of some kind in order to have access to competitive bid information, and the ability to measure how it could negotiate a new contract. Powell and Myron Selznick eventually agreed to a forty-week contract with a pay cut to $4,000 a week, which allowed Powell to appear in four pictures with the option of one of the pictures being produced at another studio. *Variety* in May 1933 announced that the pay cut amounted to $40,000 per picture, down from $100,000 per picture.

Alongside Warners' diminishing financial prospects in the spring of 1933 was the departure of Darryl F. Zanuck from the studio. Not only was Powell's salary cut, but all Hollywood studio employees had their paychecks cut by 50 percent for eight weeks as an emergency measure. While Zanuck was initially incensed by the plan, which had been approved by the Academy of Motion Picture Arts and Science Emergency Committee, he acquiesced to the cut. What rankled him, however, was the lack of advance notice. When Price Waterhouse told the Academy that salaries should be restored to their previous levels at the end of the eight-week period, all the studio heads agreed, except for Harry Warner. He and his brother Jack never reduced their own salaries. Zanuck left the studio in a huff in April 1933 and formed 20th Century Pictures with Joe Schenck, a longtime production veteran then with United Artists. Only two years later the new outfit merged with the dying Fox Film and became one of the Big Five studios in a flash (Schatz, 1989).

After Zanuck left Warner Bros., his assistant Hal B. Wallis took over as production chief. He was no "Yes Man," but the change in regime meant that cost savings became a high priority at Warners, and Powell could not have felt particularly comfortable. In fact, Myron Selznick had already begun to work to move Powell to MGM, since the installment of Myron's brother David as a producer there had created an obvious connection.

Powell's long-term future at Warners was in serious doubt, and his next two movies represented a return to the comfortable—at least in terms of content—by returning him to his talkie roots as a sleuth in his next two films, *Private Detective 62* and the *Kennel Murder Case*. Both were directed by Michael Curtiz, Warner's top director alongside Mervyn LeRoy and by this time an unquestioned master of the Warners style of tightly constructed, efficient, muscular narratives. In *Private Detective 62* (the number is never really explained), Powell is Donald Free, a disgraced, seemingly unemployable former spy who desperately needs cash and stoops to working with hugely unethical private detective Dan Hogan (Arthur Hohl). Donald then winds up embroiled in a plot to rob a lucky gambler (Margaret Lindsay) of her winnings, but then falls in love with her. The usual plot complications ensue.

At a tight sixty-six minutes, the film is a fine return to the detective genre for Powell and an example of how effortless these early Warners productions appear to the modern eye. The fact that Donald is working for a detective agency run by a crook makes for some enjoyable plot twists. Powell gets to play some romantic scenes with newcomer Lindsay and play the noble hero trying to overcome the machinations of the rotten detective agency for which he works. Curtiz keeps things moving at a fast clip, and by this time Zanuck's formula is well-worn, comfortable, and efficient, even if the viewer can't remember the film for very long after watching it.

The second Curtiz film, *The Kennel Murder Case*, was the fourth and final time Powell played Philo Vance. It is vastly superior to the Vance films at Paramount in every way. Powell is far more comfortable in the role, which has been softened even further from the insufferable lout in the original novels. Now, Vance is the amiable kind of sophisticated fellow who displays his dog in dog shows. There is no sense of an inner personal life in Vance, but Powell makes for an appealing, charming, sophisticated detective.

It helps that Curtiz and Warners had assembled the usual crack supporting cast, including the welcome return of Eugene Pallette in the role of Sergeant Heath. Pallette too is far more comfortable in his voluminous skin than he ever was in the early Paramounts, and the supporting cast includes Mary Astor and Ralph Morgan and the highly amusing Etienne Girardot as a coroner incensed that the murders keep interrupting his meals. It is an efficiently constructed mystery that opens with scene after scene establishing the victim Archer Coe (Robert Barrat) as a despicable human being whom anyone would want to murder, and then kills him in a room with the lock bolted on the inside.

The Kennel Murder Case is a classic locked-room mystery that never stops for breath to develop characters, and it's all very good fun. Powell's confidence and screen presence establishes a strong foundation, and he makes a fine traditional screen detective. It's a mistake, however, to think of Vance as a kind of embryonic Nick Charles. While Nick was a reluctant detective who would rather drink himself into a happy stupor, Vance cancels a vacation to Italy simply because he thinks a so-called suicide sounds fishy. Vance is an eager, enthusiastic amateur detective in the traditional manner, and if there's anything in the storytelling that's eccentric, it's that the police are perfectly willing to let Vance help out without complaint.

Released in October 1933, *The Kennel Murder Case* would be a critical and box office success, grossing $682,000 on a budget of $272,000. While its grosses were well below Warners' biggest hit of the season—*Gold Diggers of 1933* grossed $2.4 million—it still portended a bright future for Powell. It wasn't long before Warners announced that he would revive the character again in *The Dragon Murder Case*. However, Powell wasn't interested. As popular as the character seemed to be with audiences, he could not have been that interesting to play as an actor. His reticence would not have gone over particularly well.

Released in February 1934, *Fashions of 1934* was Powell's penultimate film with Warner Bros. Here Powell played Sherwood Nash, a con man assisted by Snap (Frank McHugh) and Lynn (Bette Davis). It was the first and only time Powell played opposite Bette Davis, who plays practically the same role as she did opposite James Cagney in *Jimmy the Gent* that same year: the disapproving, scolding, and yet secretly adoring assistant. Here, she reluctantly follows Powell and Frank McHugh as they plot a con to copy expensive clothes by Paris fashion designers and sell them as their own. The con evolves into more and more elaborate schemes until somehow, implausibly, Powell becomes the producer of an elaborate stage show choreographed by Busby Berkeley. Berkeley's lengthy sequence, featuring barely dressed pre-Code chorines, reaches its climax with the appearance of human harps.

It's a marvelous spectacle, of course, but that the sequence is clumsily shoehorned into the film underlines the central problem with the film. While Powell, McHugh, and Davis make a game trio, they're eventually lost amid the spectacle because none of them participate in any of the song and dance. Powell shows some great energy when he's at the height of his con, but once the extravagance takes over, he's lost. Bette Davis at this time was rightly frustrated with these thankless roles, and she rather glumly makes her way through the film. A lame love triangle results when a character named Jimmy (Phillip Reed) falls in love with Davis and implores her to give up Powell and join him on his trip to Berlin. The fact that Davis's character actually struggles with the decision of whether to stay with William Powell or follow this man to Berlin in 1934, after Hitler has taken power in Germany, underscores how little effort was put into the writing of this film.

By the time *Fashions of 1934* was released in February, Powell was just about to be loaned out to MGM to film *The Thin Man*, based on Dashiell Hammett's brand-new smash hit novel. When filming was delayed, Powell was cast in *Manhattan Melodrama*, not coincidentally produced by David O. Selznick, which was such a hit that Powell was signed to a long-term contract with the studio; all it took for Powell to get released from his Warners commitment was a check for $16,333.33 (Walsh, 2013). Warners was more than happy to let the expensive star go, with a sigh of relief that no doubt would lead to a sense of regret once *The Thin Man* became an all-time classic.

Powell did have one final film at Warners before filming *Manhattan Melodrama* at MGM. Filmed in February 1934 and released in June—after both *Manhattan Melodrama* and *The Thin Man* were in theaters—*The Key* was a rather lefthand turn by Warners, a studio never known for politically charged period pieces. Directed by Michael Curtiz, *The Key* was based on *Isle of Fury*, a London play set against the backdrop of the Irish rebellion in 1920. Powell returns to the role of charming cad.

This time he is Captain Bill Tennant, a British officer assigned to Dublin during the Irish rebellion whose chief concern is finding dancers to seduce. In the film Tennant is introduced by hopping off a carriage and encountering a flower girl to whom he is dashing and honorable; once he arrives in the officers' quarters to see the general about his assignment, he is equally dashing. Powell by this point is able to pull off the charm with ease, and he's as comfortable in his own skin as he's ever been. It's hard to imagine he's the same actor who composed himself so stiffly in early talkies.

At seventy-one minutes, this is another typically fast-paced Warner Bros. affair. When Captain Tennant finds lodgings after he is assigned to help find Irish leader Peador Conlan (Donald Crisp), he is pleased to learn his upstairs neighbor is Andy Kerr (Colin Clive), a British spy helping to uncover Conlan. Tennant is less pleased to learn that Kerr's wife, Norah (Edna Best), is a woman with whom he had an affair three years earlier.

Powell acquits himself well with Clive and Best, two British actors who were newcomers to the Warner Bros. lot. Clive, best known as the doomed doctor in James Whale's *Frankenstein*, plays an impassioned advocate against Irish rebellion in contrast to Powell's "professional hero," who will fight anyone for money. Best, in a very rare American appearance, is made up to look as much like Warners' Ruth Chatterton as possible. Popularly known for her role in Alfred Hitchcock's first version of *The Man Who Knew Too Much* that year, Best works well with Powell, and their chemistry successfully recalls Powell and Kay Francis's doomed love in *One Way Passage*. Upon rediscovering his lost love, Powell transforms his character from the fun-loving character we met at the opening of the film to the ardent lover.

Some of Powell's best acting in the film comes in the scenes with Andy and Norah, in which he attempts to hide his longing for Norah, all the while playing the part of fun fellow for Andy's benefit. Curtiz's finest moment as director, meanwhile, comes with some beautifully executed fog-shrouded camera movements, particularly in the moment when Tennant and Norah reconsummate their love affair. Here, while Andy has gone out for another mission at night, Bill and Norah are left in the latter's apartment, standing achingly close to one another as the camera pulls further and further back, out the window and into a dissolve to a brief flashback three years earlier when the two of them are in a passionate embrace. It convincingly provides the message that the same scenario is presenting itself in the here and now, without having to clearly show adultery and rankling the censors.

Eventually, despite their plans to run away together, Norah realizes that it's Andy she loves (imagine choosing Colin Clive over William Powell!), and once Andy is captured by the rebels, who will only release him in return for the release of Conlan, who's due to hang, Tennant sacrifices his career and freedom to forge the general's signature ordering Conlan free.

A June 5, 1934, *Variety* article stated:

William Powell is starred, but the acting honors go to Colin Clive. Fault doesn't lie with Powell. It's a role that's as wooden as the central plot itself. In the early phase of the narrative, when the characterization calls for a debonair, glib fellow with a flair for getting himself out of femme complications, the Powell personality clicks on all cylinders. Later, when the tale gives way to self-sacrificing, Powell becomes no longer a focal point of attention. From then on he's a puppet moving this way and that to the tug of the strings. To the femme following the Powell assignment here will likely prove disappointing.

The unnamed reviewer for *Variety* is being a little unfair, since the appearance of his great love motivates Powell's change in character, but the film was bound to disappoint as a picture released just a couple of weeks after *The Thin Man* positively blew everyone away. *The Key* turned out to be a bit of an anticlimactic end to William Powell's time at Warner Bros. In all likelihood, he would never have succeeded at MGM if not for nine films at Warners, where he proved he had more range than anyone likely expected, and his turns in *High Pressure* and *Jewel Robbery* especially showed that he did have the capacity for comedy. How extraordinary that capacity was had yet to be seen, but without those films, Powell's potential in that arena would have been completely unknown, and perhaps his success in *The Thin Man* would never have been possible.

6

BECOMING NICK AND NORA

Manhattan Melodrama *brought William Powell to Metro against the protests of some of the executives, who thought I was making a serious mistake in engaging a washed-up star instead of using one of their stock players.*

—David O. Selznick (Selznick, 1972)

In the summer of 1934, industry-wide self-censorship reared its judgmental head following a summer of boycotts organized by the Catholic Legion of Decency, protesting what they perceived was an epidemic of low morals in Hollywood films. While the studios had in theory begun practicing self-censorship with its "Code to Govern the Making of Motion Pictures" in 1930 in an effort to avoid government control of the industry, the studios themselves were the final arbiters of what content was acceptable on their screens. However, during that summer four years later, with their backs against the wall in the face of the legion's successful boycott in Catholic centers like Philadelphia, Boston, and Chicago, the studios capitulated with the creation of the Production Code Administration (PCA) under the auspices of Will Hays's Motion Picture Producers and Distributors of America (MP-PDA). Headed by Joseph Breen, a lifelong Catholic and virulent anti-Semite, the PCA would judge all major studio films fit or unfit to release based on their moral content. For years going forward, married couples would sleep in separate beds, criminals always paid the penalty for their crimes, and a litany of other rules had to be followed.

The year 1934 also saw the dawn of a new age of romantic comedy. Released in February by Columbia Pictures, Frank Capra's *It Happened One Night* featured Clark Gable and Claudette Colbert in the story of a newspaper reporter greedily seeking the reward money for a spoiled runaway heiress, and how the two fall in love on the road. The first of three films to win Academy Awards in every one of the five major categories, *It Happened One Night* was one of the progenitors of the "screwball comedy," a fast-talking variation on the romantic comedy featuring the male star in the straight role dealing with a comic leading lady, usually a spoiled member of the upper class. Class played an enormous part in the screwball comedy as the nation emerged from the Great Depression, and the wealthy class was a desirable target for mockery.

Aside from beginning a golden age of romantic comedy, *It Happened One Night* cemented forever the wisecracking, immoral, but ultimately kind-hearted lug displaying a hearty Rooseveltian masculinity that would define Clark Gable's persona for decades to come. Gable had signed with MGM in 1930, and the following year he went through a gauntlet of twelve features in supporting and leading roles before his breakthrough in Victor Fleming's *Red Dust*, which paired him with a white-hot Jean Harlow and made them both top stars at the studio.

After the loan-out to Columbia Pictures for *It Happened One Night*, Gable returned to his home studio to star in an adaptation of Sidney Kingsley's Pulitzer Prize–winning play, *Men in White*. The play was a look at the professional and personal lives of doctors as they face their roles as heroic "men in white" in contrast to their personal difficulties. Starring alongside Gable, with her name above the title for the very first time, was Myrna Loy. The fact that Loy would co-star with one of MGM's biggest stars in the adaptation of such a prestigious play reflected how much her star had risen at MGM over the prior year.

In *Men in White*, Loy plays a vain and selfish society girl named Laura Hudson, the fiancée of Dr. George Ferguson (Gable). Ferguson is a young hospital intern working eighteen to twenty hours a day saving lives. Meanwhile, Laura relentlessly berates him because she resents the time he spends at the hospital. Laura is an unbearably selfish character that would be hard to watch in the hands of a lesser performer, and it is a testament to how much Loy had grown as an actor that she does not play her like a dastardly shrew. There is a sense that she legitimately misses him as opposed to just being philosophically opposed to the idea of hospitals. The script makes it difficult, however, for Loy to salvage much audience sympathy for Laura.

Director Richard Boleslavsky does the best he can with the seventy-three-minute film that seems much longer, bathing the set with unmotivated shadows to add some sense of artistry, but the picture is not a success, primarily because Loy and Gable's characters are so thinly drawn. Censorship issues revolving around a botched abortion in the original play hurt the adaptation, but it is clear that the story was simplified considerably given the short running time. The original play was three acts long.

So while Myrna Loy now appeared above the title and was a definitive star at MGM, she still lacked actual star power. Ads in trade magazines for *Men in White* only spotlighted Gable as the star, and while Loy clearly was on the upswing, it was also clear to some observers that her tremendous potential had yet to be fully tapped.

Cecelia Ager wrote in her "Going Places" column in *Variety*:

> The career of Myrna Loy, which has lately taken on promise and scope, pauses in its advance for "Men in White," rests a spell, finds in "Men in White" scant opportunity to foster its development.
>
> Granted here a strictly conventional role, Miss Loy brings to it her own qualities of understanding and regularness, expands it with her own personality, makes a stock characterization something more than that, but it is still routine work done by an actress who rates more interesting material. It doesn't tap Miss Loy's capabilities. (Ager, 1934)

While Loy was filming *Men in White*, Powell signed *The Thin Man* contract, and almost immediately the pieces fell into place to bring his star power to a whole new level. When MGM decided to delay filming to fit *Manhattan Melodrama* into its production schedule, that picture turned out to be Powell's first with the studio, his first with Myrna Loy, and his first with W. S. Van Dyke. It also reunited both stars with David O. Selznick.

Produced by Selznick, who had a smash hit at the struggling RKO the year before in the studio-saving *King Kong* before moving to MGM, *Manhattan Melodrama* was a prestige production with much larger scope and ambition than anything Powell had done at Warner Bros. The film featured a giant riverboat fire and a Bolshevik-flamed riot in the first two scenes alone. Directed by Van Dyke and shot by James Wong Howe, *Manhattan Melodrama* reflects Selznick's aesthetic of enormous set pieces, giant stakes, and high melodrama.

In the film, Powell and Gable play lifelong friends Jim Wade and Blackie Gallagher, the former rising through the ranks to district attorney and eventual governor of New York and the latter rising through the ranks of the criminal underworld. The two remain best friends despite falling on different sides of the law. The whole thing plays like a rough draft of Michael Curtiz's 1938 masterpiece *Angels with Dirty Faces*, in which Pat O'Brien and James Cagney play

Myrna Loy and William Powell in *Manhattan Melodrama* (1934). Directed by W. S. Van Dyke. *Author's Collection*

lifelong friends who would face off in adulthood as priest and criminal. While Cagney could articulate the inner-coiled rage that made him such a believable and terrifying criminal in his best gangster pictures, Gable's threat was more on the surface. His innate charm was too strong for him truly to be terrifying the way Cagney was.

What also separated *Manhattan Melodrama* and *Angels with Dirty Faces* was the wedge that would come between the opposing best friends. In the former film, we have Myrna Loy as Gable's lover and Powell's eventual wife, and in the latter we have the hero-worshiping East Side Kids. Loy acquits herself admirably in what could have been a thankless role.

The big moment in *Manhattan Melodrama* is the first time Loy's Eleanor and Powell's Jim Wade meet. In a rather implausible plot machination, Gable's Blackie tells Eleanor to go with Jim to a nightclub to wait for him while he runs off on some criminal commitment. While Jim is in the car waiting for the driver to hit the pedal, Eleanor jumps in, trips, and falls right onto an astonished Jim's lap.

The sequence in the car is one of the few organic moments in a film weighed down by the requirements of melodrama. Powell and Loy immediately fall into a patter they would soon perfect as Nick and Nora Charles. Their chemistry, in fact, is so strong that the scene almost seems like it's from a different picture. It's impossible that W. S. Van Dyke, who would direct the two in *The Thin Man*, could not have noticed the ease with which the two traded lines.

The chemistry between the two actors was extraordinary and immediate. It all comes down to the simple act of acknowledging and listening to your partner on screen. Loy in particular had had so much thankless experience as a supporting character in dozens of films that her ability to listen had become perhaps her paramount talent. Remarkably, the first scene in *Manhattan Melodrama* in which Jim and Eleanor meet in the car was shot before Loy and Powell had even met. "When Woody called 'Action,'" Loy said, "I opened the car door, jumped in, and landed smack on William Powell's lap. He looked up nonchalantly: 'Miss Loy, I presume?' I said, 'Mr. Powell?' And that's how I met the man who would be my partner in fourteen films" (Loy, 1988).

When Eleanor winds up marrying Jim, Blackie—ever the noble gangster—blesses the union. The trio remain great friends even after Jim becomes district attorney and prepares a campaign to run for governor. Richard Snow, Jim's former assistant, threatens to tell the press that Jim has covered up Blackie's previous crimes. While the claim is false, it would do damage to Jim's campaign, and Blackie thinks he's doing a favor when he murders Snow in a public restroom. Unfortunately, a witness emerges when it turns out the blind man begging outside the restroom isn't blind at all. Jim does his civic duty and prosecutes Blackie, who's found guilty and sent to death row.

After being elected governor, Jim watches tearfully as Blackie prepares to go to the chair and refuses to commute Blackie's sentence when Eleanor begs him to. When she reveals that Blackie murdered Snow to assist Jim's run for governor, he becomes more steadfast in his resolve to see justice done no matter his personal feelings. Finally, though, he breaks down and rushes to the death house to tell Blackie he wants to commute his sentence. Blackie, who worships Jim for his ideals despite his own criminal proclivities, refuses, saying he'd rather die than serve life in prison. After Blackie's execution, Jim addresses the state assembly and nobly resigns from office, confessing that Blackie committed murder to help his gubernatorial campaign as well as revealing his own faltering sense of justice in wanting to commute Blackie's sentence.

The whole thing is even more melodramatic than you would expect from a picture with *Melodrama* in the title. Today, the picture is far less known for its own story than it is for being the picture that gangster John Dillinger was viewing at the Biograph Theater in Chicago when he was discovered by police and killed.

And while *Manhattan Melodrama* was the first time that audiences saw Powell and Loy together on screen, they were certainly not perceived as a "screen team" at the time because the relationship at the heart of the film was between Gable and Powell's characters. While some contemporary historians have claimed that Powell and Loy were cast in *The Thin Man* because director W. S. Van Dyke had noticed their chemistry in *Manhattan Melodrama*, the two were cast in *The Thin Man* first. MGM borrowed Powell from Warners to play Nick Charles based on his Philo Vance films, and Loy was cast as Nora primarily because of her work with Van Dyke in *Penthouse* and *The Prizefighter and the Lady*. In *Manhattan Melodrama*, the scene in the car in which Powell and Loy first meet was the only real inkling to audiences of the greatness of what was yet to come.

The real couple in the picture—Powell and Gable—are wonderful together, and it is a shame the two never got to work together again. Their polar-opposite screen energies work perfectly together to support the counterpoints between their characters. Powell channels his noble, self-sacrificing persona from earlier films like *Street of Chance*, *One Way Passage*, and *The Key*, and Gable is remarkably successful as the seemingly contradictory character who worships Powell's passion for the law and yet continues to fully embrace the criminal life.

The picture brought in $1.2 million on a budget of $355,000, and while it was a hit with audiences, reviews were mixed. While all rhapsodized about the performances of Gable, Powell, and Loy, some found the implausible and unmotivated melodrama more than a little tiresome. Mordaunt Hall in the *New York Times* (May 5, 1934) criticized "a mechanical plot which is scarcely worthy of the cast," and *Variety* (May 8, 1934), after enthusing over the picture's box office prospects, said the picture "is possibly a bit verbose in its unfolding; that the basic situation is obviously not an entirely original thought; that the melodramatics are at times synthetic."

By the time *Manhattan Melodrama* completed filming in the first week of April, *The Thin Man* was ready to shoot. Based on Dashiell Hammett's sixth (and final) novel, *The Thin Man* was the tale of a retired detective named Nick Charles and his wife Nora. On vacation for Christmas, they encounter Dorothy Winant, a young woman whose father Clyde, an eccentric scientist, has been missing for two months after hiding away to work on a secret invention. When his mistress Julia Wolf winds up dead, Clyde Winant is the main suspect and a manhunt begins. Nick, who would rather spend his days and nights drinking to excess, finally consents to investigate the matter thanks to threats from the people involved and Nora's own sense of adventure.

There is no sign of Winant, the "Thin Man" of the title, in Hammett's original novel. It opens with Dorothy informing Nick of his disappearance, and other characters merely refer to him, so his legitimacy as a murder suspect is not adequately established, since the reader has no way to form an opinion about his character. The film's introduction improves on the novel significantly by planting the seed of misgiving in the audience against Winant, the prime suspect in the two murders following his suspicious disappearance.

The opening scene of *The Thin Man* is a triumph of studio screenwriting by Albert Hackett and Frances Goodrich, a husband-and-wife team that would later co-write Frank Capra's *It's a Wonderful Life* and eventually win the Pulitzer Prize for Drama in 1956 for *The Diary of Anne Frank*. Here, they introduce Winant immediately as this cruel, eccentric scientist in an eerie laboratory, who fires his assistant for distracting him. Only a few shots later, Maureen O'Sullivan enters as daughter Dorothy. O'Sullivan, best known then as Jane in the MGM *Tarzan* movies, possessed a luminescent, spritely presence whose perky announcement of her engagement and introduction to her fiancé brings out Winant's humanity. Within three minutes, Hackett, Goodrich, Van Dyke, and Howe establish Winant not only as a plausible murder suspect prone to fits of uncontrollable temper, but also as a kind and loving father.

In fact, we don't even see Nick or Nora Charles until the eleven-minute mark of the film, turning the tradition of the detective novel on its ear. Hammett, the inventor of the modern form, opens stories like *The Maltese Falcon* with the introduction of the detective, followed almost immediately by the introduction of a woman approaching him to seek his help. The crime to be solved is provided by the new clients' simple explanation of their problem and the services they need the detective to provide.

Hackett and Goodrich, on the other hand, establish the world of the murder suspect (and victim) Clyde Winant first, giving the audience a crystal-clear picture of all the major players in the mystery to come. With the hindsight of nearly eighty-five years, it's easy to underestimate the simple and elegant brilliance in this approach, but by investing the audience in the players in the mystery before introducing the mystery itself, *The Thin Man* screenplay can concentrate next on establishing Nick and Nora's relationship. A brief scene with Dorothy seeking Nick's help is necessary to establish first, that they know each other and second, that Nick is a former detective, but by getting all the exposition regarding the mystery out of the way, now the filmmakers can concentrate on the most important part of the film: the relationship between Nick and Nora Charles.

That relationship was then and remains today an extraordinary outlier for romantic comedies. The well-known tradition for the genre is for our two protagonists to begin the story with an adversarial relationship loaded with sexual tension and move on to the inevitable conflicts that arise: a prior existing relationship, perhaps some kind of class difference, a moment of revelation (the first kiss!) followed by a misunderstanding, until finally one of the protagonists must declare undying love as the other is just about to utter "I do" to the wrong person in a crowded church.

In *The Thin Man*, the entire plot of a typical romantic comedy is in the past. Nick and Nora are an established married couple, and there is absolutely no sign whatsoever of any marital problems. The conflict that one would deem missing, that unreleased tension on which the form relies so heavily, here is replaced by the murder mystery. Nick, the wary ex-detective, and Nora, the eager would-be-adventuress, are able to engage in witty wordplay, annoy, tease, and cajole each other, without the fear of the relationship dissolving into pointless conflict. The conflict already exists in the mystery.

Powell plays Nick Charles as a playboy without the unsavory womanizing elements one associates with the trope. He's a wastrel and a drinker who un-apologetically lives off his wife's wealth and has little desire to work a day in his life. But he adores his wife. He loves her. She fascinates him. She's his best friend. What Powell brings to the role is a kind of restrained elegance, but not the unattainable elegance that someone like Cary Grant possessed. As luminous and excellent as he was as an actor, Grant was a superman on screen, the man every man wanted to be, while William Powell represented the man that every man already was. His heavy-set eyes, rakish mustache, and receding hairline belie the image of the classic movie star.

Introduced on screen for the first time, Nick and Nora's best-known trait is immediately established: their drinking. Rarely does a single frame appear without a drink in either Nick or Nora's hands. When such a frame does appear, it is because one of the two is waiting for a drink to be poured. Nick and Nora's devotion to drinking remains intact from Hammett's original novel. Written in 1933, when the Twenty-First Amendment repealing Prohibition was introduced in Congress, the drinking in the novel and the relationship between the couple reflected the inebriated lifestyle embraced by Hammett and his paramour, Lillian Hellman. The film only enhanced the glamour of drinking. Screenwriters Hackett and Goodrich wrote the screenplay for *The Thin Man* in February 1934, only three months after the ratification of the Twenty-First Amendment, and the film is soaked to the brim in the glory of drinking, reflecting a celebratory environment that had washed over the country in those first months after repeal. While Hollywood films during the years of Prohibition had often shamelessly depicted drinking in speakeasies and the criminal element that resulted from bootlegging, *The Thin Man* opens with a scene in a nightclub that will never be raided because the whole thing is completely legal.

The words "Nick and Nora" will forever be associated with drinking. Even the cocktail glasses from which we see Nick and Nora drinking in the first scene of the film have in the decades since been branded "Nick and Nora" glasses and are still sold today with that label. Young people who drink from the small glasses during the cocktail revival of the twenty-first century know what "Nick and Nora" represent, even if they've never seen *The Thin Man*.

When we first see Nick Charles, we're at an unnamed nightclub on Christmas Eve, where Dorothy Winant and her fiancé Tommy are dancing. Dorothy expresses disappointment that she hasn't heard from her father in months and Tommy attempts to allay her fear that's something happened to him. Van Dyke and Howe follow their dancing with a gracefully moving camera. They dance off frame and the camera moves through the other couples to see the back of Nick Charles, vigorously shaking a cocktail shaker in an attempt to instruct the three bartenders how to do so.

"See, the important thing is the rhythm," he lectures the skeptical bartenders, "always have a rhythm to your shaking. A Manhattan you shake to a fox trot. A Bronx to a two-step time. A dry martini you always shake to waltzes." He places the completed martini on a tray and immediately picks it up again, sniffs it happily, and drinks as Dorothy Winant notices him.

The staging of the introduction of Nick Charles is perfection. We're establishing several things at the outset. Nick, adorned in a tux, is a drunk. But he's a charming drunk. He's also a drunk who possesses a certain pride in his drunkenness. He feels obliged to educate professionals on the proper way to mix a drink. He does not do so arrogantly, however. He's charming, funny, handsome, lazy. Nora's introduction, which comes as she is dragged into the bar by their dog, Asta, echoes the introduction Hammett created for the novel. As Nick stands at the bar speaking with Dorothy Winant, Asta suddenly pops up out of nowhere. In the novel, told in the first person from Nick's perspective:

> Asta jumped up and punched me in the belly with her front feet. Nora, at the other end of the leash, said: "She's had a swell afternoon—knocked over a table of toys at Lord & Taylor's, scared a fat woman silly by licking her leg in Saks, and's been patted by three policemen."

Shot by James Wong Howe, near the beginning of a legendary decades-long career that would see him win two Academy Awards for Best Cinematography, *The Thin Man* displays little of the young cinematographer's gift for dramatic, low-key lighting he had displayed in films like William K. Howard's *Transatlantic* in 1931.

Still, Howe does manage to fit in a few stylistic flourishes. The opening shot consists of the giant cast shadow on a wall of eccentric scientist Winant operating a mysterious invention that is never identified, and when the camera tilts down from the shadow, we see the old man surrounded by apparati, deep dark shadows, and a droning sound from the mystery machine, all echoing the sound and look of the Universal horror pictures of the time.

In the film version of Nora's first appearance in the nightclub, Howe's camera gracefully follows her from behind in a lengthy tracking shot as she's dragged into the bar by Asta, holding piles of giftboxes, and finally, when we cut to a front view, she takes a spill that would make Buster Keaton proud. The introduction of Nora in this seemingly meaningless bit of physical comedy does provide a key function for the story: It establishes Nora as *active*. She's the go-getter, the mover, the engine that drives the relationship and the marriage. It also establishes a new type of screen persona for Myrna Loy. While Loy, as actor and star, had successfully and finally shaken off the indignity of the exotic characters, she never had a chance to shine in a comic role, and here she even engages in slapstick. The playful tone of their relationship is immediately set when Nick shows little concern for Nora after her pratfall, and she shows little concern either. As she realizes why Asta was pulling on the leash so hard:

NORA: Ohhh, so it's YOU he was after!

NICK: (smiles) Hello, Sugar!

NORA: He's dragged me into every gin mill on the block!

NICK: Yeah, I had him out this morning.

NORA: I thought so.

Goodrich and Hackett completely dispensed with Hammett's lengthy little diatribe about Asta's behavior (and changed her gender on top of it all!) and focused instead on establishing Nick and Nora's witty, affectionate wordplay:

WAITER: Madam, I am afraid we must take the dog out.

NICK: Oh it's all right, Joe. It's all right. It's my dog . . . and, uh, my wife.

NORA: Well you might have mentioned me first on the billing!

And after Nora meets Dorothy:

NORA: Pretty girl!

NICK: Yes she's a very nice type.

NORA: Oh, you got types?

NICK: Only you, darling. Lanky brunettes with wicked jaws. (beat) Leo. Compliments for this evening.

NORA: Who is she?

NICK: Darling, I was hoping I wouldn't have to answer that.

NORA: Come on.

NICK: Well, Dorothy is really my daughter. You see, it was spring in Venice and I was so young I didn't know what I was doing. We're all like that on my father's side.

NORA: By the way, how is your father's side?

NICK: It's much better thanks, and yours?

NORA: Say, how many drinks have you had?

(Leo approaches with drinks.)

NICK: This will make six martinis.

NORA: All right. Will you bring me five more martinis, Leo, line them right up here.

LEO: Yes ma'am.

NICK: (Smiling) Hmmmm . . .

Myrna Loy and William Powell in *The Thin Man* (1934). Directed by W. S. Van Dyke. *Author's Collection*

The only line in the above exchange that belonged to Hammett's original novel was the reference to lanky brunettes with wicked jaws. All the other lines were Goodrich and Hackett's creation. And the rest was all William Powell and Myrna Loy.

"When we did a scene together," Powell wrote,

we forgot about technique, camera angles and microphones. We weren't acting. We were just two people in perfect harmony. Many times I've played with an actress who seemed to be separated from me by a plate-glass window; there was no contact at all. But Myrna, unlike some actresses who think only of themselves, has the happy faculty of being able to listen while the other fellow says his lines. She has the give and take of acting that brings out the best. (Loy, 1988)

Nick and Nora's conversation takes place over the course of a single, forty-seven-second shot as we witness this clever interplay that has nothing to do with the mystery but everything to do with showing us this marvelous relationship. The single shot is very economical, as this was a film that had to be shot quickly, and filming any close-ups or over-the-shoulder shots as coverage would have taken precious time. However, it also winds up being absolutely the correct approach from a narrative standpoint. By holding both Nick and Nora in the frame, we're able to see them both speaking, and both listening, at the same time. Nora, adorned in a fur coat with her chin resting in her hand, perpetually amused by the sight of her besotted and blotto husband, has her focus entirely on him. Nick, with his arms resting on the table, his hands inches away from hers, has his focus entirely on her.

Looking strictly at the dialogue, one could easily interpret Nora's entrance and her comment about gin mills as a gentle scolding, but Loy delivers it flirtatiously with that spectacular lilt in her voice. The line establishes the potential for a nagging wife who disapproves of her husband's dipsomania, but it's quickly undercut by Nora's order of five martinis in a row to allow her to catch up with Nick. That moment at the table is remarkable, one that captures the essence of their relationship. They're almost always playing, and they're equals on top of it all. That latter trait is a major contributor to the continuing appeal of Nick and Nora Charles over eighty-five years later. While the surface elements of male-female relationships and sexual politics has transformed entirely since the film was produced, and the world's population has almost entirely turned over (as morbid as it is to consider, everyone in the film and nearly everyone who saw it in the theaters in 1934 is now dead), there is one incontrovertible appeal about Nick and Nora Charles that will never change: They like each other. It is the friendliest, most fun marriage ever captured on screen.

Another key moment is in the next scene when MacCaulay, Winant's lawyer (the great character actor Porter Hall in his first credited role), shows up to the couple's hotel room to gauge Nick's interest in the missing mad scientist. At one point MacCaulay receives a phone call and he stands on the right side of the frame talking on the phone, seemingly learning about Winant's whereabouts. While he does so, Nick and Nora goof off with seemingly childish games—Nick booping Nora on the nose when she looks down to see him poking her with a finger in her chest—heightening their charm, their game-playing, and their friendship.

These first two scenes alone created a legendary screen partnership that would last for another dozen films over the next thirteen years. When released in June 1934, *The Thin Man* was the beneficiary of an extraordinarily efficient studio system. Stories of old Hollywood abound regarding how many immortal, classic films were never anticipated to be immortal, classic films. It can be difficult in these days of prerelease hype to imagine how that can be true, but it was. Today's studios are under pressure to deliver blockbuster hit after blockbuster hit because they only produce a dozen or fewer notable feature films a year, spending years developing properties, cobbling together committees to write screenplays, and finally spending hundreds and hundreds of millions of dollars on production, postproduction, and marketing.

In 1934, MGM was producing dozens of features every year, gobbling up properties en masse in the hope that at least a few would hit the mark. On paper, Dashiell Hammett's latest novel, *The Thin Man*, seemed like a surefire property, and the speed with which the picture was produced and released looks astonishing by today's careful, marketing-aware standards. Hammett's novel was first published in full form in the December 1933 issue of *Redbook* magazine and published in book form the following month. It was an immediate smash success thanks in part to Alexander Woollcott's effusive endorsement on his radio show, *The Town Crier*. It didn't take long for studios, ravenous for new material, to take notice.

The extent of any bidding war is unknown, but if there was one, it was extraordinarily brief. *Film Daily* announced MGM's acquisition of the novel on January 24, 1934. A week later, the trade publication announced that W. S. Van Dyke was assigned to direct the film. Two weeks after that, on February 14, the publication announced MGM would be borrowing William Powell from Warner Bros. (where he was still under contract until April 15) to team him up with Myrna Loy for the picture. Frances Goodrich and Albert Hackett were assigned to write the screenplay, which they completed by March 29, and filming began on April 12. On May 23, the film received an enthusiastic review in *Film Daily*, which noted, "the screen seldom presents a more thoroughly interesting piece of entertainment than this adaptation of Dashiell Hammett's popular novel." Two days later, the picture opened and was an immediate smash hit.

Only six months after the publication of the novel in *Redbook*, the novel was purchased, a screenplay was written, and the film was shot, edited, and released. Most remarkably, this also included the brief delay in production during which *Manhattan Melodrama* was filmed. Much has been made of the speed with which director Van Dyke, known affectionately as "One Take Woody," shot *The Thin Man*. He completed filming in around eighteen days, but this was not an outrageous speed for the studio system. Because everyone was under contract to the studio at all times, crew members could be assigned to a film in a flash, so Hackett, Goodrich, Van Dyke, Howe, and the dozens of other MGM employees would be plucked from the sidelines and assigned to a production in a matter of days.

In many ways, the quality of a picture was up to chance. Van Dyke was a fine, efficient craftsman during the studio era, able to shoot a picture on time and under budget. In 1934, MGM released five features helmed by Van Dyke: *Manhattan Melodrama* and *The Thin Man* were the highlights, *Forsaking All Others* was a competent melodrama featuring another chemistry-laden pair in Joan Crawford and Clark Gable, and two all-but-forgotten films in *Hide-Out* with Robert Montgomery and Maureen O'Sullivan and the flop *Laughing Boy* with Ramon Novarro and Lupe Velez. The success of the studio system was simply mathematical. Statistically, if you release fifty to sixty features a year, you have to get a few of them right.

Co-screenwriter Albert Hackett said of *The Thin Man*, which he and wife Frances Goodrich were inexplicably not proud of, "Neither of us had ever read a mystery story, so we didn't know what to do. And Van Dyke said, 'I don't care anything about the mystery stuff—just give me dive scenes between Nick and Nora. . . . Forget about the mystery, let that come in when you want" (Goodrich, 2001). The mystery, however, is there and, thanks to Winant's presence in the film's opening, is far more dynamic and interesting than in the novel, primarily because of Goodrich and Hackett's adept setups of all the players in the mystery. After Julia Wolf is murdered and Winant's ex-wife Mimi finds the body, we go through the routine of the police questioning the ex, and we see her hiding a piece of evidence that implicates Winant and then enter the great comic setpiece of the film: Nick and Nora's Christmas party.

It is a Christmas party rife with eccentrics, ex-cons, and shady friends of Nick, who, while definitely a detective and not a crook, appears clearly comfortable in the atmosphere of the underworld. There is absolutely no dark side

Nick is caught embracing another woman . . . *Author's Collection*

to his personality. Powell was obviously adept at projecting a dark side, but he chooses instead to project only a serious side when he (and especially Nora) are in danger. He is not flippant; he's just clever. No, Nick's underworld is a glamorous, attractive world, as stated by one partygoer at the beginning of the scene when she stops Nick, awestruck, to ask, "Who are these amazing people?" There's the manager who bullies his boxer, the fat man uncontrollably crying when he calls his mother long distance, and an ex-con named Face Peppler who attends the party and respects and loves Nick even though Nick was the one who sent him up the river. Nora plays the part of the supporting wife, also serving cocktails, perpetually amused by the goings-on of the nefarious goons enjoying the couple's hospitality.

When Dorothy Winant arrives at the party to confess to the murder to protect her father, Nick immediately figures out she's lying, and when she embraces him, it sets up one of the great little moments of the film. Van Dyke stages it as if it would become one of those dramatic incidents in which a wife sees her husband with another woman in her arms. In the medium shot, Nick and Dorothy embrace and, before we cut away, we hear the door open and see a medium shot of Nora with an expression of shock. Howe then does a quick pan back to Nick and Dorothy to show Nick making a goofy face at Nora. The camera then pans

. . . and Nora couldn't care less. *Author's Collection*

quickly back to Nora, who responds with her patented nose crinkle. It pans yet again back to Nick and Dorothy when the latter responds apologetically before cutting back to Nora entering the room with even more drinks.

There is no recrimination, no suspicion. By panning between the embrace and Nora's reaction rather than cutting between them, again we have Nick and Nora as one unit rather than being edited apart from each other, and we establish again that this married couple trusts each other completely. Films in 1934 (not to mention in the eighty-eight years since) were rife with melodramatic misunderstandings between spouses. Those misunderstandings and the melodramas that arose from them were primarily plot-driven devices in which one character keeps a piece of information from another character. *Manhattan Melodrama*, for example, was a melodrama primarily because Myrna Loy's character Eleanor knows Gable's Blackie has committed murder to advance the political career of her husband, Powell's Jim Wade. Eleanor withholds this information from Jim to protect him because she knows he will do something irritatingly noble if he learns the truth.

The audience gets the impression, however, that Nick and Nora would hide nothing from each other. Nothing important anyway. The other key moment in the scene is when Nick very compassionately dismisses Dorothy's attempted confession. He doesn't even believe it in the first place and immediately questions her on the details of the shooting death of Julia Wolf. She gets it all wrong, of course, leading him to ask whom she's protecting. This establishes Nick fairly early in the film as a compassionate man who does care about people, and as a keen detective who can clearly spot someone's motivations. This was a moment absent from the novel, in which Dorothy is a swinging drunk without a fiancé and is merely a device to get Nick involved in the mystery of her father's disappearance. Here, in this very brief scene, Hackett and Goodrich establish Dorothy's inherent goodness and create sympathy in the audience for her conundrum.

The party scene is genius. It plays with Nick and Nora's lifestyle, the trust in their relationship, and gives us forward movement in the mystery. A drunken sing-along to "O Tannenbaum" ends the scene, with brief shots of all of Nick's reprobate friends being drunk and silly, followed by one of the great moments of the film when Nora turns to her husband and says with great joy and exhaustion: "Oh Nicky, I love you . . . because you know such lovely people!" Fade out. And thus Powell and Loy's immortal appeal as a couple was perfectly established after about thirty-eight minutes of *The Thin Man*.

Despite its emphasis on the relationship between Nick and Nora, *The Thin Man* does not so much ignore its mystery as deftly weave it into scenes that emphasize the witty wordplay between the couple even in moments of extreme danger. The scene following the party, for example, features Nick and Nora in bed (separate beds, of course). The scene starts with Nora asking Nick whether he'd want to just do some "detecting for fun," and they engage in some witty repartee about drinking and Christmas gifts. When a small-time hood named Morelli enters their bedroom, Nick merely raises an eyebrow, to which Nora retorts before she sees the hood, "You've got the funniest look on your face I ever saw in my life."

NICK: Would you mind putting that gun away? My wife doesn't mind, but I'm a very timid fellow.

NORA: You idiot.

NICK: All right, shoot . . . I mean, what's on your mind?

Even as they face a gunman, the emphasis is still on wordplay. The plot of the mystery moves forward, and while the danger is evident—Nick has to punch Nora to get her out of the way of Morelli's shot and is shot himself—there is a casual joy to the aftermath.

NORA: You darn fool, you didn't have to knock me out. I knew you'd take him, but I wanted to see you do it!

The bedroom is bathed in deep shadow, an opportunity for cinematographer James Wong Howe to display his mastery with low-key lighting, visually creating a potentially suspenseful setting. Here Nick and Nora are confronted by a criminal with a gun in their own room, a moment that could easily have been handled dramatically. Somehow, someway, however, Powell and Loy's chemistry and humor belie the audience's expectations of a dramatic moment of high danger and mystery.

Perhaps the most remarkable part of *The Thin Man* is how William Powell and Myrna Loy rather instantly became comic legends together. Neither of them had ever displayed such a high sense of comic timing before. The closest Powell had ever come was in *High Pressure* and *Jewel Robbery* at Warners, and Loy's sole moment of comic triumph took place in Paramount's *Love Me Tonight*. Audiences could not have anticipated the hijinks of their MGM films together based on their previous films. Powell's character was always debonair, always one step ahead of the other fellow, sometimes a rake, but always a romantic figure, someone idealized. Even when playing a criminal in *One Way Passage*, Powell still possesses that quality of arch, knowing sophistication. There was no way for the old William Powell to play the fool.

Loy's prior characters, first the vamps and then the brats, could never gain the audience sympathy that comes from a self-aware, smart sense of humor. The Myrna Loy that developed alongside William Powell allowed her to utilize her truly underappreciated skill of listening to underplay Powell's wisecracks. And not only listening. Few looks of amusement elicit laughter like Nora Charles watching her husband shooting balloons off a Christmas tree on Christmas morning. The scene's editing is masterful. All we need are frequent cuts to Nora's amused glare, almost unmoving, in reaction to Nick's shenanigans.

"Well, I hope you're satisfied," she murmurs after a minute or two, at which point she begins reading telegrams and pushes him to take the case of Julia Wolf's murder when she sees a telegram allegedly from Winant in Philadelphia. Again, the genius here of Goodrich and Hackett's screenplay is moving the plot of the mystery forward, all wrapped up in their witty wordplay. When Winant's lawyer MacCaulay receives a call from the police saying Winant has attempted suicide and decides that's admission of guilt, Nick is prompted to start sleuthing because he has a hunch Winant didn't commit the murder. It's typical for a detective to be suspicious when everything appears to be tied up with a bow, and fifty minutes into the picture, Nick's investigation actually begins.

The rest of *The Thin Man* unfolds as more of a traditional detective story, with Nick investigating the mystery accompanied by police lieutenant Guild (Nat Pendleton). While Pendleton's Guild isn't quite as buffoonish as Eugene

Pallette's Sergeant Heath in the Vance movies, he is still one or two steps behind Nick Charles and makes a fine counterpoint to William Powell's sophistication. Pendleton, a former wrestler, played genial lunkheads to perfection. As Guild interrogates Nunheim in his apartment, we go to a brief shot of Nick lackadaisically blowing smoke rings. It's a shot that has nothing to do with what's actually happening in the scene, but it does capture Nick's airy confidence and humor. When Mrs. Jorgenson confesses to Guild that she took Winant's watch chain from Julia Wolf's dead hand, the cop is convinced it proves Winant's guilt, but Nick, the detective who can't help but be smarter than everyone else in the room, clearly doubts the obvious conclusion.

The next key scene between Nick and Nora is when Nick decides he's going to go to Winant's shop to see why he closed it. While the eccentric old scientist was prone to leaving town for long stretches, Nick observes that Winant has never actually locked up the shop before. It leads to one of the best scenes between Nick and Nora in the film.

NICK: He won't kill me. I've got Asta to protect me.

NORA: All right. Go ahead, go on. See if I care. But I think it's a dirty trick to bring me all the way to New York just to make a widow of me.

NICK: You wouldn't be a widow long.

NORA: You bet I wouldn't!

NICK: Not with all your money. (Reaches to embrace her)

NORA: Fool. (Avoids kiss)

NICK: Well, any port in a storm. (Kisses her) Goodbye! Sugar!

(Nick and Asta walk toward the door. Nora chases after them.)

NORA: Nicky! Nicky!

NICK: Huh?

NORA: Take care of yourself.

NICK: Oh ho ho! Sure I will!

NORA: Don't say it like that. Say it as if you meant it!

NICK: Well, I do believe the little woman cares.

NORA: I don't care! It's just that I'm used to you, that's all.

(Pause. She gives him a long kiss.) (to Asta) If you ever let anything happen to him, you'll never wag that tail again!

Here, Nora is expressing her sincere worry about Nick's safety, even after she spent much of the film goading him into being a detective again. It's one thing for two characters to engage in witty repartee, but it's another thing for Hackett and Goodrich to establish that these two sparkling personalities are actually deeply in love with each other. It's Myrna Loy who shines particularly in this brief scene, communicating through body language and that twinkle in her voice the difficulty she's having pretending to be blasé about Nick's crime-fighting trip, until she finally breaks down and delivers a wallop of a kiss to the amusingly startled Nick. It's another, deeper level to their relationship and to Powell and Loy's chemistry that we haven't seen yet in the film.

During the investigation in Winant's lab—another opportunity for Howe to bathe the set in shadows—Nick discovers a body and concludes that Winant is the victim and not the murderer. While the decomposed body is buried under the floor along with the clothes of a man much larger than Winant, Nick realizes that the body is Winant himself when the skeleton shows shrapnel in the same place Winant had his war wound. It's a fine piece of detective storytelling.

REPORTER: Can't you tell us anything about the case?

NICK: Yes, it's putting me way behind on my drinking.

When Nick reveals to Nora that it's Winant's body in the shop and he couldn't have committed those other murders, it is in part a scene that could have been placed in any old detective story in which the genius detective reveals his findings to his hapless assistant, but little touches distinguish it, particularly Nora's little game of keeping Nick's drink away from him in order to get him to keep telling the tale of the murder.

NORA: You're not going to get another swallow until you open up.

NICK: I happened to remember that Winant had some shrapnel in his shin and it used to bother him and I looked for it and I found it. Gimme.

NORA: (Gives him the drink) How long has he been dead?

NICK: A couple of months anyway.

NORA: Then he couldn't have committed those murders!

NICK: (Taps her cheek) Smart gal.

Some viewers might detect a sense of condescension in Nick's treatment of Nora. Tricking her into taking a cab to keep her away from the investigation, tapping her on the cheek. But what elevates the material is Powell's performance. There is a self-aware amusement on his part, the sense that this is a game between him and Nora rather than squashing her ambitions to become an investigator, and there is little sense that Nora would ever let him get away with trying to make her a housewife.

The scene leads into a classic sequence in which Nick holds a dinner party and invites all the suspects. From today's perspective, it's one of the supreme clichés in the detective genre for our hero to gather every possible suspect into one room to confront the guilty, but the scene didn't exist in Hammett's novel. In the novel, Nick simply concluded that Winant's lawyer MacCaulay was the murderer and revealed it when he, MacCaulay, and several other characters were in Mimi's home. Nora was hardly a part of that reveal scene.

Hackett and Goodrich's scene is far superior, presents a wonderful setup for W. S. Van Dyke and James Wong Howe and, again, never lets us forget that the highlight of the story is Nick and Nora's relationship even as we're discovering the identity of the murderer. It also provides a far more cinematic resolution than the scene Hammett wrote, with the dining room table providing not only a fine anchor for Howe's compositions but a perfect opportunity for the speedy Van Dyke to capture plentiful coverage with a veritable cornucopia of reaction shots from all the eccentric characters gathered for the grand reveal. Nick and Nora begin the scene deciding where to place the suspects at the table, after

The cast of *The Thin Man* (1934). Directed by W. S. Van Dyke. *Author's Collection*

which point Nick reveals to Nora that he doesn't really know who the murderer is.

NORA: Which one of them did it? I wish you would tell me.
NICK: I wish you would tell *me*.

He punctuates the line with an affectionate kiss. The seemingly dramatic revelation of a murderer is just another excuse to flirt with his wife. And even without the added delight of Nick and Nora, the dinner party is a classic sequence. Nick's goon friends act as the waitstaff. And each suspect is accompanied by a detective as they file through the door. The dinner party also serves as a great way to compress some of the plot details of the novel, which features a much larger role for Chris Jorgenson, the second husband of Mimi Wynant, and a mystery involving his own first wife from whom he never received a divorce. The character most changed from the novel, Dorothy Winant, is here estranged from the fiancé Tommy (who doesn't exist in the book) and present with a blotto date, giving the proceedings some chance for action when Tommy clubs the guy.

While Nick and Nora's relationship is overshadowed by the throng of characters gathered in the dinner party, there are small moments of flirtation between the two ("You give such charming parties, Mr. Charles!" "Thank you, Mrs. Charles.") Nora, however, gets the high comic moment on her own in the scene: "Waiter, will you serve the nuts? I mean, will you serve the guests the nuts?"

During Nick's lengthy explanation of what must have happened in the past three months since Clyde Winant was murdered, Nora grows impatient and snappy, desperate for him to get to the point. But because their relationship is so well established and the foundation for their love is clearly solid, her annoyance ("You're driving me CRAZY!") come across less as nagging and more as the excitement and eagerness of an equal partner. Much of the scene is framed with Nick at the head of the table in the background, and we see Lieutenant Guild's back in the foreground at the other end of the table. It's a perfect marriage of speedy efficiency in shooting and well-motivated framing. Here, we're able to see all the players laid out in front of us so we don't lose track of them. It also creates an appealing composition.

The scene is expertly staged and makes for a successful conclusion. Nick rambles through his story, thinking out loud as he eventually comes to the conclusion that the lawyer MacCaulay is the murderer, and punches him out just as MacCaulay pulls a gun. It's a dramatic end to the scene, but the last bit belongs to Nora and Nick. Nora embraces him in a moment of relief.

NORA: Nicky, he might have killed you!

NICK: What's the matter, you sorry he didn't?

NORA: Oh I'm glad you're not a detective!

The Thin Man was an immediate smash hit, with rapturous reviews and even an endorsement from Dashiell Hammett, who told MGM officials it was the only film adaptation that preserved the mood of his work. Which was true, to an extent. However, the film went much further than his original novel in celebrating the partnership in marriage and mystery of Nick and Nora Charles.

Critics were gleeful. *Photoplay* (August 1934) exclaimed, "The picture spells entertainment plus—a humdinger!" while the *Hollywood Reporter* (May 10, 1934) said: "A smart honey, a sophisticated wow. A murder story with a brilliant cast, a brilliant script, brilliant direction, and photography that tells the story in no mean terms." *Film Daily* (May 23, 1934) wrote: "The screen seldom presents a more thoroughly interesting piece of entertainment that this adaptation of Dashiell Hammett's popular novel. The rapid-fire dialogue is about the best heard since talkies, and it is delivered by Powell and Miss Loy to perfection." Mordaunt Hall in the *New York Times* (June 30, 1934) called the film "an excellent combination of comedy and excitement."

The Thin Man would go on to be nominated for four Academy Awards (Best Picture, Best Actor, Best Director, Best Screenplay). But even before then, based on boffo box office, superb audience tracking, and enthusiastic reviews, MGM knew what it had immediately. At the end of June, the studio announced William Powell would play Philo Vance yet again, this time with Myrna Loy by his side, in *The Casino Murder Case* (*Motion Picture Herald*, July 28, 1934). As he did the previous year when Warners tried to get him to do another Philo Vance picture after *Kennel Murder Case*, Powell refused the assignment. He had had quite enough of Mr. Vance, thank you very much.

In March 1934, while filming *The Thin Man*, MGM announced that it had purchased the rights to W. E. Woodward's novel *Evelyn Prentice* as a potential vehicle for Loy. In August, MGM announced that Powell would join her. Released in November, *Evelyn Prentice* must have been puzzling to audiences who loved Powell and Loy in *The Thin Man*, and it remains puzzling today. Clearly not developed for the two as a screen couple, the project was simply a way to get William Powell and Myrna Loy's names back together on a marquee as quickly as possible.

It's obvious at first glance why MGM thought it was an apt project for Myrna Loy. While her picture *Men in White* earlier in 1934 cast her as a woman who bemoans the long working hours of her physician fiancé Clark Gable,

Evelyn Prentice (1934). Directed by William K. Howard. From left: William Powell, Cora Sue Collins, Myrna Loy. *MGM/Photofest © MGM*

Evelyn Prentice casts her as a woman who bemoans the long working hours of her lawyer husband William Powell. While it isn't fair to compare the two characters—Evelyn is far more sympathetic—it showed how MGM saw Loy's screen persona developing before *The Thin Man* catapulted her into an unexpected and completely different direction.

The picture is a typical melodrama of the era, with all kinds of plot twists dependent on the married couple at the center of the action never honestly communicating with each other. Evelyn Prentice (Loy) begins a flirtatious and yet innocent friendship with gigolo Lawrence Kennard (Harvey Stephens) because her husband John (Powell) is spending all his hours, day and night, working on a defense of socialite Nancy Harrison (Rosalind Russell, in her screen debut) against a charge of manslaughter. Mrs. Harrison, though, wants John to be far more than just her defense attorney and frames him to make Evelyn believe the two are having an affair. When a devastated Evelyn visits Kennard again, rather than giving her comfort, he tries to blackmail her by saying he'll give John three letters she wrote to him. Even though the letters are innocent enough, Evelyn grabs a gun from a drawer and the film cuts to Kennard's girlfriend Judith (Isabel Jewell) entering his apartment, hearing a gunshot, and witnessing Evelyn running out the door.

When Judith ends up being accused of Kennard's murder, Evelyn pleads with John to defend her. He does so, and then John learns that Kennard kept a secret diary that revealed the name of a prominent married woman with whom he had a relationship. When John sends his investigator to seek the diary, Evelyn is tormented over what it could contain, and it's only in the middle of the trial in front of everyone in the courtroom that John receives the diary and sees Evelyn's name inside it. Evelyn demands to be heard and confesses that she and Kennard struggled over the gun and it went off, but in an extraordinarily implausible twist, it turns out that the shot didn't hit Kennard. John then puts Judith on the stand and forces his own client to admit she picked up the gun after Evelyn exited and shot Kennard dead. After John convinces the jury that Judith shot Kennard in self-defense, all is well, and John and Evelyn are able to move on happily with their lives.

The picture was an opportunity for Loy to reunite with *Transatlantic* director William K. Howard, who had come over from Fox to work with MGM. Unfortunately, the relative freedom he enjoyed at his previous studio was nowhere to be found at the tightly controlled Culver City studio, and he was unable to replicate the creative success he experienced at Fox. There is little to distinguish the picture from any other MGM melodrama produced at the time. *Evelyn Prentice* is difficult to view objectively nearly ninety years later without the hindsight that Powell and Loy's success together was dependent primarily on comedy. It is a rather turgid little melodrama that would not have been terribly different if a different screen couple had starred in it.

Of course, both Powell and Loy are quite good in it. This sort of thing was old hat to William Powell at this point, and he comports himself with the usual combination of charm, sophistication, and overall decency that he had established as his trademarks at Paramount. He really just has to be noble and wonderful. In most ways, *Evelyn Prentice* is far more of an opportunity for Myrna Loy to stretch, because she had not had the opportunity to star in a women's picture of this sort before. She does a fine job communicating the inner turmoil that Evelyn is going through without descending to any of the lip-quivering that one might associate with early twentieth-century melodrama. Not once does she seem like anything but a genuine human being who is terrified at the prospect of losing the husband she loves.

From today's perspective, it seems ridiculous that William Powell or Myrna Loy could ever be accused of being the slightest bit tempted by anyone else. While both had appeared in *Manhattan Melodrama*, the heart of that film was in Powell and Clark Gable's relationship, so *Evelyn Prentice* is the only true film focused on the screen couple that turns out to be anything but a comedy. For MGM, it confirmed that the two of them together presented an unmistakable cash cow. On a budget of just less than $500,000, the picture brought in a worldwide gross of $1.17 million.

Meanwhile, reviews were somewhat mixed but agreed that the couple had elevated the material far beyond what another pair of actors could do. Andre Sennwald in the *New York Times* said, "Myrna Loy and William Powell continue to be the most engaging of the current cinema teams. . . . Agreeable rather than stimulating, it manages, with the exception of a surprise climax, to be predictable at almost any given point. Without the handsome assistance of its leading players, *Evelyn Prentice* would be one more item in the less than exhilarating melodramas which are always cropping up when the season settles into its stride and ideas begin to be scarce" (Sennwald, 1934).

While not a resounding success on the level of *The Thin Man*, the picture was the third opportunity for audiences to see William Powell and Myrna Loy as a screen couple in 1934. They were now an established screen team, both finally genuine stars, and MGM wasted no time planning more pictures for the two of them.

Of course, the best laid plans . . .

THE MOVIE STARS

At the beginning of 1935, MGM was eager to pair William Powell and Myrna Loy over and over again, but Loy was rightfully impatient with the studio for not rewarding her for her new status as a star and equal to Powell after three successful films together. With her inaugural 1931 MGM contract paying her about $1,500 a week, half of Powell's salary, Loy expressed her desire simply to be paid equal to Powell. "I wanted what Bill was getting, that's all," Loy wrote in her autobiography (Loy, 1988).

The studio not only refused her request for a pay raise but, following the successful release of *Evelyn Prentice*, decided to pair her with Powell for a fourth time in a film called *Escapade*, which was set to be a shot-for-shot remake of the Austrian film *Maskerade*, in which Loy was cast in what she saw as a thankless role as a "wistful little girl selling flowers on the streets of Vienna."

Loy thought it was a terrible script and felt the part was far inferior to Powell's, but acquiesced after MGM head Louis B. Mayer pleaded with her to take the role. After a week of shooting, however, Loy learned the studio had begun testing Austrian newcomer Luise Rainer for the role, and was livid when studio manager Eddie Mannix said they realized Loy was wrong for the part.

"I told you not to put me in the damn thing in the first place, and after I go through all the preliminaries you put some new girl into it," Loy said. When MGM wanted Loy to step down as "sick," she kept reporting to the set anyway until she could get a formal release from the studio, and when they finally capitulated, Loy was off to Europe, where she stayed for months on a self-imposed strike (Loy, 1988).

Escapade has been impossible to view for decades, beset by rights issues that have never been satisfactorily defined. Playing the role that so offended Loy,

Luise Rainer was a success and would appear with Powell in two more pictures, as well as win back-to-back Best Actress Academy Awards in 1937 and 1938 before her career quickly declined and she descended back into obscurity.

After *Escapade*, MGM had little choice to pair William Powell with substitute leading ladies. Between Powell and Loy's teaming in *Evelyn Prentice*, released in November 1934, and *Libeled Lady*, released exactly two years later, Powell appeared in six films with six different leading ladies, not including the epic *The Great Ziegfeld*, which—while Powell and Loy appear together—cannot really be considered a "Powell and Loy" picture, since their time together runs less than fifteen minutes in the final act of the film.

The first film in this period attempted to get some publicity out of William Powell's new real-life romance. By the time *The Thin Man* was released in June 1934, Powell had started seeing the MGM star Jean Harlow. The twenty-four-year-old Harlow had just formally separated from her husband, Harold Rosson, on May 5, 1934, and she and Powell quickly struck up a romance. Powell was careful to note he that knew Harlow casually on the Culver City lot but "never had any dates with her 'til I learned she was leaving Hal" (Stenn, 1993).

Always keen for new ways to promote his stars, Louis B. Mayer couldn't resist casting a picture solely to promote Harlow and Powell's affair. He removed Joan Crawford from the lead role for a picture titled *A Woman Called Cheap*, replaced her with Harlow, whom he paired with Powell, and retitled it *Reckless*. It was a canny move. MGM was in the midst of struggling to find a new screen persona for Harlow, who had been under contract to the studio since 1931 and had established herself as a playfully sexual screen presence in films like Victor Fleming's *Red Dust* in 1932. Unfortunately, in the Production Code era, Sexual Harlow had to go, and MGM was left to experiment with new approaches for their star. *Reckless* was the studio's least successful. While Mayer's decision to cast Harlow in the role reflected his expert sense of publicity, it certainly didn't reflect any skill for casting a movie properly. Harlow, who could neither sing nor dance, was cast as a singing and dancing showgirl named Mona Leslie in a story loosely based on a 1932 scandal that erupted when torch singer Libby Holman's husband, Zachary Smith Reynolds, died of a self-inflicted gunshot wound seven months after their wedding.

Harlow's one production number features awkward cutting to mask her lack of dancing acumen, along with often-amusing blocking of other performers conveniently preventing the audience from seeing her (or her dancing double) in full. Fortunately, the number is early in the picture, and Harlow fares better afterwards. In dramatic scenes, she is effective as the misunderstood showgirl who falls for miserable alcoholic heir Bob Harrison (Franchot Tone) and is blamed mercilessly by high society when he commits suicide. Rather cruelly, Harlow had to play scenes mourning the suicide of her on-screen husband just three years after her real-life husband Paul Bern committed suicide.

Powell, meanwhile, plays sports promoter Ned Riley, who is constantly hanging around Mona and her grandmother (May Robson) and pines for Mona, unable to find the courage to tell her how he really feels about her. While Powell is a fine actor, he projects far too much confidence for the audience to buy the crippling shyness his character is supposed to harbor. And curiously, probably because of this, he and Harlow lack the chemistry on screen they apparently shared in real life. More suited to play opposite actors like the earthy Clark Gable, Harlow's brashness clashed with Powell's easygoing sophistication. The two would fare much better together in the following year's *Libeled Lady*.

Released in November 1935 by MGM and directed by William K. Howard, *Rendezvous* was another film that was originally intended to be a Powell-Loy vehicle. With Loy still absent, newcomer Rosalind Russell stepped in as the lovestruck niece of an assistant secretary of war who chases decoding expert Powell. Russell has a certain charm, although she was still a few years away from the career-defining performances in *His Girl Friday* and *My Sister Eileen* that established her as Hollywood's best fast-talking professional woman. It was, unfortunately, a no-win situation for the young Russell, whom critics called a "second-string Myrna Loy." Which, of course, she was.

In her autobiography, Russell had nothing but good things to say about the experience, and found Powell an encouraging presence who dismissed her attempts to apologize for not being Myrna Loy. He said to her, "I love Myrna, but I think this is good for you, and I'm glad we're doing it together." Russell recalled:

> He was not only dear, he was cool. If an actor thought he could get any place by having tantrums, watching Bill Powell would have altered his opinion. I remember a story conference during which he objected to a scene that he felt wasn't right for him. He was at once imperious and lucid. "It's beyond my histrionic ability to do this," he said. I thought that was delicious. (Chase, 1977)

Viewing the film, it's hard to argue with Loy's decision to strike from MGM if she was only going to be cast in lesser supporting roles opposite Powell. Russell is merely shoehorned into scenes of espionage melodrama as the lovestruck woman constantly interrupting Powell's attempts to uncover a German plot to break an American code during World War I. The attempts to inject romance and comedy into the proceedings don't work particularly well, although Russell and Powell display a level of chemistry that makes one regret that the pair never got a chance to work together in a better film. It is to Russell's credit that, even at this stage in her career, she projects the skill to overcome the weaknesses of her character as the meddling woman, so desperate for attention from the man she loves that she ignores the necessities of wartime. It is a rather weak attempt at replicating the role of Nora Charles trying to ingratiate herself into mysteries. At least Nora had some common sense. And while there is that element of Nora in the character that may have appealed to Loy, the sparseness of the part would not have pleased her. It is a part meant for a developing actor like Russell, not a star like Loy.

Powell himself is pleasant enough as former newspaperman William Gordon, who is stuck in Washington, DC, breaking codes when what he really wants is to head to the front lines in Europe. It feels mostly, however, like a bit of a throwback to his mostly one-dimensional Paramount and Warner Bros. roles, when the only demand on him was to enunciate well and appear distinguished. It seemed like a step backwards for Powell as star and actor. He was in fact a bit of a conundrum for the studio at the time. William Powell at MGM in 1935 suffered from the malady every actor eventually faces when he's found the absolutely perfect role: He couldn't play Nick Charles absolutely every time. Or could he? When MGM lent Powell to RKO for two pictures in 1935 and 1936, the latter studio chose simply to cast Powell as an amateur sleuth in two mystery-comedies opposite up-and-coming leading ladies.

The first, *Star of Midnight*, released in April 1935 and directed by Stephen Roberts, paired Powell with Ginger Rogers. Based on a novel by Arthur Somers Roche, this comedy-mystery featured Powell as Clay "Dal" Dalzell, a New York lawyer who is famous around town as an amateur sleuth. Rogers is Donna Mantell, a much younger woman who has been in love with Dal since she was ten years old. Rogers possesses a simple youthful charm that works nicely as a counterpoint to Powell's sophistication, but the film tries too hard to be a *Thin Man* knockoff. Scenes of Powell drinking cocktails (including eight sidecars!) seem like mere afterthoughts, and other small bits of business from *The Thin Man* are clumsily inserted. There's a moment in which he slugs Rogers to get her out of the line of fire and is grazed by a bullet, and there's even a moment in which he orders multiple cocktails and Rogers orders the same number.

Rogers has brief moments of amusement, but the film has the ponderous plot-heaviness that afflicted the Paramount Philo Vance movies, and even Powell himself seems more reserved than usual at this point in his career. He doesn't even seem to enjoy drinking like Nick Charles does; he just orders and drinks. One problem is the lack of definition in Dal's character. We never even learn what kind of lawyer he is, or how he's famous as an amateur sleuth. With the lack of exposition, *Star of Midnight* feels at times like a sequel to a missing film.

The plot is muddy as well. One important plot development is that a woman named Agnes disappeared, posed as a masked and anonymous showgirl named Mary Smith, and disappeared again. For some reason, she never appears on screen at all, so the audience never cares about her disappearance. If there was one thing *The Thin Man* screenplay vastly improved on the original novel, it was that murder suspect Clyde Winant had screen time and the audience was able to be invested in the mystery. Here, we lack that investment.

The second RKO picture, *The Ex-Mrs. Bradford*, was released in May 1936 and featured Jean Arthur. Arthur had been in pictures since 1923 and had finally achieved stardom in Frank Capra's *Mr. Deeds Goes to Town*. She had come a long way since her days as a generic supporting actor in early Paramount talkies and, like Powell, it was her departure from that studio that finally provided the opportunities that allowed her talents to thrive. She could play both the professional and the romantic woman in one fell swoop.

In the film, Powell plays Dr. Lawrence "Brad" Bradford, a famous surgeon who has divorced his wife Paula (Arthur), a wealthy mystery story writer, due to her penchant for dragging him into life-threatening, real-life murder mysteries. When a jockey dies of an apparent heart attack during a big race, Paula suspects foul play and, of course, she drags Brad into yet another mystery. This second attempt at a *Thin Man* knockoff by RKO and director Stephen Roberts is a bit more successful than the first, primarily because Arthur's character is far more actively involved in the mystery, driving the reluctant doctor into the adventure with a zest for crime-solving even greater than that of Nora Charles. Also helping matters is a superior supporting cast featuring the ever-reliable James Gleason as a police inspector, *King Kong*'s Robert Armstrong as a gangster, and Eric Blore as Brad's butler.

Powell is also better in this role than he was in *Star of Midnight*, likely more confident with Arthur, an actor with whom he was already familiar and much closer to his own age than Rogers. At age thirty-five when filming, Arthur was just approaching her peak as a romantic comedy leading lady at an age when many actresses of the time were heading into matronly roles. There is an easygoing banter between the two that makes it absurd that they were divorced in the first place, so this never follows the typical course of a romance and works well enough as a minor comedy-mystery. It also helps that Brad is a better-defined character than Dal, and that his skill as a doctor actually contributes to his crime-solving.

The one undisputed masterpiece among the films Powell made with Loy substitutes was *My Man Godfrey*, in which Powell was paired for the third time with Carole Lombard. Just as Powell's fortunes had changed since his days at Paramount, so had Lombard's. Previously another victim of that studio's ineptitude in properly developing its contract players in the early sound years, Lombard's genius for comedy had seemingly burst out of nowhere with an extraordinary performance in Howard Hawks's 1934 film *Twentieth Century* opposite John Barrymore for Columbia Pictures. As Lily Garland, Lombard dueled with a volcanically funny Barrymore in one of the greatest tête-à-têtes in film comedy history. Displaying a comic brilliance and energy and an electric screen presence that had never been remotely hinted at in her previous films, Lombard immediately became a comedy icon.

My Man Godfrey brought about Lombard's second immortal role as daffy heiress Irene Bullock, who takes on Powell's Godfrey as her protégé when she finds him homeless on an ash heap. Gregory La Cava's film is one of the great screwball comedies of the '30s, and may well be the greatest of them all in its un-flinching criticism of the wealthy class. The opening scenes depict the wealthy conducting a scavenger hunt in which one of the objects to be found is a "forgot-ten man," perfectly encapsulating the cruel dichotomies of the Depression years and setting up one of the great satires in American film. As the wealthy continue to become wealthier, the film has remained timely and has aged extraordinarily well, particularly because the cruelties of the class system remain alive today.

Powell, who would receive his first Best Actor Oscar nomination for the performance, was never better. It is his perfect role and, given Powell's personal reticence about publicity and his own well-known modesty, could well have been his most personal. He is a model of stillness and quiet dignity, the con-summate straight man in a sea of zanies. He underplays absolutely everything to perfection, allowing Lombard and the other comic actors—Alice Brady, Eugene Pallette, and Mischa Auer—to thrive. And while those actors do thrive, it would be remiss to underrate Powell's achievement in the film.

Powell had a magnificent face and, with his experience in silent cinema, manages to express multiple emotions in a few glances. In the opening scav-enger hunt scene, he displays both utter bemusement and disgust in a single expression. Director La Cava knew what he had, and simple reaction shots by Powell throughout the film get big laughs. There is one moment in which Mischa Auer's Carlo is climbing around the house pretending to be a monkey to cheer up Irene, hamming it up intolerably and climbing the curtains in the living room. The biggest laugh in the scene comes from a several-second shot of Powell holding a tray and simply looking up at Carlo. There was no astonished outrage, simply a look. La Cava knew not to hold onto the shot too long, and Powell knew how to simply react with stillness.

Released in September 1936, the film was an immediate smash hit with critics and audiences alike. It is easy to overlook Powell's skill in this film, since Lombard's performance as Irene Bullock remains one of the greatest comic per-

My Man Godfrey (1936). Directed by Gregory La Cava. From left: Carole Lombard (as Irene Bullock), William Powell (as Godfrey Smith/Godfrey "Duke" Parke). *Universal Pictures/Photofest © Universal Pictures*

formances by a woman in American cinema. But he is the consummate straight man here, and a profoundly generous actor. Along with Powell's nomination for Best Actor, the film received Oscar nominations for Best Original Screenplay, Best Director, and Best Actress, and was somehow not nominated for Best Picture. It was the first film in the awards' brief history to receive nominations for all the top awards except for Best Picture.

Despite the Best Picture snub, *My Man Godfrey* has proven to be a well-remembered masterpiece, while the one film that was nominated for and awarded the Best Picture Oscar for that year has been nearly forgotten by the general public. MGM's *The Great Ziegfeld* would carry away that trophy. The film took a circuitous route to production. In late 1933, Universal Pictures purchased the life rights to legendary Broadway showman Florenz Ziegfeld Jr. from his widow, Billie Burke, and assigned the screenplay and production duties to Ziegfeld protégé William Anthony McGuire. In June 1934, McGuire announced in *Variety* that William Powell would play Ziegfeld and that he planned to start shooting that September. Preproduction dragged on for months, with McGuire attempting to sustain interest with publicity boasting that more than 5,000 candidates for 300 roles as Ziegfeld Girls were considered for parts (Wilk, November 5, 1934). By December 1934, news broke that Carl Laemmle, the founder of Universal, was offering Roy Del Ruth the "highest figure ever offered a director in the history of motion pictures" to direct the picture (Wilk, December 27, 1934). After finally announcing in February 1935 that Edward Sutherland was going to direct the picture (Bureau, 1935), it was just a few weeks later that MGM purchased the whole package—lock, stock, and barrel—from Universal for a sum reported to be $250,000 (Wilk, February 25, 1935).

At Universal, studio head Carl Laemmle Jr.'s strategy to boost Universal's reputation and box office heft by moving from dozens of super-cheap B-movies a year to fewer, bigger prestige productions was proving to be a financial disaster. With the studio short of cash, selling all the rights to *The Great Ziegfeld* was the only available option. For MGM, the production was a perfect fit. The studio had always prioritized big-budget prestige productions and already had mega-productions of *Mutiny on the Bounty*, *Anna Karenina*, *A Tale of Two Cities*, and *David Copperfield* just around the corner. Even better, Powell had become a significantly bigger star since Universal originally cast him as Florenz Ziegfeld, and he was already the property of MGM. This was also a chance to reunite him with Myrna Loy, who had finally ended her strike and who was cast as Ziegfeld's final wife, Billie Burke.

Loy's casting as Burke has been the subject of some speculation, primarily regarding Burke's own reaction to Loy's casting. Billie Burke had become a very successful character actress under contract at MGM, and many accounts cite Burke's rage at not being cast as herself. However, Burke's biographer said she knew she shouldn't play a twenty-years-younger version of herself. While Burke preferred Miriam Hopkins to play the role, MGM was extremely eager to have

The Great Ziegfeld (1936). Directed by Robert Z. Leonard. From left: Nat Pendleton and William Powell (as Florenz Ziegfeld Jr.). *MGM/Photofest* © *MGM*

the opportunity to finally reunite Loy with Powell, and gave her second billing despite her not appearing in the massive film until two hours and fifteen minutes into the run time. Up until that point, Luise Rainer played opposite Powell as Ziegfeld's previous wife, Anna Held.

As Flo Ziegfeld in the mostly fictional depiction of the showman's life, Powell acquits himself admirably amid the spectacle, although he seems most at home in the opening scenes of the picture, in which he gets to play Ziegfeld as an ambitious carnival barker at the 1893 World's Fair in Chicago, reunited with Nat Pendleton playing Sandor the Strong Man. The two men seem more at home with each other than Powell and Rainer ever do, and the scenes are even more enjoyable thanks to Powell's friendly yet cutthroat competition with Frank Morgan, in one of his first big MGM roles, as a fellow carnival barker.

It is a strange picture, a hodgepodge of vignettes and musical numbers that would hold up well today if they were presented as individual short films. But when the scenes are strung together with only Powell as the connecting thread over what quickly seems like an interminable 180 minutes, the lack of structure just makes the entire narrative house implode. It's a slog to get through. Loy is charming, of course, but she has little to do but look at Powell adoringly and offer him platitudes to buck him up when he's feeling low.

However, their chemistry is evident in the few scenes they share, even though they aren't given very much interesting to say or do, and it must have been a thrill for audiences—and especially MGM—to get the two on screen at the same time for the first time in seventeen months. At any rate, the movie received raves globally, with a cornucopia of pull quotes that must have made the MGM publicists cry with glee. MGM circulated quotes from its Paris office to the rest of Europe when the film was released in France in October 1936: "Simply dazzling!" "Magnificent spectacle." "The Biggest Production Ever Given on the Screen."

The Great Ziegfeld was released in March 1936, the fourth picture released since Myrna Loy's return to MGM. Her strike had ended following the announcement in the summer of 1935 that she had signed a contract with acclaimed writers Ben Hecht and Charles MacArthur to appear in their film, *Soak the Rich*. After MGM learned Loy would be paid $75,000 for five weeks' work on the film, the studio capitulated, and Loy returned. In September, headlines everywhere announced that Loy had mended fences with the studio with no change to her contract, but in truth, she was handed a bonus lump sum of $25,000 and was able to get significantly better terms when her contract came up for renewal in 1937 (Leider, 2011).

Released in December 1935, *Whipsaw* was Loy's first picture back at MGM. Featuring Loy as a sophisticated moll working with jewel thieves, it paired her for the first time with Spencer Tracy, who played a federal agent accompanying her on the road, intending to be there when she meets her fellow criminals. It was a variation on the road-trip romance in *It Happened One Night*, and while it was not an enormous success as a film, it gave Loy another co-star option in Tracy.

Her second picture back was particularly significant. Released in February 1936, *Wife vs. Secretary* paired her with Clark Gable for the third time. Since they had previously appeared together in *Manhattan Melodrama*, Gable's popularity had exploded. In 1935, he was the third most popular movie star in Hollywood in terms of box office, behind only Shirley Temple and the recently deceased Will Rogers. He had won the Academy Award for *It Happened One Night,* and his latest film, *Mutiny on the Bounty*, was a smash hit with both audiences and critics on its way to a Best Picture Oscar. Gable was huge, the most popular living male movie star on the planet.

Between 1936 and 1938, Loy's star would ascend at least as high as Gable's; she would appear in four films with him, establishing him as her second most favored co-star behind Powell. She saw Gable as a different kind of foil than Powell. "[Gable] kept very reserved, afraid to be sensitive for fear it would counteract his masculine image," Loy said. "I always played it a little bit tough with him, giving him what-for to bring him out, because he liked girls like that—Carole Lombard [Gable's future wife] had a tough quality" (Loy, 1988).

And despite all the complaints about how MGM would work the actors to death, throwing them into picture after picture with hardly a rest, Loy said "one of the benefits of the studio system was that you worked repeatedly with the same people, as I did with Spence and Bill Powell and Clark Gable. Consequently, I enjoyed great friendships with these men."

When Loy was cast in *Wife vs. Secretary*, however, she was slightly guarded because when she had last worked with Gable, several years earlier, she had to swat him out of a drunken, amorous mood. He clearly had no memory of it, though. "He was very sweet, very warm," she said. "He'd probably forgotten all about it. He brought me coffee in the morning, and we began to be friends."

As Loy recounted, Gable was an extraordinarily sensitive man who was terrified of showing that side of himself.

> He loved poetry, and read beautifully, with great sensitivity, but he wouldn't dare let anybody else know it. He was afraid people would think him weak or effeminate and not the tough guy who liked to fish and hunt. I was the only one

he trusted. We have an awful macho thing in this country and he was cursed by it. (Loy, 1988)

The defining moment of Gable's screen career would come two years later in his portrayal of Rhett Butler in *Gone with the Wind*, in which he carries his noncompliant new bride Scarlett O'Hara up the stairs to forcibly consummate their marriage if need be. William Powell would never do any such thing. And, certainly, no character played by Myrna Loy would stand such a thing from anyone in the first place.

Loy is tougher in her films with Gable because she has to be, and their films together—while hardly morose—are devoid of the screwball humor that defines so many of the films Powell and Loy made together. Even though Gable starred in comedies, he was not the kind of actor who was as willing to make himself look foolish as William Powell could.

Based on a story by Faith Baldwin published in the May 1935 issue of *Cosmopolitan*, *Wife vs. Secretary* also reunited Loy with producer Hunt Stromberg and director Clarence Brown, and was her first chance to work with Jean Harlow. As late as October, Ralph Wilk announced William Powell as the male lead to co-star with Loy and Harlow (Wilk, October 31, 1935), but three weeks later, Wilk wrote that filming would begin the next day and said "the name of the fortunate male lead to play opposite [Loy and Harlow] will not be announced until the MGM megaphonist completes making tests of several prominent players on the studio roster" (Wilk, November 19, 1935).

The fortunate male lead was, of course, Clark Gable. He played Van "V. S." Stanhope, a magazine publishing magnate (and in a bizarre continuity error, referred to as Jake multiple times in the first scene) who is celebrating his third wedding anniversary with the perfect Linda (Loy). Meanwhile, everyone but Linda seems to believe that Van must be having an affair with Van's extraordinarily efficient and dependable secretary "Whitey" (Harlow) because she's a knockout. Even Van's own mother (May Robson) assumes Van is having a little on the side and tells Linda she should insist that Van fire Whitey.

The first scene sets up Gable and Loy's relationship as an ideal, sexy married couple (albeit a couple that has separate bedrooms in order to satisfy the Production Code). Director Brown does a fine job of visually inferring that these two pretty much have sex all the time, shooting them together in tight close-ups as Gable holds Loy's body impossibly close and showers her with little kisses. They're a far more exuberantly sexual couple on screen than Powell and Loy were, and it reflects Gable's emphasis on aggressive masculinity as opposed to Powell's flirtatious gentlemanliness. Loy matches Gable note for note, writhing, giggling, and blushing like a schoolgirl.

"Actually we did kind of a reversal in that picture," Loy would recount. "Jean, supposedly the other woman, stayed very proper, while I had one foot in bed throughout. That's the sexiest wife I've ever played. In one scene, Clark stands outside my bedroom door and we banter, nothing more, but there's just no question about what they've done the night before" (Loy, 1988).

Wife vs. Secretary (1936). Directed by Clarence Brown. Shown on the set from left: Jean Harlow, Clark Gable, Myrna Loy. *MGM/Photofest* © *MGM*

MGM's struggle to redefine Harlow had continued since her appearance in *Reckless* opposite Powell, and *Wife vs. Secretary* was the best effort yet in softening her screen image, even going so far as to dye her blonde hair a little darker. Harlow is actually quite wonderful as the innocent Whitey, who lives with her parents, has an impossibly sweet boyfriend (James Stewart), is unflinchingly dedicated to her job, and is perhaps a little in love with her boss. The trick of the film is for the audience to actually buy that Harlow would never try anything with Gable, especially given the sparks that had flown between them in prior films like *Red Dust*, and Harlow manages to pull it off. If anything, her lack of flashiness in the picture almost hinders the narrative legitimacy of so many supporting characters assuming that there's some hanky-panky going on.

Inevitably, given the nonstop insinuations everywhere around her, Linda begins to wonder whether something truly inappropriate is going on. As it is with most melodrama, *Wife vs. Secretary* creates conflict by forcing its characters not to communicate things simply to each other. Van decides he needs to keep his attempt at acquiring the five-cent *National Weekly* secret from everyone, including Linda, and rather than just telling her that he's got a secret deal he's working on and can't say anything more, he instead lies about where he is at any given moment. When Van goes to a convention in Havana and he realizes that he needs to close the deal there, he calls Whitey to come join him, they spend all day and all night drafting a contract, Van forgets to call Linda, and when she tries to reach him at 2:00 a.m. and Whitey answers the phone, Linda decides to end the marriage. Eventually, Whitey convinces Linda to return to Van because while she would happily take Van on the rebound and he could almost be happy with her, it would only be second best to what he has with Linda.

Wife vs. Secretary was a box office hit, grossing over $2 million on a budget of $567,000, and forever cementing Loy as Hollywood's perfect wife and bringing her star power to another level. With this new screen couple at its disposal, MGM paired them next in perhaps the most infamous of MGM's flops of the 1930s, a curiously wrongheaded epic that somehow manages to take two of the studio's biggest stars and make them completely uninteresting.

Released in June 1937, *Parnell* was based on a play by Elsie Schoeffler about Irish patriot Charles Stewart Parnell, who in the 1880s had become famous for passionately advocating for Irish Home Rule. His political career was ultimately ruined following the scandal erupting from his long-term affair with the married Katie O'Shea, and he died at age forty-five in 1891.

After MGM purchased the play in January 1936, announcing it as a potential project for young MGM contract player Brian Ahearne, Gable won the role and was set to be paired with his frequent co-star Joan Crawford as Katie, but

Crawford asked to be replaced after reading the completed script and deciding the part as written was unsuited to her. Later accounts said she decided she didn't want to appear in another costume picture after her recent appearance in *The Gorgeous Hussy*. Either way, Loy was taken out of the upcoming remake of *The Last of Mrs. Cheyney*, in which she was slated to appear once again with William Powell (AFI Catalog of Feature Films, n.d.). Crawford replaced Loy in *Cheyney* and Loy was inserted into *Parnell*. Shooting began in December 1936 (Leider, 2011).

Producer and director John M. Stahl had seen considerable success in recent years at Universal Pictures, where he directed the melodramas *Imitation of Life* and *Magnificent Obsession*, both enormously successful six-hanky women's pictures. Given his dual credit, an extreme rarity at MGM, it's hard to blame the failure of the picture on anyone but him. In many ways, it was a no-win situation, and one wonders if Crawford dropped out simply because the script was bad.

If she did so for that reason, it was the correct decision. It is a dreadful script that attempts to create interest in Charles Stewart Parnell by repeatedly communicating to the audience he is interesting. The film opens with Parnell returning to Ireland from a trip to New York greeting adoring crowds, and the audience has little to no information on why he's adored so much or what he's done to earn it. While Gable is unquestionably miscast, he was an extraordinarily charismatic actor and could have overcome the miscasting with the force of his personality, even without an Irish accent. Unfortunately, Gable is subdued here, almost sleepy, as if he's trying to play a quiet, sleepy Irish Jesus without an Irish accent. Parnell was a legendary orator, but here Gable delivers his speeches quietly, almost as if he is embarrassed to be there. When Parnell meets the already-married Katie O'Shea (Loy), the two actors portraying them somehow manage to surgically remove all the chemistry that audiences know they possess given the other films in which they appeared together. Loy is overly restrained, and there is little evidence of the great love that is supposed to exist between the two characters.

Not helping matters was the Production Code, which limited how much the film could delve into Parnell's long affair with O'Shea, which in real life resulted in several children. With a run time of two hours and far too many speeches in Parliament referring to events the audience did not get to see, such as the notorious Phoenix Park murders, it may not be one of the worst pictures ever made if only because of its technical excellence, but it's certainly one of the dullest big-budget films produced during the studio era. Audiences at the time agreed. The film lost $637,000 at the box office. Gable decided to eschew appearances in costume pictures, and even hesitated to take the part of Rhett Butler in *Gone with the Wind* until it was obvious that no other human being on Earth could possibly play the role.

Fortunately, both Gable and Loy more than survived the failure of *Parnell,* and in December 1937 they were named "King" and "Queen" of Hollywood. Results from a survey of twenty million readers conducted by fifty-five metropolitan newspapers were announced that month by the Chicago Tribune–News Syndicate. Columnist Ed Sullivan even presented the amused Gable and Loy with crowns. The real crown for Loy, however, was that the contract she had denounced had finally expired and she won a new one for $4,000 a week, which included a bigger dressing room and a promise of a less punishing working pace (Leider, 2011).

The first picture for Loy under that new contract was *Test Pilot,* co-starring Gable and Spencer Tracy. Filming began in December 1937. Based on a manuscript called *Wings of Tomorrow* by aviator-turned-writer Frank "Spig" Wead, the film was directed by Victor Fleming, who had been Gable's favorite director for years.

Gable plays Jim Lane, a hard-drinking, womanizing test pilot who's attempting to set a new coast-to-coast speed record for airline manufacturer Howard Drake (Lionel Barrymore), always supported by his deeply devoted pal Gunner Morse (Tracy). When in the middle of the journey he is forced to land on a Kansas farm, he encounters sprightly farm girl Ann Barton (Loy), and their meet-cute is a perfect example of how Loy worked so well with Gable. They flirt, and his annoyance at his situation quickly grows until he takes on the frustrated obstinacy that audiences found so familiar in Gable. Loy, however, has the gall to interrupt his rant: "I know you! You're the prince! A nice charming prince right out of the sky. A young girl's dream. And I've been waiting for you all my life. That's why no other man touched the tip of my finger! I have lived for a prince," she says.

It is dialogue that reads sarcastically, but such was Loy's immense skill at this point that with her twinkling voice, she both berates and flirts with Gable simultaneously. She's playing with the blowhard pilot, and he doesn't really know how to respond because he can't quite figure out whether he's being insulted or built up. He's never met a woman like this before. It's a beautiful line reading because a lesser actor could have made the choice to berate or flirt, but Loy knew better.

It is perhaps the best moment in the film, after which point the two spend a rapturously enjoyable day together in Wichita waiting for Gunner to fly in and help Jim repair his plane. Ann shows Jim the simple pleasures of life in

Wichita, including a rollicking Minor League baseball game in which Loy lets her enthusiasm run rampant. Loy is so completely effective and adorable in the part that the film falters when the narrative attempts to make Jim struggle with whether to commit to her. There really is no choice—it's Myrna Loy! And once they finally do get married after a day's courtship, Gunner accompanies the two everywhere, including a pointlessly unfunny sequence in which the two men attempt to take Loy shopping for a nightgown.

After an air race in which Jim nearly dies and another pilot meets his inevitable doom after we meet his sympathetic wife and adorable children, Jim goes on a cross-country bender, and once Gunner brings him back home, Loy laments: "Oh, Jim, if only I could hate you!" The film takes a turn as Ann vainly attempts to be over-the-top supportive of Jim's dangerous and foolhardy profession, even as it's tearing her up inside. Fleming and cameraman Ray June give Loy plenty of close-ups as she silently suffers while watching Jim lose control of a plane and parachute to safety. She, of course, faints in Gunner's arms. If there's one part of the story that seems somewhat peculiar, it's that Gunner never leaves the couple's side; it's difficult not to see the gay subtext in Gunner having absolutely nothing in his life but his loyalty and love for Jim.

If there was one ironclad rule for aviation pictures featuring a male best friend during the Hollywood studio era, it's that the best friend has to die. And so it happens here when Gunner goes up with Jim in a test plane and winds up getting crushed by some cargo that has fallen loose. When Jim returns home, heartbroken, Ann screams that she wishes he was the one who died, and it hits Jim (and the audience) hard, because we all know it's true. While the film has a saggy middle, it's probably the best of the films Loy made with Gable. They worked well as a team primarily because their dynamic was so radically different from Powell and Loy's.

After *Test Pilot*, Loy made one more picture with Gable. MGM commissioned an original screenplay by Laurence Stallings about newsreel cameramen, then called *Let 'Em All Talk*, in September 1937. Eventually retitled *Too Hot to Handle*, MGM first announced that Gable would co-star with Spencer Tracy and Margaret Sullavan before settling on Walter Pidgeon and Myrna Loy.

In the film, Chris Hunter (Gable) and Bill Dennis (Pidgeon) are cameramen for competing newsreel outfits who are always trying to out-scoop each other, even if it requires resorting to fakery. When Dennis enlists his friend, famed aviator Alma Harding (Loy), to pretend to fly in for a dramatic delivery of cholera serum in China, Hunter and his trusty assistant Joselito (Leo Carrillo) accidentally crash into Alma's plane. After Chris rescues Alma from the fiery crash, romance blooms until Alma is disgraced when her fake medicine delivery is exposed. Her disgrace ruins her plans to raise funds to go to South America to rescue her brother Harry (George Peter Lynn). Guilt-stricken, Chris and Dennis sell their cameras to get her the funds and wind up going to the continent themselves to help her find her brother. An adventure involving the usual racist depictions of indigenous peoples ensues, Harry is rescued, and Alma and Chris are reunited in love.

Despite once again having to romance and be romanced by Gable, Loy's role here is far more interesting. She's a bold and fearless adventuress in the mold of legendary female aviator Amelia Earhart, who had just tragically disappeared over the Pacific Ocean in June 1937. Loy once again adjusts her performance to match Gable's energy, and here she is an even more significantly independent woman who, while falling in love with the big lug, will not take his guff for one instant. Her obsessive drive to find her brother whom everyone else presumes is long since dead inadvertently makes Alma a more modern character. While she falls in love with Gable (of course), she does not falter in her single-minded mission.

Watching *Test Pilot* and *Too Hot to Handle* back-to-back really showcases Loy's range. She was more than just a perfect wife—she had the uncanny ability to remain authentic to herself even as she embodied different types of characters with completely different objectives. The former film is superior because the latter's narrative lurches everywhere, especially in the far-too-long rescue sequence that finishes the film. True, the race-based humor throughout the sequence is nearly impossible for modern audiences to enjoy, but beyond that, from a structural standpoint, the sequence suffers by putting Gable and Pidgeon at the center of the action and removing Loy.

Too Hot to Handle was less successful than *Test Pilot*, coming in for a small loss, and it would prove to be Loy's final picture with Gable. In August 1938, now-independent producer David O. Selznick signed with MGM to distribute his mammoth production of Margaret Mitchell's *Gone with the Wind*, a deal that included borrowing Gable for a $50,000 signing bonus and a weekly salary of $4,500 to play Rhett Butler. Gable would be tied up for most of 1939 making the picture, William Powell would return from a long convalescence battling cancer, and the team of Powell and Loy returned to prominence.

Although the chemistry of William Powell and Myrna Loy remained unmatched, Loy's films with Clark Gable showcased her extraordinary ability to tune her performances to her co-star. While she always remained Myrna Loy, watching her with Powell and Gable was like watching two different, extraordinarily charismatic and talented performers with those legendary movie stars.

8

THE SCREWBALLS

In 1936, Hollywood's perfect wife was finally married. It would be a harsh irony for Myrna Loy that she was perceived for decades as the personification of American womanhood and marriage when she never managed to be part of a successful marriage. Her marriage to Arthur Hornblow Jr. would be the first of four trips down the aisle. Her June 27 marriage to the producer that year was not the kind of event that was well-publicized like the marriage of William Powell and Carole Lombard (and Clark Gable and Lombard less than three years later) because Hornblow was not a celebrity, and Loy was still considered to be a very private person.

Many audiences would think she was married to William Powell in real life, and 1936 represented the renewal of those vows, at least on screen. After Loy's self-imposed exile from MGM was finally over and Powell was able to complete his prior commitments, Nick and Nora Charles would soon live again. It had been an awfully long time for audiences to wait to see the beloved couple.

Almost immediately after *The Thin Man* was released in June 1934, producer Hunt Stromberg launched into development for a sequel. While MGM was able to get the first film in theaters less than five months after purchasing the rights to Dashiell Hammett's novel, the development phase for a sequel was going to be significantly longer, even without Loy's contract skirmish. First, Hammett didn't have any other Nick and Nora stories on hand and second, he owned the characters, so MGM was going to have to get him involved somehow, despite the fact that, as Louis B. Mayer would warn, the alcoholic Hammett had "irregular habits."

The bare bones of a premise was already in mind: The sequel would begin immediately after the conclusion of the first film, and be set in Nick and Nora's home base in San Francisco. A memo from producer Hunt Stromberg dated August 29, 1934, also suggests the sequence in the final film in which Nick and Nora are driven home from the train station on New Year's Eve:

"Down Market Street all the cops wave to Nick. And some truck drivers too—and all the doormen and nightclubs—Nick's a popular figure—and the whole feeling behind this scene is to keep up that delightful humanness of the man, and the joy of living with him and around him."

Stromberg also suggests that Nick and Nora get surprised by a party, although he then suggests they sit there quietly before the guests pop out and yell surprise. The later variation—Nick and Nora arriving as the party is in full swing and nary a soul actually knows who they are—is ingenious, providing a mirror to the party in the first film. Beyond that, Stromberg has little notion of what the plot would entail, except he proposes the sequel retain all the supporting characters from the original, complete with the entire Winant family. He suggests Joe Morelli call from New York with news that another crime has been unfairly pinned on him, and then . . . and then the producer doesn't really know. He needed Hammett (Stromberg, 1934).

On October 23, 1934, Dashiell Hammett signed an agreement to work on a treatment for *After the Thin Man* at $2,000 a week. He turned in a first draft on January 8, 1935, that tossed the idea of retaining the original film's characters and instead gave the audience the opportunity to meet Nora's eccentric, wealthy family as a humorous counterpoint to Nick's underworld life (Hammett, n.d.). After completing the screen story in September 1935, Hammett fell into an alcoholic binge and was committed to a sanitarium. Fortunately, despite Hammett's dipsomania, he managed to come up with something MGM could use as a screen story, and the studio rehired Frances Goodrich and Albert Hackett to work their magic on the screenplay, along with director W. S. Van Dyke (Hammett, 2012).

Goodrich and Hackett had serious misgivings about the project, not the least of which was having to "grope back through three years of time to catch the same characteristic idioms, voiced by Bill and Myrna in the first story," as Van Dyke later put it. The writers had such misgivings about working on the new script that they inserted a final scene intended to squash any possibility of further sequels: the moment on the train in which Nora tells Nick she's pregnant (without, of course, saying the offensive word). The Hacketts simply thought that a baby would put an end to their adventurous life, and Goodrich even claimed to her friend Leah Salisbury later that she and Hackett were so adamant about not writing a third movie that they wanted to make a particularly bold move with the ending of the sequel. "We wanted to kill both of them at the end [of *After the Thin Man*] just to be sure, but Hunt wouldn't let us," Goodrich wrote to Salisbury (Goodrich, 2001).

Following all the delays, *After the Thin Man* started filming in September 1936. By this point, Nick and Nora Charles were already the most famous and beloved married couple on screen, and MGM put all its resources into putting together a sequel to satisfy fans and critics. With a $673,000 budget, nearly triple the $231,000 budget of the original film, *After the Thin Man* would even go on location in the actual San Francisco to shoot exterior scenes. Once there, Myrna Loy discovered how much she and Powell were attached in the public mind. "At the St. Francis in San Francisco, they had reserved the Flyshaker Suite for Bill and me," Loy said later. "The management assumed we were married. Already they considered us a couple after only five [*sic*] pictures together! Well, of course it was hysterical" (Loy, 1988).

After the Thin Man opens on the same train where the original movie ended, as Nick and Nora arrive in San Francisco on New Year's Eve to enjoy a respite from the murder mystery in which they were embroiled during the Christmas

After the Thin Man (1936). Directed by W. S. Van Dyke. From left: Unknown, Unknown, William Powell, Myrna Loy. *Author's Collection*

holiday in New York. As with all sequels to popular films, there is the narrative convenience of the audience's existing familiarity with the main characters, so exposition is not required and the film immediately delves into comfortable territory as we watch Nick and Nora act out a little scene of domesticity as the train arrives in San Francisco and they pack up their belongings.

It's a deft, efficient, and quite funny opening as screenwriters Goodrich and Hackett quickly remind the audience of who Nick and Nora are, their fondness for drinking, and their friendly, teasing repartee. Particularly ingenious is an encounter in the train station with "Fingers," a purse snatcher and old acquaintance of Nick who is mortified when he learns Nick is married to the woman whose purse he just stole. It was a scene in Hammett's original screen story, and it's a charming moment that reminds us immediately of the different worlds from which Nick and Nora come, providing Nora with a callback line—"Dear, you do know the nicest people"—that provides an early moment of genuine fan service, the first of a number of in-jokes for people familiar with the first film. The real capper, however, is when Nick and Nora are being driven home by their chauffeur and Nora spots two of her upper-class friends in another car; they exchange pleasantries, after which Nora tells Nick: "You wouldn't know them, dear. They're respectable."

Loy's genius as an actor is her ability to deliver this not merely as a cutting line, but as a joke that Nick is always in on. While she's seemingly exasperated at the griminess of Nick's associates, we already know from the first film that she thirsts for elements of the unsavory lives they lead. Also important to realize is that Nora's line would never have worked in the first film. It is the audience's existing familiarity with the characters, earned through the length of the first film, that enables the joke to succeed.

After the Thin Man is full of references to the first film, the most obvious of which is a second party sequence mirroring that of the first film, a New Year's Eve surprise party thrown for Nick and Nora that the two manage to crash without being recognized by one guest after another, who have no idea of who they are. While it emulates the first party in some respects, it's significantly bigger, complete with a woman singing a zippy show tune to the accompaniment of a ragtag band made up of revelers.

Here is where *After the Thin Man* sets the template for the Hollywood Sequel. Everything is bigger. And longer. The film runs 112 minutes compared to *The Thin Man*'s 91 minutes. We now have lovely exterior location shots, including a historically interesting shot of the uncompleted Golden Gate Bridge in the background, while the rapid-fire shoot of the first film was completely studio-bound. A huge nightclub is now one of the settings, complete with a couple of superfluous production numbers that MGM simply loved to pointlessly insert in their "A" pictures during that era.

At the party, Nora receives a call from her hysterical cousin Selma (Elissa Landi), terrified because her rotten husband Robert Landis (Alan Marshall) has disappeared. When Nora's stuffy and elderly Aunt Katherine (Jessie Ralph) interrupts the phone call and invites Nora and Nick to a formal dinner, Nora agrees to attend, much to Nick's chagrin. When they arrive at Aunt Katherine's home, they are greeted by an impossibly old butler who nearly topples over when Nick places his coat on the old man's arm. For the first time, the audience is privy to Nora's background, and the film ruthlessly skewers the upper class (as many Great Depression–era comedies were apt to do) by making Nora's entirely family consist of stuffy fossils. One of the most amusing moments of the sequence is Nick carrying on a conversation with himself in the smoking room while the other men, all antiques, have fallen asleep.

The scene is eventually set for the mystery, featuring various nightclub hooligans as well as David (James Stewart), Selma's friend who has harbored an unrequited love for her for years. Eventually, Nick and Nora find Robert, who is presented as just the kind of lout that one could imagine anyone wanting to murder. Then, of course, he is murdered, Selma is found standing over his body holding a gun, and the mystery begins. That mystery is weaker than the mystery of the first film, featuring too many potential suspects and a plot that is unnecessarily convoluted, especially when one realizes in the final scene that the murderer is simply revealed by making a mistake in identifying one of his victims. As with the first film, it's the relationship between Nick and Nora that provides the great highlights, but the difference is even more stark here because the mystery is weaker.

An exchange in Nick and Nora's bedroom provides a beautiful comic moment that has nothing to do with the mystery. True, they're absurdly placed in separate single beds, now that it's 1936 and the Production Code Administration doesn't want us to think the movies' happiest married couple might actually have sex, but even so, Powell and Loy inhabit a simple and lovely intimacy. They're sleepy, it's the middle of the night, Nora mentions scrambled eggs, Nick obligingly asks whether she wants him to make any, Nora says he shouldn't bother, and Nick lies down to go back to sleep.

NORA: Nicky, can you reach the water?

(Nick reaches for the water on the nightstand and hands it to her.)

Oh no, I don't want it. I just wanted to be sure you could reach it.

(Beat)

NICK: Come on, I'll scramble those eggs.

Few films have ever managed to capture that kind of playful intimacy between two married people. It's a simple little scene that has no bearing on the narrative, and in the hands of lesser writers could have descended into a series of petty wisecracks. Instead, Nora's passive-aggressive attempt to get Nick to get up to make scrambled eggs is almost a sexy moment. She's teasing him, and he knows she's teasing him, and while he rolls his eyes when he realizes he just has to get out of bed, there is no argument. This is just the way that it is. It's beautiful.

Of course, for the younger set, the movie also had to give us more of the dog. Asta gets his own comic subplot in which he learns of his mate's infidelity with the next-door dog, but his best moment is when he playfully steals a piece of evidence that has been thrown through the window, and Nick and Nora go through some slapstick machinations in order to retrieve it from the mutt, a fun bit of domestic comedy.

The final scene in the film echoes that of the first, in which Nick simply gathers every character in a single room hoping that he'll discover who the murderer is, and of course he does. James Stewart provides the film a delightfully unhinged moment when he's discovered, and while his role as the villain has often been cited as an example of MGM tinkering with their new discovery in order to find the right fit, there's something fascinating about seeing young Stewart foreshadowing the darker side that would emerge in his postwar career in films like the Westerns of Anthony Mann.

While the mystery itself is saddled with too much plot, this last scene is just as delightful as that of the first film, rife with wisecracks and asides from Nick and Nora. By the time we've reached the final moment of the film, when it suddenly occurs to Nick that Nora is knitting booties because she's pregnant, the two have become old friends to the audience. While Goodrich and Hackett may have been fed up with writing these two characters and thought their becoming parents would prevent future adventures, their strategy seriously backfired. Audiences did not (and do not) really care about the mysteries. They care about Nick and Nora, and it almost didn't matter what they were doing. Powell and Loy's chemistry had created an institution, and there was nothing that was going to stop it.

That being said, MGM did have a quandary with Nick and Nora. The studio wanted to feature the smash box office combination of William Powell and Myrna Loy together, and the natural thing to do in that scenario was to churn out as many Nick and Nora films as possible. The bread and butter of studios in the 1930s were the "B"-movie series that were cheap and quick to produce. Two of the most popular such series that MGM would launch in the next two years were the *Andy Hardy* pictures starring Mickey Rooney and the *Dr. Kildare* movies starring Lew Ayres and Lionel Barrymore.

However, Powell and Loy were too expensive at this point for B movies, and it's not a stretch to imagine neither would remotely tolerate starring in four to six cheap *Thin Man* quickies a year, and aside from that, the characters were still the property of Dashiell Hammett. The natural answer would be to star Powell and Loy together in other "A" pictures throughout the year. Both stars, who clearly loved to work together, would be satisfied by not having to be Nick and Nora every single time, plus it would make each *Thin Man* picture a true event. The pair's other three pictures released up to this point—*Manhattan Melodrama, Evelyn Prentice,* and *The Great Ziegfeld*—had been all serious dramas not tailored for the pair, and now MGM had the opportunity to explore the possibility of Powell and Loy together in more traditional romantic comedies in which they were not already married.

Their first venture into traditional romantic comedy was *Libeled Lady*. While released in November 1936, one month before *After the Thin Man*, its development began long after work on the Nick and Nora sequel commenced and was the studio's first attempt at tailoring a new romance for the popular pair. The challenges were clear. While *The Thin Man* seemed to most people to fall into the romantic comedy genre, Nick and Nora were already together at the opening of the film, and the traditional romantic comedy of the 1930s required antagonism of some kind existing between the two characters at the opening of the film. At least in the traditional romantic scenario, the male character was the pursuer, which meant that the female character would have to be the one with antagonistic feelings.

While masterpieces like *My Man Godfrey* and *Bringing Up Baby* would brilliantly flip this societal assumption on its head, MGM was the most conservative of the major studios, so the traditional male-female roles would be retained with Powell as pursuer and Loy as pursued. Structurally, it was always more interesting for a romantic comedy to pile on as many conflicts as possible between the two future lovers besides just the fact that one doesn't like the other at the opening of the film. The most common was the existing love interest, often a man wildly unsuited to the lead female character. Think Ralph Bellamy in *The Awful Truth* or *His Girl Friday*, or Jameson Thomas as the doomed "King" Westley in *It Happened One Night*. Interestingly, Powell and Loy's traditional romantic comedies lacked this character. Neither Powell nor Loy was ever already attached to anyone else in any of their traditional romantic comedies, perhaps because even in an age when implausible narratives were the norm, the idea that either William Powell or Myrna Loy could ever be in love with anyone else was so wildly implausible, it wasn't even worth considering.

Another very common plot element was a difference in class between the two protagonists. As seen in *It Happened One Night*, Clark Gable's Peter Warne is a newspaper reporter and Claudette Colbert's Ellie Andrews is a spoiled heiress. Their conflict is Gable's disdain for the rich, an emotional theme that fit right into Depression-era audiences' mindsets. Powell and Loy each fit nicely into those class-based roles, since Loy had portrayed spoiled heiresses and other assorted spoiled upper-class characters almost since the beginning of her screen career. Powell had portrayed either upper-class characters or tuxedoed gentlemen as well, but Nick Charles—despite already being married to an upper-class woman and a new entrant into that world—provided a window for a continuing refinement of Powell's screen persona.

Nick's underworld connections and the comedy that resulted from his time in that world gave MGM the freedom to build on that role. In *Libeled Lady*, he's a kind of semi-lowlife fixer for a newspaper, and in *Double Wedding* he is a bohemian artist living in a trailer. Both roles seem like departures from Nick Charles, but they wind up being natural evolutions of his underworld connections.

Libeled Lady was an original script by Wallace Sullivan, purchased by MGM in March 1936 and originally promoted as a project for Powell, Loy, and fifteen-year-old Mickey Rooney (Cunningham, 1936). Whatever Rooney's role was supposed to be, there is nary a teenage boy to be seen in the final film, and eventually two other marquee stars would be added to the mix. Jean Harlow would get top billing and another opportunity to play opposite Powell to redeem their screen partnership from the misstep of *Reckless*, and Spencer Tracy was assigned as the fourth-billed lead. Production began in mid-July 1936 and by all accounts was a breezy shoot, with even the alcoholic Tracy, who was renowned for occasionally abandoning shoots to go on multiday binges, behaving himself. It could be his good behavior was for Loy's benefit. A crush he developed during the production of *Whipsaw* was still evident, certainly to the recently married Loy. "[Tracy] moped around pretending to pout, playing the wronged suitor," she wrote. "He set up a 'Hate Hornblow Table' in the commissary, announcing that only men I had spurned could sit there. So all these men joined him who were supposed to have crushes on me, which they didn't have at all. It was just a gag, but Spence made his point" (Loy, 1988).

Libeled Lady (1936). Directed by Jack Conway. From left: Myrna Loy, William Powell, Jean Harlow, Spencer Tracy. *MGM/Photofest © MGM*

Libeled Lady is one of the more peculiarly structured of the great romantic comedies of the 1930s, with four characters embroiled in the romance. Tracy is Warren Haggerty, editor of the *New York Evening Star*, who runs into a crisis when his paper cannot stop the presses fast enough to kill a false story claiming famous heiress Connie Allenbury (Loy) is a "husband stealer." Allenbury's father, J. B. (Walter Connolly), a man whose attempts to seek political office have been thwarted at every turn by the *Evening Star*, immediately sues for libel, seeking $5 million.

Knowing the story is false and he can't possibly win the suit, Haggerty recruits his nemesis, the paper's former fixer Bill Chandler (Powell) to marry Haggerty's fiancée Gladys (Harlow) and then manipulate Connie into some kind of a compromising and potentially scandalous position. By constructing a real-life "husband stealer" scenario, Haggerty believes he can squash the libel suit. Things go awry, however, when Gladys falls in love with Bill, and Bill and Connie fall in love with each other.

Considering the plot features a sham marriage and generally treats the institution with derision, it is remarkable it got past Joseph Breen, head of the Production Code Administration. While Breen huffed and puffed over parts of the script reflecting "unfavorable upon marriage and the sanctity of the home," relatively minor changes passed enough muster for the script to be approved. It's quite possible that the plot was so convoluted that Breen didn't understand it completely. It is indeed very convoluted and certainly cannot possibly hold up under the least bit of scrutiny. What is remarkable about the film is how good it is considering the ridiculous plot. The screenplay, credited to Maurine Dallas Watkins, Howard Emmett Rogers, and George Oppenheimer, does not give the audience a single moment to scrutinize the plot, moving from point to point with the speed of a locomotive. It takes almost no time at all to get to the point in which Powell has sailed to Europe in order to sail back to New York with the Allenburys and having the utmost confidence that he will be able to lure Connie into that compromising position, ready to be witnessed by outside observers to create an immediate scandal.

Before leaving on the boat, however, Bill and Gladys have to share a hotel room and stage a tearful farewell for the benefit of witnesses to vouch for the legitimacy of their marriage. The scene of William Powell and Jean Harlow overdoing it—"I'll miss my Billikins" and "I'll miss my little fuzzy face"—provides not only some comic relief, but also delivers a real sign of chemistry between real-life lovers Powell and Harlow. Broad comedy was clearly the key to making the pair work on screen, and while Powell is very funny as a droll Nick Charles dropping bemused observations about drinking and the mysteries in which he finds himself unwillingly embroiled, *Libeled Lady* was the first opportunity in his entire career to descend into truly broad and sometimes genuinely slapstick comedy.

When Harlow chomps down on his hand to prevent a kiss as part of their staged departure scene, it is William Powell's first genuine moment of slapstick. The scene works in large part due to Harlow's growing confidence as an actor, and her performance shows no signs of the health problems that plagued her. During *Libeled Lady*'s shoot, for example, production had to be halted for a few days because she suffered a terrible sunburn. Harlow's early and needless death was a terrible shame for the obvious reasons, and watching her opposite Powell in this picture magnifies the missed opportunity of their screen partnership. Going forward, their teaming could have been a fine, more comedic counterpoint to the Powell-Loy pictures.

Apparently, Harlow wanted script changes because she wanted to end the picture with Powell, but MGM wanted Powell and Loy to wind up together (Stenn, 1993). It couldn't be any other way. When he finally boards the ship in Europe, Bill attempts to ingratiate himself with Connie and her father by educating himself on angling, a flatfooted attempt that nonetheless results in J. B. being besotted with Bill's seeming passion for the sport and extending an invitation for a weekend of angling at his cabin with Connie. As Connie, Loy is splendid in a role that requires her to begin as a haughty and cynical heiress, but be likable enough to make the transition to her falling in love with Bill completely plausible. The audience's familiarity with Powell and Loy helps, of course.

Powell, meanwhile, gets to indulge in more slapstick as he accidentally catches a legendary trout, stumbling into the water multiple times, showing all the willingness to get into harm's way. It becomes clear it was a terrible shame he didn't get to flex his comic muscles in this way before in his screen career. The romance eventually climaxes after Bill and Connie take a moonlight swim, the two sharing a lovely, quiet moment in an otherwise loud comedy. She apologizes for thinking he was a fortune hunter and, while the two don't embrace, the realization on Powell's face that she has fallen in love with him simply because she apologized is a beautiful thing. Bill then decides to waylay Haggerty as much as possible, and of course, he and Connie wind up together. There was no other possible conclusion, as audiences well knew.

The film is one of the shining lights in the golden age of the romantic comedy, and it was a smash hit. If there was ever any doubt that the Academy Awards have always been ridiculous for nearly a century, the 1937 roster of nominations should erase them. While *My Man Godfrey* would be nominated for Best Director, Best Screenplay, Best Actor, Best Actress, Best Supporting Actor, and Best Supporting Actress awards and not receive a Best Picture nomination, *Libeled Lady* received a nomination for Best Picture and absolutely nothing else. It may seem strange that Academy membership determined *Libeled Lady* was one of the ten nominees for best picture of the year even though not one single element in the film merited recognition, but that peculiar disconnect may represent an example of the unique greatness of the studio system, that blending of disparate, seemingly unremarkable individual elements that somehow add up to something wonderful. After all, no one has ever called *Libeled Lady*'s director Jack Conway a great auteur, and he delivered a near-masterpiece.

As Vincent Canby would write in a retrospective review over forty years later:

> The success of *Libeled Lady* can't easily be attributed to the genius of the writers or the director, based on their other work. Nor can it be attributed solely to the four stars who, though they are among the most gifted of their time, did not write the material or direct themselves, nor, probably, did they even choose their material. As was the custom with contract stars in those days, they were assigned the work, which they had to do or face suspension. (Canby, 1981)

"There's no convenient way to justify *Libeled Lady*," Canby continues. "The only thing we can do is speculate, and then credit the relentless studio system that every now and again transformed base elements into gold."

By the end of 1936, the team of William Powell and Myrna Loy was an entrenched institution. The year was unquestionably the peak in Powell's career. While the reputation of *The Great Ziegfeld* has suffered over the past eighty-five years, *My Man Godfrey*, *Libeled Lady*, and *After the Thin Man* are still among the most beloved comedies of the 1930s, all of which have been consistently revived, aired on Turner Classic Movies, and released on Blu-rays. They represent the real flowering of William Powell's career as a truly comic actor. No longer the heavy, no longer the dignified respectable gentleman, Powell was now one of the shining lights of MGM as a genuinely brilliant comic performer.

Loy, meanwhile, cemented her screen persona as the movies' "perfect wife" with her turns in *Wife vs. Secretary* and *After the Thin Man*. This persona would carry her career through to *The Best Years of Our Lives* ten years later, when William Wyler chose her to represent every American wife who was left at home during World War II.

The year 1937 would begin with Powell and Loy separated. Loy was paired with Gable again in the disastrous *Parnell,* and Powell, meanwhile, would be given a curiously puny supporting role in *The Last of Mrs. Cheyney*, the remake of the Norma Shearer–starring 1929 adaptation of the Frederick Lonsdale play, with Joan Crawford taking over the role Loy had originally been set to play. Fay Cheyney (Crawford), with the assistance of her mentor Charlie (Powell) and three other gang members, spends months ingratiating herself into the society of Lord Kelton (Frank Morgan). Kelton and Lord Arthur (Robert Montgomery) immediately fall in love with Fay, and she struggles with going through with the theft as she becomes not only fond of her two paramours, but of all of the characters in the circle. Marvelous character actors Nigel Bruce and Jessie Ralph are also in the mix.

Powell, however, has almost nothing to do in a curious backwards step for his career. He plays a refined gentleman thief and his role feels like a tired retread of his early talkie roles at Paramount, although, as always, he acquits himself well enough. The production, frustratingly, feels like an early talkie. A number of early talking productions were primitive enough that studios often remade them within a decade because the original versions had already become dated. This remake, however, feels just as primitive cinematically as the original. It's possible it seems this way because of the disasters that befell its directors. Original director Richard Boleslawski died during production and was replaced by George Fitzmaurice, and then *he* fell ill and Dorothy Arzner completed the shoot (AFI Catalog of Feature Films, n.d.). The picture generally gives the impression of a lazily shot film that all participants seemed anxious to complete as soon as possible.

Powell's second film of 1937 was *The Emperor's Candlesticks*, which would team him once again with Luise Rainer. The film, based on an 1899 novel by *Scarlet Pimpernel* author Baroness Orczy, features Powell as Baron Stephan Wolensky, a spy for Polish nationalists in pre-revolutionary Russia who heads to St. Petersburg to deliver a ransom demanding the release of a fellow nationalist in exchange for the Tsar's kidnapped son. He hides the demand in one of two antique candlesticks, while Countess Olga Mironova hides papers revealing the Baron as a spy in the other candlestick. The two become unwilling allies when the candlesticks go missing and, of course, they fall in love.

While Powell and Rainer are appealing as always, the plot is cumbersome and their story only begins after the half-hour mark, a troubling sign for an eighty-nine-minute picture. Most of the opening of the film is devoted to a long big-budget sequence of a masquerade ball featuring Frank Morgan, Robert Young, and Maureen O'Sullivan, which is amusing but ultimately has no function except to kick off the plot; under ordinary circumstances it should have wound up on the cutting-room floor. Remove those scenes, and the spy story lasts a paltry hour. Critics and audiences were unimpressed, and the film earned $733,000 in the United States and Canada on a $1.1-million budget.

Rainer's career would quickly falter, but Powell's would thrive, thanks in large part to not starring in this kind of film anymore. While *The Emperor's Candlesticks* would squeak out a profit in international markets and avoid the massive loss that Gable and Loy's *Parnell* would experience, it was immediately clear that audiences did not necessarily want to see William Powell and Myrna Loy apart, and certainly not in turgid big-budget costume epics.

MGM soon reteamed Loy with Powell to provide some guaranteed box office success. The film would be *Double Wedding*, produced by Joseph L. Mankiewicz and adapted by Jo Swerling from an unproduced Ferenc Molnar play called *Great Love*. Swerling had written a plethora of fast, efficient, and entertaining pictures over the past few years, most for Columbia Pictures and some of which were directed by Frank Capra, including *Ladies of Leisure*, *The Miracle Worker*, and *Platinum Blonde*, one of Jean Harlow's first big successes. Playing opposite Powell and Loy would be young MGM contract players Florence Rice and John Beal. Beal in particular would enjoy a very long career, ending with an appearance in Sydney Pollack's adaptation of John Grisham's *The Firm* in 1993.

Double Wedding today may be best known as the film that William Powell was shooting when Jean Harlow died. Harlow, who had been beset by head-aches and bouts of poor health for years, experienced a complete collapse in early June 1937. She suffered for days due to undiagnosed kidney failure, which biographer David Stenn attributed to a teenage bout of scarlet fever followed by a kidney infection. Because her condition was never properly diagnosed and because Harlow's obsessively controlling mother had constantly changed doc-tors, Harlow needlessly suffered an agonizing death. Powell's relationship with Harlow had soured in recent months, according to Stenn, and he had started dat-ing Bernadine Hayes. When he visited the sick Harlow on Sunday, June 6, he was unaware of the gravity of her condition. No one was (Stenn, 1993).

But Harlow was gone the next day, and Powell was inconsolable. Loy said later, "He blamed himself for Jean's death. He had loved her but hadn't married her and taken her away from her mother." After a break from production, Powell could barely continue, but he gamely finished shooting. Both he and Loy would forever associate the film with the tragedy and would dismiss it under the cloud of the terrible circumstances that occurred during production (Loy, 1988).

William Powell and Myrna Loy in *Double Wedding* (1937). Directed by Richard Thorpe. *Author's Collection*

That cloud has somewhat obscured views about the film, which, while far from the level of other comic masterpieces of the 1930s, is still an immensely amusing little farce highlighted by a memorable comic performance by a supporting actor. As Waldo Beaver, John Beal gives a bravura performance in one of the most comically exaggerated portrayals of a completely agreeable person ever captured on screen.

In the film, Powell plays Charlie Lodge, a bohemian who lives in a trailer across the street from a joint called Spike's Place. He spends his evenings rehearsing a ridiculous script with Waldo as a lusty Arabian in the spirit of Rudolph Valentino, with his fiancée Irene Adler (Florence Rice) as the swooning damsel. Waldo and Irene live with Irene's controlling older sister and dress shop manager Margit (Loy), who raised Irene and decided four years ago that Waldo and Irene were right for each other.

When explaining how Margit decided on their engagement, the ever-agreeable Waldo tells Charlie, "I should have thought of it myself, but Margit explained that Irene was the only girl for me, and I should love her. So I did." When Irene eventually gets frustrated with Waldo's passivity, she pretends to fall in love with Charlie, and when an outraged Margit confronts Charlie, he plays along and says he'll only let go of Irene if Margit sits for him for a portrait for three weeks. She reluctantly agrees to the condition, and of course Charlie and Margit fall in love during those three weeks, although Margit refuses to acknowledge it.

All the while, Charlie attempts to teach Waldo how be strong to win Irene back. Charlie plans to take Irene to lunch and coaches Waldo to storm into the restaurant in a fit of jealousy and punch Charlie, but Waldo ultimately fails to muster up the required outrage. Both the coaching and the restaurant scene are significant highlights, and Powell and Beal's comic chemistry is perfect.

In a desperate gambit, Charlie decides to schedule a wedding with Irene at his trailer at 3:00 p.m., hoping that both Waldo and Irene will finally make the required bold choices and show up to stop the wedding so that Waldo and Irene and then Charlie and Margit can properly tie the knot. The film flounders a bit as the trailer becomes packed with guests, a weak regurgitation of the Marx Brothers' masterful stateroom scene in *A Night at the Opera* two years earlier, but ultimately our two pairs are matched up as they should be.

As Charlie and Margit, Powell and Loy recycle their dynamic from *Libeled Lady*. Powell is the pursuer, and here he plays the eccentric bohemian to the hilt. Loy plays the bossy antagonist whose obsession with Irene and Waldo's relationship is so perverse, it requires Loy to amp up the absurdity of her character. As a result, she plays Margit more harshly than she played Connie in *Libeled Lady*. Combined with John Beal's hilariously absurd affability as Waldo, Florence Rice as Irene is left as the only straight character, and even she is required to cry a lot. The film plays as broad farce, and succeeds much of the time.

Interestingly, it is the Powell and Loy picture that depends the least on their chemistry. They don't share a great deal of screen time together, and the most appealing pair for most of the run time is Powell and John Beal. Charlie's attempts at building Waldo's courage (or "Yumph!" as the picture constantly reminds us) provide the comic high points of the film. Still, the picture needs William Powell and Myrna Loy as its foundation. A scene of the two picnicking together after a portrait, followed by Margit playfully stealing Charlie's trailer when she wakes from a nap before he does, is a fine example of the old chemistry and a rare moment of lovely quiet intimacy in the frenzied film.

Unfortunately, the film and its production would always remain a sad memory for both Powell and Loy. Powell retreated from the limelight even more following Harlow's death and went off on a European vacation. Upon his return, Powell shot *The Baroness and the Butler* for 20th Century Fox in December 1937 and January 1938. Directed by Walter Lang, the adaptation of Ladislaus Bus-Fekete's play cast Powell as Johann Porok, butler to conservative Hungarian prime minister Count Sandor (Henry Stephenson) and his daughter, the Baroness Katrina (French actress Annabella in her first English-language role). Quiet mayhem results when Johann is elected as a Social Progressive candidate for the Hungarian parliament and chooses to continue to serve as butler to the very man he attacks on its floor. Daughter Katrina takes every offense to Johann's words, while Count Sandor is the most easygoing politician ever, who takes delight in his butler's vicious rhetoric.

Almost entirely unknown, the film is a minor little gem, as Powell essentially gets to play both Godfrey again and a passionate politician in a single role. Henry Stephenson, a ubiquitous character actor who specialized in old British fuddy-duddies, is surprisingly charming as that most endangered species, the civilized politician. Naturally, Johann and Katrina wind up falling in love despite her marriage to the slimy little toad Baron Georg (Joseph Schildkraut). While the film staggers whenever Annabella speaks—director Lang unwisely allows her to deliver her dialogue far too quickly for someone who's never spoken English on film before—Powell himself is delightful in a kind of mirror image of Godfrey. He's far more passionate and romantic than that iconic character, and the absurd premise that he would continue to serve as a butler when he joins parliament somehow works, primarily due to Powell managing to convey a completely plausible commitment to the idea.

The film is an enjoyable little trifle, although there is a sense of lost opportunity in this one of a category of films of the era that attempted to ape the style of director Ernst Lubitsch, but could not quite pull off.

While *The Baroness and the Butler* didn't make much of an impression when it was released in February 1938, that was the least of Powell's concerns shortly after its release. Already still mourning the loss of Harlow, a visit to the doctor in March revealed that Powell had rectal cancer, and while he would eventually recover thanks to a combination of multiple surgeries and platinum needles containing radium pellets, he would remain off the screen for nearly two years (*Los Angeles Times*, May 1, 1963). Audiences would spend most of 1938 and 1939 without a William Powell movie, and while by today's standards that hardly seems like an epic period, during the studio era it was an eternity.

It was not until his reappearance as Nick Charles in *Another Thin Man* in November 1939 that the public would have a chance to see Powell on screen again, accompanied by breathless publicity announcing his return. His absence from the screen represented a real turning point for Powell, who would withdraw even further from the public eye. Press reports at the time made vague references to hospitalizations and surgeries without mentioning the C-word, and Powell didn't reveal the diagnosis and recovery details until his 1963 interview with the *Los Angeles Times*.

While Powell was away and the industry's most beloved screen couple seemed to be in jeopardy, Loy would appear in five films, including her final two appearances with Clark Gable. Aside from those, Loy's other two MGM films were reflective of the studio's struggles following the death of Irving Thalberg. *Man-Proof*, released in January 1938, featured Loy as Mimi Swift, whose great love Alan (Walter Pidgeon) has left to marry younger society girl Elizabeth (Rosalind Russell). During the interminable seventy-four-minute running time, Mimi pursues the married Alan, catches him, and then he changes his mind again. Meanwhile, Franchot Tone plays a friend of the family with whom Loy has no chemistry or sexual tension until Mimi's mother announces she believes they're in love with each other, they quietly agree and nod, and the film fades out.

Lucky Night, released in May 1939, features Loy as an heiress who decides she wants to make good outside her father's influence and stumbles into Bill (Robert Taylor), an inveterate gambler with whom she shares an amazing evening. When the two wake up sober and find out they're married, they have to face the consequences.

Both films have game casts, but both feel extremely thin, featuring first-draft script material on which any competent producer would have demanded significantly more work. While *Man-Proof* is almost entirely forgettable (aside from Russell's extraordinary wedding dress that makes her look like a nun from space), *Lucky Night* features a very entertaining first half hour as Loy and Taylor spend a magical evening making fifty cents grow through a series of comically lucky breaks. The second half of the latter film drags terribly, to such an extent that it feels like work on the script just stopped halfway through.

Considering Loy had gone on strike not too many years before this in order to get better roles, it is a real shame that she was thoughtlessly thrown into these films that reflected the declining creative fortunes of Hollywood's most iconic studio. While 1939 is touted as a magical year for Hollywood, it was also the beginning of the end for MGM. Notwithstanding *The Wizard of Oz* and the welcome coup of distribution rights for David O. Selznick's giant production of *Gone with the Wind*, the number of truly entertaining pictures out of Culver City was experiencing a significant decline. Also declining was the studio's lead over the other majors in box office receipts.

After the untimely death of production chief Irving Thalberg in September 1936, Louis B. Mayer had complete control of the studio, and while the studio's slate for 1937 was impressive enough and brought in $14.3 million in net receipts (due primarily to projects that Thalberg had initiated), Mayer's lack of imagination was clearly harmful. As Thomas Schatz puts it in his definitive history of the studio era, *The Genius of the System*:

> While Mayer was an administrator, Thalberg was a creative executive; while Mayer was cautious and conservative, Thalberg was a risk-taker and innovator. Mayer was straightforward and pragmatic, while Thalberg had a subtle, complex mind. Both favored love stories, but Thalberg was a romantic and cynic, while Mayer was hopelessly sentimental. And both favored "quality" pictures, but Thalberg gauged quality in terms of style and inventive technique, while for Mayer it was a function of glamour, polish and production costs. Thalberg also had supreme confidence in his own abilities and instincts as a filmmaker and he was willing to bet the studio's money on them. (Schatz, 1989)

One only has to look at the sad differences in the set lighting in Powell and Loy's MGM pictures before and after Thalberg's death to see the loss of creative muscle. While *The Thin Man* had the great James Wong Howe behind the camera making creative choices with light and shadow during a lightning-fast shoot, by the time 1939 came around, nary a shadow could be seen anywhere in the frame as all the MGM pictures displayed a house style featuring incredibly flat, high-key lighting. While Mayer certainly wasn't involved in the day-to-day operation of productions, his style of micromanagement through endless committees permeated every facet of production, and just about every MGM picture began to look exactly the same.

Meanwhile, the other studios, especially Warner Bros. and 20th Century Fox, were benefiting from the continuity of their creative executives and their improving sense of how to make pictures, make them good, and make them the kinds of films that people wanted to see. As a prime example of how the other studios were catching up with MGM, the best of Myrna Loy's pictures during Powell's absence from the screen was *The Rains Came*. Released in September 1939 by 20th Century Fox, the film adaptation of the novel by Pulitzer Prize–winning author Louis Bromfield reunited Loy with her old Warners boss, Darryl F. Zanuck. Loy was loaned for the film by MGM along with director Clarence Brown in exchange for Tyrone Power, who would appear opposite Norma Shearer in MGM's *Marie Antoinette*. Over ten years after he wrote *Noah's Ark* for Warners, here Zanuck was able to oversee another enormous flood, with the extra bonus disasters of an earthquake and a plague.

It is a spectacular, big-budget affair set in the mythical Indian city of Ranchipur on the eve of the earthquake, flood, and subsequent plague. Loy plays the recently arrived Lady Edwina Esketh, unhappily married to the cruel Lord Esketh (Nigel Bruce, brilliantly cast against type) and desperate for some naughty fun with old flame Tom Ransome (George Brent) until she encounters the brilliant Indian surgeon Major Rama Safti (Power) and blatantly pursues him. When the disasters hit, Edwina changes her ways and volunteers to help the plague-afflicted citizens, falls deeply in love with Major Rama, and eventually dies after accidentally drinking some plague-contaminated water.

Notwithstanding the absurd casting of actors of every possible nationality as Indians except for actual Indians, *The Rains Came* makes for effective studio-era drama and at times transcends the disaster movie genre. Loy is excellent in the role and gets to stretch herself in ways that MGM would never allow during this time. As Edwina, Loy channels her early '30s screen persona of the man-chasing aristocrat, but Loy is a much better actor by this point, and the script and the casting of Bruce as her wicked husband provide some needed motivation for her desperate search for tender love. George Brent is his usual dependably bland self, and Power displays the screen magnetism and innate talent that made him Fox's marquee star beginning in the late '30s.

While Loy in her MGM films does manage to transform her point of view, often in romantic comedies or dramas, that point of view is almost extraordinarily narrow: It is simply her view of a man, whether it is William Powell or Clark Gable. Loy's characters rarely, if ever, fundamentally change. Edwina, on the other hand, undergoes a total transformation from a bored, selfish, and amoral aristocrat to a woman who would scrub dirty floors in a plague-infected hospital.

Ironically, years after she was typecast as a bad girl, Loy's new typecasting as the "perfect wife" required her to justify to the press her casting as a bad girl again. After casting was announced Loy said, "I want to be wicked for a change" (Leider, 2011). She is extraordinarily effective in the role, and it represents one of her very best overall performances. The film itself would be nominated for six Academy Awards, an impressive achievement for a film produced in 1939, and won a deserved Oscar for Best Visual Effects.

After *The Rains Came* was released, Loy reunited with Powell to film *Another Thin Man*. During Powell's time away from the screen, MGM mulled over what they would do with Nick and Nora Charles. At the beginning of 1938, the Powell and Loy screen team was ranked by *Variety* as the biggest box office champs in Hollywood behind only Greta Garbo and Gary Cooper. The seriousness of Powell's condition must have been clear to producer Hunt Stromberg, because he was thinking of substitute Nicks. An announcement in *Variety* on October 26, 1938, revealed that Reginald Gardner or Melvyn Douglas would play Nick in the next *Thin Man* picture opposite Virginia Bruce as Nora, since Loy did not want to portray Nora opposite anyone other than Powell.

Thankfully for posterity's sake, that film never saw the light of day (although Melvyn Douglas probably could have pulled off Nick Charles rather nicely). Fortunately, Powell had recovered enough by the summer of 1939 that MGM could move forward with their dream team again for a third *Thin Man* picture. It had been under development almost immediately after it was clear that *After the Thin Man* was going to be another smash hit for MGM, and Hunt Stromberg was clearly intent on bringing together all the parties that had been so instrumental in the success of the first two films.

This even included the always-unpredictable Hammett, whose involvement in the series was assumed to be over in February 1937. That month he sold all rights to Nick and Nora Charles and Asta to MGM in perpetuity for $40,000 (just under $775,000 in 2022 dollars), meaning the studio could keep producing *Thin Man* movies forever without any interference from Hammett or his future estate (Hammett, 2012). However, despite the sale of the rights, Stromberg still employed Hammett to come up with the screen story for what would become *Another Thin Man*. Hammett did manage to do so, delivering a screen story in May 1938 and then immediately falling off the wagon again. By July 1938, Hammett and MGM finally came to the terms of a divorce and he sold the studio a one-year option on all his writings for $5,000 (Hammett, 2012).

Keeping the team entirely intact, Stromberg once again hired Frances Goodrich and Albert Hackett to write the screenplay, which they agreed to do despite all their best efforts to bring the series to a conclusion by introducing a baby into the mix in the second film. Hackett said to a reporter, "You get a little punchy [doing] the same kind of thing. We thought the second *Thin Man* picture would be the last when we hinted they were going to have a baby . . . but the reviews [said] there must be a third picture planned, because they were going to have a baby. We just made it doubly hard for ourselves" (Goodrich, 2001).

The screenwriters' contempt for their assignment comes through in their description of baby Nick Jr. in the screenplay as a "fat, year-old boy who is interested in very little besides eating and sleeping. He eats anything that comes to hand and can sleep anywhere. He seldom laughs and never cries and doesn't think his parents are amusing." Regardless of its writers' distaste for the material they were assigned, *Another Thin Man* started shooting in July 1939, and Stromberg ordered a number of allowances made for Powell, who while cancer-free was still recovering and low on stamina. The production only shot for six hours a day, working on four soundstages that were already set up with a crew double the usual size and more doubles for the supporting actors so Powell could get through his scenes quickly with little fuss.

Speaking of fuss, Powell made it clear to Van Dyke and Loy that he did not want to have any kind of big, emotional "Welcome Back" on the first day of the

Another Thin Man (1939). Directed by W. S. Van Dyke. From left: Myrna Loy, William A. Poulsen, William Powell, unknown. *Author's Collection*

shoot, which they both honored, although the crew spontaneously gave him a standing ovation on his first morning back. With the renowned "One Take Woody" in the director's chair, the need for a quick, painless shoot for the weakened Powell went off without a hitch (Leider, 2011). The actual movie, however, was another matter.

Another Thin Man opens with Nick and Nora Charles (and Nick Jr. and Asta) arriving in New York City by train, only to be summoned for a mandatory weekend with Colonel MacFay (C. Aubrey Smith), an old business partner of Nora's father. The Colonel believes he's going to be murdered by fiendish Phil Church (Sheldon Leonard). Church purports to be a psychic and has been warning the Colonel that he's been dreaming the old man was going to be murdered.

We are then introduced to a truly dizzying throng of characters, including the Colonel's adopted daughter, Lois (Virginia Grey); her two suitors, Dudley (Patric Knowles) and Freddie (Tom Neal); Church's partners, Smitty (Muriel Hutchinson) and Dum-Dum (Abner Biberman); the maid, Mrs. Bellam (Phyllis Gordon); young Nick Jr.'s mysterious new maid, Dorothy Waters (Ruth Hussey), who flees once Colonel MacFay really does get murdered; a mysterious Peeping Tom named "Diamond Back" Vogel (Don Costello); and finally cops Van Slack (Otto Kruger) and Lieutenant Guild (Nat Pendleton), the latter a welcome familiar face from the first movie.

To go through the screenplay blow-by-blow would be a futile effort given its complete impenetrability, and for most of the time, Powell and Loy don't get to have very much fun at all. Perhaps it's reflective of Hammett, Goodrich, and Hackett's overall fatigue with Nick and Nora, but the first hour very nearly brushes the two aside in favor of scenes with the bevy of suspects. Many scenes take an inordinate amount of time simply establishing the relationships of these characters we don't care about. One such scene, for example, features Church, Smitty, and Dum-Dum in a hotel room to allow the audience to see that Church and Smitty's professional relationship has become personal, a scene that could have been omitted if Goodrich and Hackett simply established their relationship in advance with a line or two of dialogue.

Scenes like this featuring neither Nick nor Nora seem like a terrible waste. The other problem with the overall mystery is by restricting Nick and Nora to this mythical Long Island mansion, we keep them from the outside world and lose the couple's reactions to that world. The one item that sets things up for the first truly fun scene is the cops' interrogation of Nora in which they mention a list of Nick's marvelously named old flames, including Bella Spruce and Lettie Finhatten, which gives Nora an opportunity to tease Nick in a very amusing nightclub scene.

The sequence in the West Indies Nightclub is set up as Nick and Nora are separately following their own leads in the disappearance of Phil Church. Surrounded by a group of young ladies attracted to Nick like moths to a flame, Nick receives a note: "Sweetheart, if you still remember poor little me and my coal years in Cleveland, won't you come over and have a drinkie for old times' sake. Adoringly, Bella Spruce."

Of course when Nick ambles over to "Bella's" table, it's Nora sitting there surrounded by young men attracted to her like moths to a flame. It's by far the best scene in the picture, and the only one in which Nick and Nora are truly able to resurrect their old repartee. When Nora learns of Nick's past conquests, she is far from jealous—she's delighted because she gets to play a funny little trick on him. Things do pick up a bit after that point, toward some kind of a resolution to the mystery, although it's all so impenetrable it makes *The Big Sleep* seem like a simple Dr. Seuss narrative. A first birthday party for Nick Jr. thrown by "Creeps" Binder with a bunch of Nick's old crook acquaintances is fun, but it seems too little too late, even though the solution to the mystery (involving a homemade contraption to cause a delayed gunshot) is fun and creative.

Speaking of Nick Jr., Goodrich and Hackett's desire to kill the series by introducing a baby seems to have nearly worked. Too much attention is given to Nick and Nora interacting with the baby, especially in the first hour, and in retrospect it would have better served the film to eliminate the baby's presence by making a relative babysit while Nick and Nora go off to Long Island. The red herring of Ruth Hussey's ex-con nurse could be sacrificed with little fuss.

Reviews were decidedly mixed, if respectful, but as Frank S. Nugent put it in his *New York Times* review, "Some of the bloom is off the rose":

> The law of diminishing returns tends to put any comedy on a reducing diet and it may, unless his next script is considerably brighter, confound us with a *Thin Man* thinned to the point of emaciation. It hasn't happened yet, mark! We're merely getting in our warning early, notifying Metro-Goldwyn-Mayer that there's a limit to everything—including the charm of the delightful Mr. and Mrs. Charles. (Nugent, 1939)

One wonders if the mystery Hammett conceived would have been more effective had it been played completely straight and featured his other great creation, Sam Spade. It is so complex, and there are so many supporting characters, that there is little room to breathe. Goodrich and Hackett, sick and tired of writing the series, did not seem to make much effort to create that room, opting instead for a paint-by-numbers treatment of Hammett's story aside from the nightclub scene and the birthday party.

Still, the public wanted more Nick and Nora and showed their appreciation in droves. The film pulled in $2.2 million on a $1.1 million budget, and it was patently obvious to Hunt Stromberg and MGM that the *Thin Man* series was going to continue. It would have to continue, however, without Hammett, Goodrich, and Hackett, leaving the adventures of Nick and Nora to a new stable of creators, a requirement that would prove to be challenging at the declining studio.

9

THE INSTITUTIONS

As 1940 opened, Hollywood was emerging from a historically successful year, capped by the world premiere in December of *Gone with the
Wind*, produced by Powell and Loy's old boss, David O. Selznick. Selznick
had left MGM to become an independent producer some four years earlier,
and the Mitchell novel from the perspective of the antebellum South during
the American Civil War became an obsession. It would prove to be the most
financially and critically successful film in the short history of American
cinema and would represent the peak of Selznick's career. In short order
he would become obsessed with equaling his grandest project and spend
decades failing in the attempt.

The film was one of many produced in 1939 that would be perceived as
a historic classic, including *The Wizard of Oz*, John Ford's *Stagecoach*, Frank
Capra's *Mr. Smith Goes to Washington*, George Cukor's *The Women*, William
Wyler's *Wuthering Heights*, and more. The days of the technical challenges
were over, and it was the Hollywood studio system's finest hour. While MGM,
Paramount, 20th Century Fox, Warner Bros., and RKO continued to domi-
nate the industry thanks to their ownership of theater chains, even the smaller
studios like Universal and Columbia were producing throngs of great films because the demand never abated.

While neither Powell nor Loy appeared in any of the immortal films of 1939,
at its close *Another Thin Man* proved to be another success for the pair, and
with Powell's illness behind him, MGM enthusiastically prepared to feature the
two together in more films. As the year 1940 opened, however, it was forty-
seven-year-old Powell's personal life that made headlines when he surprised
colleagues and fans alike by eloping on January 5 with twenty-year-old Diana

Lewis, newly signed at MGM and known affectionately to friends as "Mousie." Lewis had previously been romantically linked with nineteen-year-old Mickey Rooney, with whom she was filming *Andy Hardy Meets Debutante*, and her marriage to Powell came as a complete shock to fans, friends, and colleagues alike.

The two hadn't even met a month before the elopement, when Powell happened to meet her while she was posing for a photo layout by his swimming pool. Fan magazines conjectured over the events that led to Powell running off with a young actress less than half his age, and *Photoplay* decided it was his long illness and convalescence that led to his bold move to marry once again: "The sick realize, more certainly than the well ever do, what an exciting, laughing, exquisite thing it is just to feel and move and think and be," wrote writer Ruth Waterbury in the March 1940 issue of *Photoplay*:

> A man returning from the shadows wants everything life holds, and wants no nonsense about correctness or conventionalities.
>
> It was in such a mood that Bill Powell looked out into his garden and saw youth and happiness there, in the saucy figure of a nice young girl. Bill had already lived several lives—and much credit to him too for he had created his own fortunate destiny out of his own being and talent and vitality—but here was a chance at another one. He strolled out into the garden—can't you see him being so casual and "Thin Man" about it—and he got himself introduced. From the introduction he worked up quickly to a dinner date, and on that date he was won by the things he learned about Diana.

Following their whirlwind courtship and surprising elopement, the two would remain married for forty-four years until Powell's death in 1984. Clearly, the marriage to Lewis brought to Powell the kind of comfort and stability that had long been absent from his life. Unfortunately, his frequent co-star was well into a marriage that she knew wasn't working.

In November 1940, Loy left Arthur Hornblow Jr., began divorce proceedings, and would return to him four months later. The two would eventually divorce for good in 1942, and the whole experience left Loy devastated. The effect it had on her was even apparent in her autobiography over four decades later.

"It shattered me, walking out on a marriage that I thought would last forever," Loy wrote. "God knows we hadn't been impetuous; we'd courted and lived together four years beforehand" (Loy, 1988). To make things worse, the famously private Loy was humiliated when Louella Parsons gleefully stopped the show at a personal appearance to announce to the delighted audience that the marriage of Hollywood's perfect wife had broken up.

Professionally, however, 1940 brought a level of comfort to both actors. Gone were the contentious contract negotiations, gone were the complaints about typecasting, and gone were the days of being forced to work on six to twelve films a year. Both were now Hollywood institutions, giant stars, and well established enough to control the pace of their movie roles. Powell and Loy would appear in one film together—*I Love You Again*—during the year, the newlywed Powell's only appearance on the screen in 1940, while Loy made only one other film, *Third Finger Left Hand*, with Melvyn Douglas. Also looming that year was the United States' likely entry into World War II following Germany's invasion of Poland the previous September, launching Loy's active, decades-long involvement in politics.

All that, however, was yet to come. Following the completion of his long honeymoon with Diana Lewis, Powell returned to the MGM set in April to begin filming *I Love You Again* with Loy, with the pair reuniting once again with director W. S. Van Dyke. The long-gestating project, based on a novel by Octavus Roy Cohen, was originally announced in October 1937 as a vehicle for Powell alone (Wilk, 1937) and the following March as Powell and Loy's latest team-up following the then-titled *The Thin Man Returns* (*Film Daily*, March 15, 1938). By March 1939, MGM still had the film on its schedule, waiting on Powell and Loy's availability, this time with a screenplay by Maurine Watkins. By the time filming finally started in April 1940, Charles Lederer, George Oppenheimer, and Harry Kurnitz were the credited screenwriters.

Lederer was best known for his brilliant screenplay for Howard Hawks's *His Girl Friday*, which changed the gender of Hildy Johnson in the play *The Front Page* to provide Rosalind Russell with one of her greatest roles. Oppenheimer had an uneven career working on duds like *Man-Proof*, and Kurnitz had successfully completed work on the scripts to three movies in MGM's "Fast" series, all *Thin Man* B-movie knockoffs about married rare-book dealers who solve crimes.

Harry Kurnitz is a name not often mentioned by film fans or scholars, but he is an important name in the history of William Powell and Myrna Loy, because after *I Love You Again*, he would be involved in the writing of the fourth and fifth *Thin Man* movies. Loy would later call Kurnitz one of the great wits, comparing him with Dorothy Parker. Also a novelist and a playwright, Kurnitz could seemingly fit into any genre at will, and among the screenplays he would co-write over the next twenty-five years would be *The Adventures of Don Juan*, *The Inspector General*, *Witness for the Prosecution* (with Billy Wilder), *Hatari!* and *How to Steal a Million*.

While much of the delay in the production of *I Love You Again* can easily be attributed to Powell's long convalescence after his cancer surgery and the priority of releasing a third *Thin Man* film before any other Powell and Loy projects, it's not hard to conjecture that the story must have been a hard nut to crack. It's completely ridiculous. Powell plays Larry Wilson, a stuffed shirt and teetotaler who, in the middle of his shipboard rescue of drunken scam artist Doc (Frank McHugh), receives a blow to the head that revives his long-dormant memory that he's really George Carey, a fast-talking, hard-drinking scam artist. Somehow, when Carey was stricken by amnesia from a criminal blow to the head nine years earlier, he was transformed into Larry Wilson, who became the general manager of a pottery works and the most respected citizen in Habersville, Pennsylvania. He then married Kay (Loy), who has grown tired of Larry's absurd level of preening morality and obsession with community involvement over the care of their marriage.

One of the most remarkable accomplishments of this film is how much it works even when the entire plot completely falls apart. George Carey got blindsided by thugs in an alley and got amnesia? How did he survive? How did the

I Love You Again (1940). Directed by W. S. Van Dyke. From left: Myrna Loy and William Powell. *Author's Collection*

entire population of a town become convince andhe was someone named Larry Wilson? How did he become convinced he was that person? How did this all happen in just nine years? The key, of course, is not to let the viewer stop to think about it for more than a few seconds.

In the first scene, the script establishes Larry Wilson as the opposite of Nick Charles, allowing Powell to earn laughs purely through the audience's familiarity with Charles. Laughing at a bushy-mustached Powell at a bar refusing liquor and instead ordering a peculiar cocktail of grape juice and ginger ale requires the audience to comprehend the significant level of irony in the sight of William Powell refusing liquor. A drunken Frank McHugh as Doc becoming incensed at Larry's refusal to drink with him only escalates the humor that relies on the audience's preconceived notions.

Powell as Larry in this early scene anticipates his work in *Life with Father* seven years later, suppressing all his natural charm in a humorous spin on his staid and formal roles in early talkies. When Doc decides to walk the railing as proof of his sobriety and falls overboard, Larry throws a life ring, the rope catches his foot, and he falls overboard as well. After an oar of a passing rescue boat strikes him in the head, Larry wakes up in a stateroom convinced he is really George Carey, a slicker and con man who got on the wrong side of gamblers, who assaulted him nine years earlier. George is astonished to learn it's now 1940, Franklin D. Roosevelt is president, and he's been leading a different life all this time. Fortunately, Doc is also a slicker and has heard of Carey, and when they discover that Larry has $147,000.83 in a checking account, they happily decide to head to Habersville, Pennsylvania, to collect it.

George/Larry is quickly distracted and delighted by the sight of Kay (Loy) meeting him when the ship disembarks, and puffs up with glee when she turns out to be Larry's wife. He soon deflates, however, when he learns Kay plans to divorce him. "A thing like a divorce can break up a marriage!" he exclaims. When he pleads for her to give him five or six weeks to convince her not to go through with it, Kay interprets the request as a scheme to avoid scandal because Larry hopes to be elected president of the chamber of commerce. Eager to marry a dud named Herbert (Don Douglas), Kay agrees to pose as a happy wife for six weeks.

Meanwhile, Larry and Doc team up with old criminal partner Duke Sheldon (Edmund Lowe) to create a fake oil boom on some of Larry's land to attract capital from some of Habersville's wealthiest and most gullible citizens. Larry quickly gets distracted by his attempt to woo Kay, much to Doc's consternation.

On the surface, this is Powell's movie. He has a ball playing a crook who's pretending to be a bland paragon of society, all the while doing everything he can to turn on the charm for Loy. The movie comes solely from his point of view, he drives all the action, and he gets the majority of the laughs as a character with a decidedly comic worldview. It's a flashy role, and Powell clearly has a ball dancing with himself at a nightclub when Kay refuses to do so, stumbling through the woods trying to get some Boy Scouts to "accidentally" discover the oil, and engaging in witty repartee with Loy.

GEORGE: You be careful, madam, or you'll turn my pretty head with your flattery.
KAY: I often wished I could turn your head—on a spit, over a slow fire.

GEORGE: The air smells different in Habersville!
KAY: That's the glue factory.

The script is classic Hollywood comedy, thanks to the cacophony of one-liners. Despite the ludicrous scenario, the writers have the good sense to establish the ridiculous scenario and then concentrate on the important thing: the relationship between the two leads. At its heart, this is simply a romantic comedy about a woman who has fallen out of love with her boring husband, and the husband's comic attempts to show he has really changed.

Loy is at her absolute best here. She has the difficult assignment of playing a woman who with every fiber of her being wants to believe Larry is the same old fuddy-duddy she wants to divorce, but finds herself falling in love with him again. She is brilliant in the movie's turning point, a scene in which Powell musters up all his charm to win her. When he coos at her like a lovebird, we can see her internal struggle as her face projects total annoyance and frustration but her eyes betray her delight at the mysterious transformation of her dullard husband.

When she finally accuses him: "The idea of giving up anything that belongs to you. You can't stand being hurt in the eyes of the public!" He pauses. And coos. And Loy breaks down crying. It is a marvelously funny and touching and sad moment that was well earned because the characters, their points of view, and the conflict were very clear and allowed the audience to become invested in the plot and ignore its inherent impossibility. Equal parts hysterical and deeply touching, the scene is one of the very best of the duo's long screen partnership.

Aside from the first two *Thin Man* films, it's hard to argue that the whole picture represented anything but the very peak of Powell and Loy's collaboration. Critics at the time agreed. Bosley Crowthers of the *New York Times* (August 16, 1940) was practically beside himself with glee:

Old family friends of the Charleses may sigh for their more suave and wordly airs, but certainly no one can complain that the new Larry Wilsons are less congenial or less delightfully full of surprises. For Mr. Powell and Miss Loy, no matter what their names, are one of our most versatile and frisky connubial comedy teams, and, given a script as daffy as the one here in evidence, they can make an hour and a half spin like a roulette wheel.

Mae Tinee in the *Chicago Daily Tribune* (September 1, 1940) said the picture "is one of those all too rare comedies with a constant mood of hilarity, an unbroken chain of impertinent dialogue without a dead gag or a wasted situation."

It didn't take long for MGM to pair Powell and Loy again. Based on an original story by David Hertz and William Ludwig, who received screenwriting credit along with Charles Lederer, *Love Crazy* cast Powell and Loy as married couple Steve and Susan Ireland, who are about to celebrate their fourth wedding anniversary by continuing their annual tradition of re-creating the events of their wedding night. Disaster strikes, however, when Steve's nosy mother-in-law Mrs. Cooper (Florence Bates) bursts in and sends Steve on an errand that gets him stuck in a broken elevator with his ex-girlfriend Isobel (Gail Patrick), leading to a series of misunderstandings that result in Susan deciding by the end of the evening to divorce Steve. Of course, Steve is still in love with Susan and does everything he can to buy some time so he can win her again, ultimately pretending to be insane in order to delay a date in divorce court.

Where *I Love You Again* worked wonders by simplifying an impossible and implausible plot, *Love Crazy* does the opposite by overcomplicating a simple plot as much as possible. The farce begins innocently enough by setting up Susan and Steve's anniversary evening with Powell singing "It's Delightful to Be Married," a sly little in-joke for audiences who remembered the song from *The Great Ziegfeld*. Powell and Loy effortlessly display the old humorous chemistry when Steve randomly suggests they re-create their wedding night backwards, the implication being that Steve wants to begin the evening the way their wedding night ended. Of course, since this is the Production Code era, no mention is made or implied of what a husband and wife do when a wedding night ends, so Steve's suggestion makes no sense dramatically. It primarily exists to establish to the audience that Steve is "eccentric," although Steve's suggestion seems more peculiar than anything else. Susan's character, meanwhile, isn't really established at all. She has no point of view. As she was in *I Love You Again*, Loy is straight man to Powell's zany character, but in the former film her point of view was immediately established: She wants to divorce her husband in order to marry another man. In *Love Crazy*, the screenwriters never give Loy a point of view; at the beginning, she's just a blank sounding board for Powell's enthusiasm.

For thirty-eight solid minutes, the script takes the audience through a long series of absurd situations to lead us to Susan at midnight announcing to Steve that she wants a divorce. It isn't until then that Susan is given any kind of point of view, so when she immediately wants a divorce because she suspects Steve of fooling around with Isobel while Susan was sent on an errand by her mother, it feels like it comes out of nowhere.

Farce is the most difficult form of comedy because (just as in melodrama) it often requires characters not to communicate what they're thinking. In the best farces, the writers take care to establish why a character would withhold that information. In *I Love You Again*, Kay does not tell Larry she's falling in love with him again because she's convinced he's only trying to avoid public humiliation, and she also believes that he's pulling an act because she's lived for years with a straight-laced bore and thinks he's faking his amorous advances. In *Love Crazy*, time and time again the characters are forced not to say what they're thinking for no narrative purpose.

The plot falls further into forced zaniness when Steve learns he can delay a divorce action by pretending to be insane, descending further and further into absurdity until finally Steve has to shave his mustache and dress in drag, pretending to be his own fictional sister in an attempt to avoid the authorities.

If anything proved how much of a beloved institution the Powell-Loy team was, it was the rapturous reception for *Love Crazy*. Bosley Crowther of the *New York Times* (June 6, 1941) gave the film a qualified rave, saying "the steady progression toward insanity which has been perceptible in the William Powell–Myrna Loy films is climaxed by a perfect consummation," and it was "one of the craziest love stories ever spread on a screen. Miss Loy never looked nattier and Mr. Powell never acted such a nut. What more could anyone want?"

Love Crazy certainly was the consummation of a gradual move into slapstick for the screen couple, and it turned out to be the final time that Powell and Loy would star in a film together as anyone other than Nick and Nora Charles. The glory days of the screwball comedy genre at which they excelled had already passed by as World War II raged, and by the standards of the era, Powell was just about reaching the age in which he was no longer plausible as a romantic comedy lead. After the next *Thin Man* picture, he would return to drama opposite Hedy Lamarr in the thriller *Crossroads*.

Contemporary accounts often split the series of six *Thin Man* films into two halves, with the first three films representing the best of the film series primarily because they were all written by Goodrich and Hackett and were adapted from original Dashiell Hammett stories. None would return for the fourth *Thin Man* movie. First, Goodrich and Hackett were well and truly fed up with the characters, and Hammett was simply too unreliable. At any rate, MGM had purchased the rights to Nick and Nora and Asta, and could now do anything they wanted with them.

Despite the exit of the screenwriting team, producer Hunt Stromberg and director W. S. Van Dyke were still on board. In May 1940, MGM announced in *Motion Picture Daily* that the next film would be entitled *The Shadow of the Thin Man*. The story by *I Love You Again* veteran Harry Kurnitz brings Nick and Nora back to San Francisco, where they become immersed in a mystery involving a dead jockey and a gambling syndicate. The script by Kurnitz and Irving Brecher provides some new wrinkles to the structure of the first three films. If anything had become a bit too repetitive from the first trio, it was the first act of the screenplay. In each of those three films, the script first establishes the group of people that Nick and Nora already know and then the hard feelings that some characters have developed for the inevitable murder victim to make them all plausible suspects. The murder itself is the inciting incident at the end

Shadow of the Thin Man (1941). Directed by W. S. Van Dyke. From left: Myrna Loy, Richard Hall, William Powell. *Author's Collection*

of the first act that catapults Nick, Nora, and the audience into the story. It is a classic, traditional structure for a murder mystery.

However, by the third film, Goodrich and Hackett's script clearly struggled to make anything new of the structure, and the relationship between Nick and Nora and the eventual suspects and the murder victim in *Another Thin Man* was far shakier than in the first two films. The emotional stakes were weak. If anything, *Shadow of the Thin Man* benefits from shaking up the structure of the first act. Kurnitz and Brecher instead turn the spotlight on something new: Nick and Nora's domestic life with their young son Nick Jr. (Richard Hall) and their Black maid, Stella (Louise Beavers).

Since there was never any maid in their home in the second film, one wonders whether it was Louis B. Mayer's growing conservative influence on the MGM style that mandated the demeaning role along with some very light domestic humor that felt more like scenes from an *Andy Hardy* movie (Mayer's favorite series), such as when Nick Jr. demands that Nick drink milk instead of a cocktail. Compared to Goodrich and Hackett's masterfully witty writing, these scenes age poorly, aside from one very amusing moment when Nick can seemingly sense a cocktail from a block away.

In addition to the antiquated scene of domestic tranquility, the other peculiar change in the screenplay is the nature of Powell's circle of admirers. In the first three films, Goodrich and Hackett mined plenty of humor from the gag of Nick running into old ex-cons whom he had helped put in jail but who still regard him warmly, leading to Nora's recurring comment, "You do know the nicest people." The running gag humorously played off Nick's underworld background against Nora's privileged background.

In *Shadow of the Thin Man*, however, after the scene at home, Nick speeds Nora to the racetrack, eager to begin a day of betting, and is pulled over for speeding by a policeman who quickly becomes starstruck by the famous detective. And once Nick and Nora arrive at the racetrack, Nick is mobbed by a large group of policemen who are similarly starstruck. Gone is the gaggle of hoods whose company Nick prefers. It is a subtle shift in the way that Nick is presented. No longer is he the object of admiration by ex-cons, but the object of admiration by law enforcement. It is another sign of the shifting emphasis at MGM that reflected Mayer's conservatism.

One clever change in the storyline, however, was Kurnitz and Brecher providing a murder at the racetrack. A jockey has been shot while showering in the locker room, and Lieutenant Abrams asks for Nick's opinion. It is the first time in a *Thin Man* movie that there's a murder victim the audience has never encountered before, and it provides a nice little sleight of hand that makes the next murder a bit of a surprise. It isn't until after the murder of the jockey that we meet our cast of characters. There's Major Sculley (Henry O'Neill) and journalist Paul Clarke (Barry Nelson), who ask Nick for help in cracking the gambling syndicate they believe is responsible for the jockey's death; Paul's girl-friend Molly (Donna Reed), who works as secretary to "Link" Stephens (Loring Smith), the head of the syndicate; "Whitey" Barrow (Alan Baxter), a crooked journalist who helps Link; and Claire Porter, Link's girlfriend. The casting of Claire is notable for being played by Stella Adler, the future legendary acting teacher in one of only three appearances on screen.

After Molly gives Paul her key to Link's office in order to retrieve some evidence, Paul is confronted by Whitey, who knocks him out and is quickly shot from an unseen hand in the doorway. Of course, Paul becomes an immediate suspect in the series' very first on-screen murder, and now with the personal connection, Nick becomes involved in the mystery. That mystery is a bit more compelling than the mystery of the third film, which was needlessly bogged down by the weak "psychic" suspect and too much focus on the suspects instead of Nick and Nora. Kurnitz and Brecher also provide a nice twist when Nick and Abrams discover that the jockey's death in the shower was accidental (albeit implausible) and decide to publicize that they believe the same person murdered both Whitey and the jockey in order to get the murderer to show his hand by framing someone else for both.

Along the way, there's a fun scene of Nick and Nora at a wrestling match, with some nice physical business from Nora getting way too much into the action and nearly strangling Nick; an amusing little scene of a radio-obsessed landlady showing Nick up to Whitey's apartment; and finally a riotous scene in a restaurant called Mario's Grotto, where Asta accidentally knocks a waiter onto someone's table and an enormous brawl breaks out. Less successful is an interminable scene at a merry-go-round featuring bratty kids calling Nick Jr. "scaredy cat" when he hesitates to climb onto one of the horsies.

Eventually, Nick for the fourth time gathers all the suspects together in one place to try to get someone to make a slip so that he can solve the murder. By this time, it's a self-aware exercise, but it works because once again, when Nick finally reveals the killer, his reasoning is plausible. The difference here is that level of self-awareness that we've all been here before, which can only be earned by a film series doing this for the fourth time. At one point, as Nick is stalling his way through another series of questions and answers before something jumps out of him, even Nora is crying, "Nicky, I can't stand it! Was it me???"

This time it's Nora who saves Nick and the rest of the attendees when Nick reveals Major Sculley as the killer and he inevitably pulls a gun on everyone, because even after doing this suspect roundup so many times before, it hadn't occurred to Nick to have suspects frisked as they enter. Still, it makes for an enjoyable finish. While the picture is imperfect and Nick and Nora's repartee has lost some of its sharpness, Goodrich and Hackett themselves had lost their zeal for the repartee by the third film they wrote, and *Shadow of the Thin Man* doesn't seem to be as much of a drop-off in quality that the film's reputation would seem to imply.

Still, *The Thin Man* series would quickly be endangered. The month after the release of the film, Japan attacked Pearl Harbor and Myrna Loy abandoned her career to assist in the war effort. In March 1942, after leaving husband Hornblow for the final time, Loy headed to the East Coast on a Navy Relief fundraising tour, impulsively married John Hertz Jr. only five days after her final divorce decree (a disastrous and abusive experience that would last only two years), and ultimately remained in New York for the remainder of the war to become assistant to the director of military and naval welfare at the American Red Cross (Loy, 1988). Myrna Loy's acting career was put on hold. In addition to Loy's sabbatical from acting, producer Hunt Stromberg left MGM in February 1942 to become an independent producer. That final stage of his career would begin with a box office smash in *Lady of Burlesque* with Barbara Stanwyck and then a series of successively less profitable films until he retired in 1951.

The other issue with continuing *The Thin Man* movies was a distinct shift in audience tastes for comedy at the opening of World War II. The kind of booze-soaked, sophisticated comedy spotlighting the lives of the wealthy had quickly gone out of fashion before the United States officially entered the war, and it was replaced with something far more simplistic and brasher. The top-grossing comedy of 1941 (and the fifth-highest grossing picture overall) was *Buck Privates*, a service comedy that featured vaudeville veterans Bud Abbott and Lou Costello in their first starring roles. A duo that notoriously despised each other in real life, Abbott and Costello were the ideal stars for movie audiences who were emotionally preparing for the extremely high likelihood that the nation was about to go to war. Their humor was based on recycled vaudeville gags—some decades old—and a level of volume and overall brashness that a nation girding itself for war seemed to desire. The picture, produced by Universal Pictures with a B-movie budget of $245,000, grossed $4 million, one of the biggest profits (by percentage) in the studio era. Slavish imitation of box office hits is hardly a symptom of twenty-first-century Hollywood alone, and other studios quickly churned out army comedies. Even the gentle, beloved duo of Stan Laurel and Oliver Hardy in their first picture for 20th Century Fox was forced to make

Great Guns, which was such an obvious attempt at copying *Buck Privates* that it actually referenced the earlier film by name.

What it all added up to was the end of the bubbling champagne of 1930s screwball comedy. The sight of Nick and Nora Charles spending their wealth on liquor and partying had quickly gone out of step with the times. Compounding this after the United States joined the conflict was the government's formation in June 1942 of the Office of War Information and its Bureau of Motion Pictures, which mandated the involvement of Hollywood's output in furthering the war effort. Affected by the loss of talent to war service, including directors John Ford and George Stevens and actors Clark Gable and James Stewart, Hollywood was more than accommodating. The war was big business, and Hollywood has always been a business. Just about every picture was about the war in some way. The idea of Nick and Nora magically becoming selfless stewards of the war effort seems absurd.

However, the series was still a moneymaker in 1942. *Shadow of the Thin Man* brought in a worldwide gross of $2.3 million against a budget of $821,000. So MGM put another *Thin Man* movie in development, now under the stewardship of Everett Riskin. Riskin was a producer who came to MGM from Columbia Pictures in 1942 after overseeing some classic comedy hits at that studio, including *Holiday* and *Here Comes Mr. Jordan*. He quickly assigned the scripting duties for *The Thin Man Comes Home* to his brother Robert (Riskin, 2019).

Robert Riskin had written the screenplays for many of Frank Capra's pictures during that director's extraordinarily successful run over the previous decade, including *It Happened One Night, Mr. Deeds Goes to Town, You Can't Take It with You*, and *Meet John Doe*. Robert quickly began to regret the assignment. While he was working in Hollywood, his new wife and former Powell co-star, Fay Wray, was working in New York. Riskin lamented his involvement in "the dreadfully dull *Thin Man*" in letters to Wray, shown in their daughter Victoria's dual biography of her parents.

"The whole thing is a weird experience for me," Riskin wrote. "I find myself as remote from the very things I, myself have written that I can't remember now, a week after the completion of the script, what the scenes are all about. Everett tries to discuss them with me and sometimes I stare at him blankly—trying to recall the scene mentioned—or its contents" (Riskin, 2019).

Hardly the attitude of an enthusiastic screenwriter. The film was originally set to go into production in June 1942, but Loy had no interest in returning to Hollywood, so MGM announced in November of that year that Irene Dunne would take over the role of Nora Charles (*New York Times*, November 2, 1942). Not surprisingly, reaction was as hostile as it was when MGM floated the idea of Melvyn Douglas and Virginia Bruce as substitutes for the third film during Powell's illness several years earlier.

Loy shared William Powell's thoughts in her autobiography forty years later: "The studio was deluged with fan letters. The fans wanted Myrna, and they didn't want anyone else. I wanted Myrna, too. Besides the favorable reception our pictures always received, I must say it was certainly a pleasure to work with her. She's—well—compatible" (Loy, 1988).

MGM simply had to wait for Myrna Loy, and complicating matters even further as the studio waited was the death of series director W. S. Van Dyke. A devout Christian Scientist who refused most treatments for the lung cancer and heart disease from which he suffered, Van Dyke said goodbye to Louis B. Mayer, his wife, and his three children and committed suicide in February 1943. He was fifty-three years old, and his deft touch would be missed not only on the remaining two *Thin Man* movies, but on countless MGM films for which his professionalism and efficiency were often then (and today) taken for granted. His death was another black mark on a studio hopelessly in decline.

In 1944, Loy was still working with the Red Cross, and while the experience was an extraordinarily positive one, her marriage to John Hertz Jr. was quickly disintegrating. The son of John Daniel Hertz Sr., an Austrian immigrant who became a giant in the transportation industry, young Hertz was plagued with mental difficulties and alcoholism and he would often become violent, quickly turning the marriage into a nightmare that truly threatened Loy's life. She left him after only two years. Hertz had been against Loy working, which she said delighted her when they first met because she had grown tired of acting, but her separation from him helped her decide to make a brief return to Hollywood to make *The Thin Man Goes Home* (Leider, 2011).

Myrna Loy's return to MGM for the first time in three years was a triumphant one. Powell recalled, "The first day of the picture, everybody wanted to kiss and hug Myrna. I've never seen a girl so popular with so many people. Everybody from wardrobe was over on the set, everybody from makeup, everybody from property, everybody from miles around, it looked like. There were big signs flamboyantly announcing, WELCOME HOME MYRNA or DON'T LEAVE US AGAIN MYRNA" (Loy, 1988).

Taking over for the late Woody Van Dyke in the director's chair was Richard Thorpe, whom Powell and Loy had worked with on *Double Wedding* seven years earlier. In the early 1940s, Thorpe had begun to specialize primarily in B-movies, including the final MGM Tarzan film, *Tarzan's New York Adventure*, and a number of pictures with Wallace Beery, who had fallen far from his peak as a movie star in the late '20s and early '30s. While hardly anything resembling an auteur, Thorpe was a solid, reliable, and efficient company man, if a couple of steps below the late Van Dyke, and his direction of *The Thin Man Goes Home* adequately reflected the style of the studio in the mid-1940s. In general, it is the first *Thin Man* movie that looks genuinely cheap and obviously studio-bound. There is never a sense that the town of Sycamore Springs is any kind of real place, with not a single establishing shot to be found. The series—and MGM—had fallen a long way from the days of location shooting in San Francisco for *After the Thin Man*.

Released in January 1945, *The Thin Man Goes Home* departs significantly from the first four films in the series. Nick and Nora resume their travels from the first three films, heading to Nick's fictional home town of Sycamore Springs. Stuck in coach on a crowded train, Nick and Nora are busted by the conductor for smuggling Asta aboard and ordered to the cattle car. Their journey there through the crowded passageway recalls the Marx Brothers' stateroom scene from *A Night at the Opera* as Nick, Nora, and Asta impossibly squeeze their way through the space clogged with bodies. It immediately establishes the humor in the picture as far more situational and broad than in the past, reflecting screenwriter Robert Riskin's preference for character-driven, situational humor than the canny dialogue and sharp wit found in Goodrich and Hackett's scripts. It is very much a fish-out-of-water scenario for Nick and Nora, stuck in a small town with nary a nightclub in sight.

The two have made the trip, and blessedly left Nick Jr. behind to continue kindergarten, in order to visit Nick's father (Harry Davenport) and mother (Lucile Watson). There are allusions to a long-simmering resentment on the part of Nick's father, who is the town doctor, because he always hoped Nick would follow in his medical footsteps. There is little to no actual sign of resentment, though, in this gentle comedy. Veteran character actor Davenport here is just as sunny and pleasant as he was as the grandfather in *Meet Me in St. Louis*, released a couple of months earlier. There is also the issue of Nick's drinking that is said to have caused his father some consternation, so the film opens up with Nick choosing to drink cider instead of liquor. But there is little evidence of actual animosity, and if that plot element feels shoehorned in, it's because it was. The truth was that producer Everett Riskin decided to eliminate liquor in the film due to wartime rationing, and reshoots were required to do so in August and September of 1944, led by director Norman Taurog.

The shadow of the war really is everywhere in the picture, in which the murder revolves around a series of paintings that conceal stolen top-secret plans for an airplane propellor. Even the murder weapon is specifically referred to as a rifle made in Japan. While the wartime elements of the story don't overwhelm the proceedings, the small town setting somehow makes them more notable. Also notable is a larger role for Nora, which perhaps could have provided some extra bait for Myrna Loy to return to Hollywood after her long sabbatical. She gets significantly more laughs than Powell who, while not entirely regressing to a Philo Vance–like state of crime-solving, is much more of a sedate character in this picture. While Nick spends his time interviewing suspects in a much more straightforward and methodical manner than audiences were accustomed to seeing him perform, Nora now is the center of the comedy. When Nora sympathizes with Nick for his strained relationship with his father, she suggests that his father might be more proud of him if he could see Nick demonstrate his crime-solving prowess.

In a bravura monologue, Nora attempts to impress Mr. Charles with the story of one of Nick's recent adventures in gory detail. Delivering it almost in the style of a '30s gangster moll as conceived by Katharine Hepburn, Nora tells how Nick uncovered the crimes of Stinky Davis, who strangled four men without leaving fingerprints, and the names of the men alone in her glorious tale are magnificent. It is a masterpiece of absurd, specific details, and while it is out of tune with the sophisticated wit of Goodrich and Hackett's screenplays, it is still the funniest part of the picture:

> But Slasher had an alibi with Squinty Burke and Studsy Green, so that took care of him. But all the time Nick was certain that Stinky Davis was the killer. Why? Because he had him pegged right away for a two-timing double-crossing rat! But did the police listen to Nick? No! They told him it was a hophead theory, wild as loco buttons, because Stinky was a cripple and couldn't navigate. So Nick got the brushoff from the police. They cold-shouldered him right out. But did that stop him? No sir! He knew the case was hot and he was all set to start cooking on the front burner. He said, "Stinky, you're the two-timing double-crossing rat who strangled Knobs McClure and Reesy Joe and Horseface Dan and Denver Mike" and then he turned his back on him. And the trick worked! Because Stinky got out of his chair and tried to strangle Nick with a piece of wire he had hidden in his mouth. But just in time, Nick turned around and gave him the old one-two and knocked Stinky colder than an ice flounder. Stinky wasn't a cripple at all! He was just using it to cover up his crimes. Now, what do you think of THAT?

We also see Nick and Nora alone together in new and unexpected ways. No longer drinking, no longer soaking in the urban nightlife, screenwriters Riskin and Taylor instead created a scene in which Nick is trying to relax in a hammock while Nora stubbornly refuses his half-hearted offers to help her put together a lawn chair. It's a light and pleasant little slapstick scene expertly executed by

Loy, who rarely got to demonstrate her flair for physical comedy. It ends with Nick suavely putting the chair together in a split second, Nora immediately falling flat on her behind after attempting to sit in it, Nick falling out of the hammock, and the scene concludes with the two lying on the ground, giggling. It is a minor little scene of comedy, but one of the more amusing moments in the entire series, demonstrating how effortless William Powell and Myrna Loy's chemistry was and validating audiences' fervent belief at the time that the two were married in real life.

Reliable MGM character actor Edward Brophy, who played Morelli in the original *Thin Man*, plays a new character named Brogan, who seems to be a secret assistant to Nick. While that is a bit of a confusing change to modern audiences who aren't accustomed to see actors switch roles in a film series, it was a frequent practice for studios eager to recycle contract players in their series.

As always, Nick has to resort to deception to keep Nora from nosing around in his murder investigation, and when Nora begins to suspect Brogan as the killer, Nick is happy to accommodate her and asks Brogan to take a walk through town so Nora can follow him and stay out of Nick's way. Unbeknownst to Nora, as she's following Brogan, legitimate suspect Edgar Draque (Leon Ames) is following her. An amusing adventure ensues, ending in Nora slapping

William Powell and Myrna Loy in *The Thin Man Goes Home* (1945). Directed by Richard Thorpe. *Author's Collection*

Edgar in a pool hall, starting a giant brawl so she can slip away and tail Brogan some more.

Nora's larger role is understandable from a narrative sense. Now in a small town, no longer drinking, there is not much for Nick to do except solve the mystery. In prior installments, he always has some kind of shady leisure activity to pursue instead of solving crimes, but here Nick exhibits zero reluctance to be involved in a mystery as he had in the previous pictures.

At the end of the picture, for the fifth time, Nick gathers all possible suspects in a room—this time his father's office—in order to suss out the murderer. This time, Nora narrates the action to Dr. Charles, letting him know what to be prepared for, including informing him that the murderer will absolutely pull a gun on everyone in the room once Nick exposes him. It is a fun bit of meta commentary on the *Thin Man* formula that is further enhanced when finally, at long last, it occurs to Nick to ask the police to frisk everyone in the room. In a rather ingenious turn of events, nearly everyone in the room is actually packing heat. It's a funny way to acknowledge the series' formula, and is also a canny way to emphasize that, truly, nearly everyone in the room could be the murderer. Of course, after Brogan enters with the Japanese-manufactured rifle as evidence that a sniper was responsible for the first murder, town coroner Dr. Bruce Clayforth (Lloyd Corrigan) grabs the weapon after Nick successfully exposes him as the killer, ending the scene in the traditional way. Naturally, Brogan had disarmed the gun so that no shot goes off, but seeing the murderer manage to grab a weapon seems peculiarly satisfying.

Despite its B-movie appearance, *The Thin Man Goes Home* still had a $1.4 million budget thanks primarily to Powell and Loy's salaries, and brought in a total of $2.8 million in global box office receipts. Reviews were respectable, but it was clear that critics saw the appeal of Nick and Nora Charles waning. Bosley Crowther in the *New York Times* (January 26, 1945) said:

> Perhaps the weather had something to do with it, but it seemed that Nick and Nora lacked the warmth we've come to expect from this sparkling team. Of course, they're the same happy pair, whose friends are legion and who, a decade ago, discovered that marriage can be merry. If, at times, their erstwhile fast pace has been slowed to a walk, blame it on the script, which takes a long time introducing Nick to crime.

Modern critics could definitely point to a loss of sophistication and wit in the series, and could easily decry the transformation of Nora into a more comic, perhaps slightly airheaded character. There is even a point in which Nick playfully spanks her in front of his own parents, probably the most offensively anachronistic moment in the *Thin Man* series. It represented the struggle of trying to breathe new life into Nick and Nora and to keep things fresh overall five pictures into the series. Objectively, they were very shallow people: wealthy alcoholics who want nothing out of life more than a good time and who manage to stumble reluctantly into crime-solving. They possess no inner conflicts, no real doubts, and their marriage is perfect.

The trouble with most long-lasting film series, and certainly long-lasting TV series, is that at some point the characters are locked into themselves. The core nature of any traditional narrative is change, and what happens when the characters stop changing? Inevitably some form of infantilism develops. The characters have nowhere to go, so the only thing to do is emphasize the plot or completely change the nature of the characters so they have somewhere to go. *Another Thin Man*, which Goodrich and Hackett had no actual desire to write, emphasized the plot. *Shadow of the Thin Man* emphasized domestic life and introduced Nick Jr. as a new element in the proceedings. *The Thin Man Goes Home* changed Nora into the comic character and straightened out Nick.

Despite the lack of sophistication and wit that embodied Goodrich and Hackett's work and the seeming infantilization of Nora's character, all that Robert Riskin and Dwight Taylor really did was heighten Nora's sense of adventure and pride in Nick. And any observers complaining of Nora being infantilized by the inability to put together a lawn chair, for example, should keep in mind that Nora was a child of immense privilege who grew up in a mansion and has lived a complete life of leisure with servants at her beck and call. When on earth would she have learned to put together a lawn chair? As much as it may seem like an infantilization of Nora's character, there is truth in that scene based on what we know of Nora's character and upbringing.

The Thin Man Goes Home does feels very little like the films that came before it, but it still feels very much more than just a familiar mystery. It still relies on the appeal of William Powell and Myrna Loy as Nick and Nora Charles, even though Nick and Nora may not be who they were at the start of the series. None of the same can be said about *Song of the Thin Man*, the final film in MGM's *Thin Man* series and the only one of the series not to make money.

By the time *Song of the Thin Man* was released in September 1947, the world, Hollywood, and Powell and Loy's careers had radically changed in the two and a half years since the previous film hit theaters. The war ended and Loy married her third husband, producer and director Gene Markey, in January 1946. She renewed her career and starred in arguably her greatest picture, *The Best Years of Our Lives*, while Powell returned to Warner Bros. to star as Father in the film adaptation of *Life with Father*, which to date is still the longest running straight play in the history of Broadway. They were both definitive roles for the stars, and it's not hard to imagine both were likely eager to move on from Nick and Nora.

Loy didn't hide her distaste for the final *Thin Man* film. "I hated it," she wrote in her autobiography. "The characters had lost their sparkle for Bill and me, and the people who knew what it was all about were all gone" (Loy, 1988). Even those people's replacements from the prior film were gone. Producer Everett Riskin was replaced by Nat Perrin, a screenwriter whose credits included several Red Skelton and Abbott & Costello pictures and *The Big Store*, the Marx Brothers' final execrable film at MGM that temporarily ended their film careers. Assigning Perrin to Nick and Nora Charles cemented their place in the studio's pantheon as B-movie heroes.

From a story by Stanley Roberts, the screenplay was credited to Perrin and Steve Fisher, a young scriptwriter whose recent credits were all crime dramas that would years later be assigned the "film noir" designation: *Johnny Angel*, *Lady in the Lake*, and *Dead Reckoning*. Often a red flag for a script by committee, "additional dialogue" was credited to James O'Hanlon and Harry Crane (the writers of *The Harvey Girls*, a Judy Garland musical). It was a strange mix of screenwriters, and if any one may have dominated, in retrospect perhaps it was Fisher, because *Song of the Thin Man* has the curious distinction of being the only film in the series that could legitimately be called film noir.

Shadowy crime dramas had quickly become the rage in the midst of a postwar malaise, with all the studios producing gritty crime dramas full of shadows and low-key lighting, even at the traditionally glamorous MGM, which produced a brilliant adaptation of James M. Cain's *The Postman Always Rings Twice* starring John Garfield and Lana Turner. At Universal, there was *The Killers* with Burt Lancaster and Ava Gardner, and at RKO there was *Out of the Past* with Robert Mitchum. Even films that have long since acquired a reputation for sentimentality, such as Frank Capra's *It's a Wonderful Life*, were far darker than Hollywood had ever produced before. Capra's masterpiece is, after all, about a man whose dreams are gradually crushed for decades until he finally decides to commit suicide.

While *The Thin Man Goes Home* radically changed the series' approach to humor by dispensing with sophisticated wit and emphasizing situational and sometimes slapstick humor, *Song of the Thin Man* goes further and dispenses with humor almost entirely. It's almost completely a straightforward, serious picture, and almost nothing about the film depends on the presence of the characters of Nick and Nora Charles. Any pair of married sleuths could have done the job just fine. Compounding this drastic change in tone was the cinematography by the great Charles Rosher. While he had recently shot Technicolor pictures at MGM, including *Kismet*, *Ziegfeld Follies*, *Yolanda and the Thief*, and *The Yearling*, Rosher was a veteran of silent pictures who got his start with Mary Pickford and eventually shot *Sunrise*, the F. W. Murnau masterpiece that was arguably the finest silent movie ever made.

Sunrise was characterized by low-key, chiaroscuro lighting favored by German directors like Murnau, and with the emergence of crime dramas in the postwar era, such as *The Killers* directed by German émigré Robert Siodmak, low-key lighting was coming back in vogue. Rosher embraced it fully for *Song of the Thin Man*. It is the first time we see so many shadows since the original *Thin Man* shot by James Wong Howe. Gone is the high-key lighting favored by MGM in the late '30s and early '40s. Now shadows were everywhere.

The picture looks great, but it's an unfortunate affair. One of the only genuine attempts at humor is a domestic scene in which Nora implores Nick to spank their son (Dean Stockwell) for misbehaving. As Nick throws Nick Jr. on his lap, images of his childhood are superimposed on an extreme close-up of the child's rear end, representing Nick wrestling with the guilt of abusing his child. To say

Song of the Thin Man (1947). Directed by Edward Buzzell. From left: Unknown, Myrna Loy, William Powell, Unknown. *Author's Collection*

it is the most embarrassingly inept attempt at humor in the series would be an understatement. The picture's only other attempts at humor come as Nick and Nora are immersed in the world of jazz, and a clarinet player (Keenan Wynn) confuses them with his unfamiliar slang, a gag stolen repeatedly from Charles Brackett and Billy Wilder's script for Howard Hawks's *Ball of Fire*.

Directed by the inconsequential Edward Buzzell, *Song of the Thin Man* brought the historic partnership of William Powell and Myrna Loy to an end with a tepid critical and financial reception that made any further entries pointless. It was also a reflection of an MGM that had fallen very far from the heights of the 1930s. Increasing operating costs and galling inefficiency had plagued the studio for years. While its dedication to spending the most on their pictures and their stars had made MGM the top studio in town, by 1946, it had suddenly become the least profitable of the five major studios. Revenues were up as much as ever, but the costs were climbing, and Nicholas Schenck was losing confidence in Louis B. Mayer and his executive committee.

Only Arthur Freed's and Joe Pasternak's MGM musicals units were reliably making any dent in the box office, but these were also by far the most expensive pictures on the lot. Worse yet, *Meet Me in St. Louis* was the last true smash hit from MGM, and that had been over three years earlier. Feeling pressure from Schenck, Mayer and his committee ended not only the *Thin Man* series in 1947, but *The Hardy Family*, *Dr. Gillespie*, and *Maisie* series were ending because their box office numbers were not justifying their costs. By 1948, Schenck wanted Mayer to find a "new Irving Thalberg" to centralize production once more. Dore Schary was hired from RKO to fill that bill, and Mayer himself was bounced out of his own studio only three years later (Schatz, 1989).

It was the end of a brief and glorious era, and a new, slimmed-down, youth-oriented Hollywood would soon take its place.

⑩

THE END

In 1957, Myrna Loy was living in New York and was offered a chance to return to Hollywood and reunite with Powell in an episode of *General Electric Theater*, one of a number of anthology series popular on television in the 1950s that featured short plays with notable actors. The half-hour tale, "Love Came Last," would have featured Powell as Professor Arthur Barris, a curmudgeon who refuses to allow student Jack Evans any leeway in his grades despite the young man having to adjust to college after leaving the army. Loy was set to play Jack's charming mother Allie, who intervenes on his behalf.

When Loy traveled to Hollywood, she was greeted by a dozen roses from Powell and an invitation to dinner at his home in Palm Springs. Suspecting bad news, she made the trip and was greeted with a shocking announcement: He was retired from acting. Powell told his old friend and co-star that he was simply sixty-five years old and tired. The arduous shoot of his final film, *Mister Roberts*, had finally done him in. "Minnie, I wouldn't even groom my mustache again, much less learn a movie role," he said. Loy was heartbroken, but said she never confronted Powell about his decision to retire, knowing he was completely content with his quiet life with Mousie (Loy, 1988). Melvyn Douglas took on the role of the professor in "Love Came Late," which aired in November 1957, and Powell would continue to refuse roles for the rest of his life. It closed the final book on a historic screen partnership.

It had been ten years since movie audiences had seen Powell and Loy on screen together. Before that final appearance, both had taken on the parts of their lives.

Near the end of World War II, Producer Samuel Goldwyn was inspired by a *Time* magazine article about Marines on furlough who were having trouble adjusting to life at the home front and commissioned a story from screenwriter and historical novelist McKinlay Kantor. When Kantor delivered a manuscript in blank verse about three servicemen back from World War II called *Glory for Me*, Goldwyn thought it was a waste of time. When director William Wyler returned home from the war and showed interest in it, Goldwyn tried to talk him out of it. It didn't work. Wyler, like many directors who found themselves overseas, found his worldview transformed and knew the effect the war had on soldiers. He thought it an important story to tell.

Pulitzer Prize–winning playwright and veteran screenwriter Robert E. Sherwood was given the assignment to adapt Kantor's manuscript into *The Best Years of Our Lives*. It was the story of three veterans and their experiences returning home from the war. Middle-aged lending agent Al Stephenson (Fredric March), soda jerk and PTSD-sufferer Fred Derry (Dana Andrews), and partial amputee Homer Parrish (Harold Russell) all face unexpected challenges in adjusting to a world that now seemed completely alien to them after four long years fighting for their lives.

While Goldwyn lobbied for Olivia de Havilland to play Al Stephenson's wife Milly, Wyler's first and only choice was Myrna Loy, the ultimate Hollywood personification of the loving wife waiting loyally for her husband to return from war. It was a testament to Loy's extraordinary status in the movie industry at this time that Wyler gave her top billing despite her limited screen time in the three-hour picture (Herman, 1995).

Loy's only reservation about doing the picture was Wyler's reputation for being tough with actors. She soon discovered that was unfounded, at least in her case:

> Despite rumors to the contrary, if he trusted actors, he gave them a chance to be creative. We could do whatever instinctively we felt like doing. Although that is perhaps my most serious film, as moving and meaningful today as it was then, Freddy (March) and I did it with great humor; otherwise, it could have been trying. Willy even gave us credit in several interviews for improvising. I've never heard of another director doing that. (Loy, 1988)

Loy is marvelous in her small role as the wife whose presence is primarily to observe, listen, and react to her husband's struggles with returning to the home front. One sequence early in the picture, in which she accompanies Al on a drunken night in the town, features Loy—often silently—expressing her annoyance and yet infinite patience with her husband's inebriated behavior. Without saying a word, she is able to express that she is tolerating the evening not only because she loves him, but because she somehow realizes what a harrowing experience the war had been for him.

Loy's most celebrated moment in the film comes when her daughter Peggy (Teresa Wright) accuses Milly and Al of not understanding her relationship troubles because their marriage has been so perfect. Milly smiles and looks up at her profoundly imperfect husband: "'We never had any trouble.' How many times have I told you I hated you and believed it in my heart? How many times have you said you were sick and tired of me; that we were all washed up? How many times have we had to fall in love all over again?" On paper, it is a very brief, simple little sentiment. But coming from the mouth of Myrna Loy, the perfect wife, it is an extraordinary sermon on the struggles of devoting oneself to another person for a lifetime. It is an astonishingly moving moment in a film that is simply stuffed with such moments. But it is Myrna Loy's finest hour, and she completely earns her top billing in that scene.

The Best Years of Our Lives would go on to win seven Academy Awards including Best Picture, Best Actor, Best Supporting Actor, Best Director, and Best Screenplay. Once again, however, Myrna Loy would not even be nominated. If she had any bitter feelings about the Academy's ineptitude regarding her talents, she kept silent about it.

Ironically, Fredric March only took on the role of Al Stephenson in *The Best Years of Our Lives* because he lost the lead role in Warner Bros.' *Life with Father*, an adaptation of the smash hit Broadway play. Produced by Oscar Serlin, written by Howard Lindsay and Russel Crouse, and based on the serialized book by Clarence Day Jr., *Life with Father* opened on Broadway in November 1939 and ran for an extraordinary 3,224 performances before finally closing in July 1947. Telling the tale of Day's stockbroker father and his family in late nineteenth-century New York, it remains the longest-running nonmusical play in Broadway history, a record it has retained for over seventy-five years and almost certainly will hold forever, since no nonmusical Broadway play since then has even approached 2,000 performances, much less 3,000.

Film rights were extremely coveted, and Jack Warner wound up outbidding all other comers with an extraordinary offer of $500,000; net profit percentages to Serlin, Lindsay, Crouse, and Day's widow Katherine; an agreement to wait to release the film until 1947; and accede the rights to the characters and play following production. Warner even acceded final authority to Katherine Day, who was named technical advisor along with Lindsay and Crouse (Rode, 2017).

Warners assigned the picture to producer Robert Buckner and director Michael Curtiz. Curtiz had come a long way since directing Powell in three pictures in the early '30s, having overseen an extraordinary litany of undisputed classics in the intervening years, including *The Adventures of Robin Hood*, *Angels with Dirty Faces*, *Yankee Doodle Dandy*, and *Casablanca*. Both he and Buckner wanted Powell for the role. Playwright Lindsay, however, had starred in the play himself with his wife Dorothy Stickney playing Clarence's wife Lavinia, and naturally thought he was perfect in the role. Buckner and Curtiz gave both screen tests out of kindness, but did not think of either seriously for their roles given their lack of motion picture experience and the star power necessary to justify the studio's enormous investment in the material.

Other screen tests were given to actors like March and Ronald Colman, primarily to satisfy Day, Lindsay, and Crouse, but ultimately Powell was the only real choice, and the price Warner had to pay is a testament to that. When cast for the role in 1946, Powell was still under contract to MGM, and Jack Warner was able to borrow him by agreeing to lend Errol Flynn to MGM for a picture two years down the road, along with an additional $200,000. The choice for Lavinia was not as obvious to Buckner and Curtiz as Powell's casting. Silent-film icon and United Artists co-founder Mary Pickford had been one of the enthusiastic bidders for the play's rights, seeing Lavinia as a perfect comeback vehicle, and even after losing that effort, she submitted to a screen test for Buckner and Curtiz, but they found her unsuitable. They also considered actors as varied as Loy, Jean Arthur, Rosalind Russell, and Rosemary DeCamp, ultimately settling on Irene Dunne (Rode, 2017).

In the July 31, 1948, issue of the *Saturday Evening Post*, Powell proclaimed the role of Father as the one he liked best. "It probably required a certain flexibility of imagination for movie-goers to accept *The Thin Man* as Father in the picture . . . but I found the transition from modern detecting to 1880 paternalism quite easy to make," he wrote.

> I always was in complete sympathy with Father. I recognized in him traits I felt I could delineate; I knew his various moods, which ranged from naïveté to pomposity to tyranny, but I also knew that basically he was a man of gentleness.
>
> During the filming of the picture, Howard Lindsay, who played Father for five seasons on Broadway, told me jokingly that I was his second choice for the role. But after the film was released, he helped make it my favorite by writing: "You'll be glad to know that you now have been promoted to my first choice for the role of Father."

Powell received his third and final Best Actor nomination for *Life with Father*, but lost out to Ronald Colman for his bravura performance as an obsessive actor portraying Othello in *A Double Life*. Powell couldn't have minded too much to accede the glory to one of his oldest and dearest friends.

Life with Father cost $4.7 million and brought in gross receipts of $6.5 million, a hit for the studio. Watching the film today, one is struck somewhat by the vivid Technicolor photography and beautiful nineteenth-century costumes and settings, along with how poorly it holds up. *Life with Father* suffers from the creative control held by Clarence Day Jr. and the playwrights despite Michael Curtiz's best efforts to inject some cinematic flair to the proceedings. If not for the three-color Technicolor, one could easily mistake the stage-bound affair for a talkie produced in 1928. With a running time of nearly two hours, the picture suffers terribly from the inability to properly adapt the play for the screen. Scenes go on far, far longer than necessary, and the religious conceits of the film have not aged well. It feels like the oldest, most outdated film of all time.

Powell, to his credit, looks like he's having a ball despite having to remain on one note throughout the picture as an unlikable control freak. One moment of Powell playing the piano brings a touch of humanity to Clarence, and it's significant that it's a moment in which Powell doesn't even have to deliver any spoken dialogue. It's a lovely peek into the sentimental side of an insufferable lout. Outside of that, the picture has aged perhaps more poorly than any other Hollywood picture of the era. The preening emphasis on religion and the formality of the characters, especially Irene Dunne in a career-worst performance, just does not pass muster. It is telling that despite being the most successful Broadway play in history, it has never been revived there.

By the beginning of 1948, the extraordinary three-decade run in which Hollywood appeared to be an unstoppable moneymaking machine was about to end. The decade-long lawsuit that the Department of Justice filed against Paramount Pictures, and by proxy the other four major studios, was about to come to a close. The charge was that the five major studios that controlled production, distribution, and exhibition had colluded to monopolize the motion picture industry.

In retrospect, the US Supreme Court's decision in favor of the United States in May of that year was predetermined, because Paramount, Warner Bros., MGM, RKO, and 20th Century Fox had been more than guilty of collusion for decades. While the Supreme Court said that the vertical integration the studios had been employing was not strictly illegal, they were guilty of violating the Sherman Antitrust Act by doing so in a calculated scheme to suppress competition.

The decision forced the major studios to divest themselves of their theater chains, a crippling blow to the industry because the theater chains represented the vast majority of assets the studios held. Coupled with the emergence of television that led to the beginning of a slow decline in movie attendance from its peak in 1946, the studios simply did not have the necessary resources to produce forty to fifty feature films each a year and carry a complement of full-time crew members and actors.

The glory days had ended. William Powell and Myrna Loy, now both freelance actors, faced a new and different kind of reality. Loy's career as a leading lady would last several more years, but her experiences during World War II radically altered her priorities. Powell's priorities had changed too. He now lived a quiet life in Palm Springs with Mousie, while the days of an actor under long-term contract blithely moving from project to project had ended. In 1950, agent Lew Wasserman negotiated a contract for his client James Stewart for the Universal production *Winchester '73*, which gave Stewart a significant cut of the profits rather than a flat fee. It transformed the industry, and power shifted from the weakened studios to actors and directors as Wasserman's agency MCA and others negotiated similar deals. Other actors such as Burt Lancaster would go further and even launch their own independent production companies to take full control over every facet of their careers.

While younger actors like Lancaster thrived under such circumstances, Powell never displayed any such ambition to run a production company. That lack of ambition in combination with the simple fact that he was aging led to his career faltering after the success of *Life with Father*. He was no longer plausible as a romantic leading man, and the kinds of comedies in which he specialized seemed to be nearly extinct. Cold reality had set in after the end of World War II, and light comedy fare about the foibles of the upper classes just didn't seem appropriate. If anything, the darker film noir tone of *Song of the Thin Man* had emphasized that Powell simply no longer fit in the new industry. He still made movies, naturally, but none entered the pantheon of classics like his films of the 1930s.

Nunnally Johnson's *Mr. Peabody and the Mermaid* (1948) was an amusingly odd and gentle comedy about a befuddled married man who reels in a mermaid while fishing, but his two films from 1949 are deservedly long forgotten: 20th Century Fox's Technicolor musical *Dancing in the Dark* and the Universal production *Take One False Step*, a film noir that required the audience to buy that fifty-seven-year-old Powell and twenty-six-year-old Shelley Winters were somehow old flames. Powell's career hit its nadir in 1952 when he starred in his final leading role in a B-movie titled *The Treasure of Lost Canyon*, based on a Robert Louis Stevenson story. The following year saw him co-starring with Elizabeth

Taylor in his final MGM picture, *The Girl Who Had Everything*, an astonishingly inept and cheap-looking remake of the studio's 1931 production of *A Free Soul*. While the series of long-forgotten films would seem to have portended a sad end to Powell's career, fortunately his final two pictures were big-budget productions with distinguished casts that gave him two fine character roles.

In 1953, Powell was cast in *How to Marry a Millionaire*, the second Cinemascope release from 20th Century Fox. Directed by Jean Negulesco, the film represented a reunion for Powell with screenwriter Nunnally Johnson, the man behind *Mr. Peabody and the Mermaid*. A showcase for the talents of Lauren Bacall, Betty Grable, and especially emerging superstar Marilyn Monroe, the picture was based in part on Zoë Akins' play, *The Greeks Had a Word for It*, along with the Dale Eunson–Katherine Albert play, *Loco*. It was the simple tale of three single women who rent a large apartment and commence a project to find and marry wealthy men. Once they find their marks, of course, they wind up finding true love with seemingly poverty-stricken heartthrobs.

Powell plays J. D. Hanley, a wealthy gentleman who quickly becomes the target of model Schatze Page (Bacall), who quickly becomes truly fond of him. Here, Powell is a silver-haired fox of a gentleman whose primary concern is the age difference between him and Bacall. He is charming in the limited role, which provides him an opportunity to recall his roles in the early '30s as a reserved and formal gentleman. By this time in his career, however, Powell no longer suffers from the stiffness of those early talking performances. Here he effortlessly glides through the supporting role, exuding charm and attractiveness that makes his character's concerns about his age ironically absurd. When he changes his mind and proposes to her, they make it to the alter just as Schatze realizes she truly loves Tom, a younger man whom she assumes is poor (but is really wealthier than Hanley). Powell's role in the film gives an impression of the kinds of roles in which he could have thrived in his later years, that of the charming older gentleman. His final role was even better, even though the experience would sour him on ever acting again.

In March 1954, legendary director John Ford was hired to adapt *Mister Roberts*, the Thomas Heggen–Joshua Logan play about Lieutenant Doug Roberts and the eccentric crew of a cargo ship during World War II. Henry Fonda had taken time off from his film career to star in the lead role on Broadway in 1948 and had won the Best Actor Tony Award, but by the time the film project was being put together six years later, he assumed he would likely not get the role because he was forty-nine years old by this point. Ford, however, refused to work with anyone but Fonda, so producer Leland Hayward cast the other senior officers older to give Fonda the impression of being younger, including

Henry Fonda and William Powell in *Mister Roberts* (1955). Directed by John Ford and Mervyn LeRoy. *Warner Bros./Photofest* © *Warner Bros.*

fifty-something James Cagney as the Captain and sixty-something Powell as Doc. Also cast as the ambitious Ensign Pulver was a young Jack Lemmon (Eyman, 1999).

Production began with location shooting on Midway Island on September 1, 1954. It immediately went off the rails as Ford became besotted with Lemmon's character and encouraged the awestruck young actor to ad-lib and steal scenes, Cold War political tensions roiled the set, and an eventual fistfight broke out between Fonda and Ford. Powell and Cagney, meanwhile, remained quietly on the sidelines, patiently awaiting their turns. When the production went back to Warner Bros. on October 12, Ford's heavy drinking would result after a few days in a gall bladder operation. Mervyn LeRoy would take over the picture and work with Joshua Logan to finally complete it, significantly over its schedule, in mid-December (Eyman, 1999).

The film is the story of the cargo ship USS *Reluctant*, and its second-in-command, Lieutenant Doug Roberts (Fonda), is despondent that in the final days of World War II, he will never get to see any actual action. Powell plays Doc, Robert's best friend and confidante and playful "den father" for the ship. It is a marvelous supporting role, and as a bonus it gives the always-dapper Powell the rare chance to appear disheveled for an entire picture. While the film has been criticized over the years for its stage-bound nature, the actors chew the scenery marvelously. One could never tell the production was embroiled in the myriad problems that caused Powell to quit show business.

Loy, on the other hand, never officially retired and would remain active for nearly the rest of her life until her health began to decline in the late 1980s. Little of that activity, however, was in motion pictures. After starring opposite Cary Grant in the marvelous comedies *The Bachelor and the Bobby-Soxer* and *Mr. Blandings Builds His Dream House* (the latter of which features perhaps Loy's greatest comic monologue in her description of desired paint colors), she would go on to play another wife and mother in Lewis Milestone's film adaptation of John Steinbeck's *The Red Pony* at Republic Pictures. Loy's final notable leading role was as Lillian Gilbreth, mother of twelve children, in the gentle 1920s-set comedies *Cheaper by the Dozen* (1950) and its sequel, *Belles on Their Toes* (1952). The first film, in which she co-starred with Clifton Webb as her husband Frank, was a smash hit for 20th Century Fox, earning $4.4 million at the box office.

However, popularity on screen meant little to Myrna Loy at this point. Her experience with the American Red Cross during World War II led to her new passion: public service. In 1948, she would become the first Hollywood movie star to become a member of the US National Commission for the United Nations Educational, Scientific, and Cultural Organization, which was a committee to the state department intended to support global humanitarian causes. It was her involvement with UNESCO that led her to meet Howland H. Sargeant, who was with the US State Department as deputy assistant secretary of state for public affairs. In June 1951, he would become Loy's fourth and final husband until their divorce in 1960.

During the 1950s, while Loy would still work occasionally in supporting roles in films and TV anthology series like *General Electric Theater*, she lived in Washington with Sargeant and devoted much of her time to service, including a lengthy stint as co-chairman of the Advisory Council of the National Committee Against Discrimination in Housing. After divorcing Sargeant in 1960 and leaving Washington, Loy's involvement in politics dipped slightly, but she would remain a dedicated Democrat and would frequently support the party's political candidates for the rest of her life.

On screen, Loy was relegated to supporting appearances, which included perhaps her finest later performance in *Lonelyhearts*, released in 1958. The first independent effort by producer Dore Schary after his own departure from MGM, the adaptation of Nathaniel West's 1933 novel *Miss Lonelyhearts* starred Montgomery Clift as struggling journalist Adam White, who takes on a columnist job as Miss Lonelyhearts at a paper edited by William Shrike (Robert Ryan). Loy is extraordinary in her role as Florence, the suffering wife of the cruel Shrike. Following that was a supporting role in *Midnight Lace*, an attempt at a Hitchcockian thriller starring Doris Day, and her first major stage appearance in a national touring company of Neil Simon's *Barefoot in the Park* in 1965.

For the rest of her life, Loy primarily concentrated on her political interests and avoided the cruel fates of contemporaries like Joan Crawford, who were forced by the mid-1960s to appear in low-budget horror films. Most of Loy's roles remained dignified if inconsequential, and she made frequent appearances on television shows during the 1970s, including *Columbo*, in which she got to work with Peter Falk and John Cassavetes. Loy also made appearances in various made-for-TV movies, including a 1971 remake of *Death Takes a Holiday*, which featured a reunion with Melvyn Douglas, and *Do Not Fold, Spindle or Mutilate*, co-starring Helen Hayes, Mildred Natwick, and Sylvia Sydney. Theatrical film appearances were few and far between. She survived the indignity of her appearance in *Airport 1975* to make two more supporting appearances before retiring from the big screen, first reuniting with her *Consolation Marriage* co-star Pat O'Brien in Burt Reynolds' film *The End* (1978), and then playing Alan King's secretary in Sidney Lumet's *Just Tell Me What You Want* (1980).

After appearing with Henry Fonda in the TV movie *Summer Solstice* (1981), Loy would make a guest appearance on Tony Randall's short-lived sitcom *Love, Sidney* before retiring from acting entirely. All that was left were the honors and the remembrances. With writer James Kotsilibas-Davis, Loy penned her autobiography, *Myrna Loy: Being and Becoming*. She was feted by the Kennedy Center Honors in 1988 and finally received a lifetime achievement Oscar in 1991 after inexplicably never being nominated for an Academy Award. Accepting the award remotely from her home, it was Loy's final public appearance before her death at age eighty-eight in 1993.

While William Powell outlived most of his contemporaries, there were no fetes and honors. There would be no television interviews, no awards show appearances, no lifetime achievement awards, and no public appearances of any kind. Powell lived a quiet life in Palm Springs for nearly three decades and would appear only occasionally in the news. In May 1963, he acquiesced to an interview with the *Los Angeles Times* and revealed publicly for the first time that the mysterious illness that kept him off-screen in the late 1930s was rectal cancer; he never had a recurrence.

The seventy-year-old Powell dismissed the idea of returning to the screen. "Why would I do it?" he asked. "For the glory? The ham in me has been pretty well burned out with the years. For the money? I'd just be put into a higher tax bracket that would eliminate most of what I earned with the job." Powell also spoke with sadness of the passing of Ronald Colman, and Richard Barthelmess's then-current battle with cancer that robbed him of his speech.

In 1968, Powell's only son, William Powell Jr., infrequently mentioned, committed suicide at the age of forty-three, and articles referenced a chronic kidney illness as the motivator. "Things are not good here," he said in a note. "I am going where things are better." The elder Powell understandably never publicly commented, and as the years went by, his name disappeared from the public record, except for Mousie's frequent appearances in the Palm Springs *Desert Sun,* billed as "Mrs. William Powell."

A *New York Times* obituary by Peter Flint published on March 6, 1984, cited an earlier interview with Powell in which he was asked how he kept trim. "I highly recommend worrying," he said. "It is much more effective than dieting." Loy was quoted in the same obituary: "I never enjoyed my work more than when I worked with William Powell. He was a brilliant actor, a delightful companion, a great friend and, above all, a true gentleman."

ACKNOWLEDGMENTS

It's been well over twenty-five years that I've wanted to write a book about movies, and for that I have to thank so many of the extraordinary authors who have kept the movies of the studio era alive, chief of whom is my personal hero Kevin Brownlow, whose 1968 book *The Parade's Gone By* and his subsequent documentary series *Hollywood* (co-directed with David Gill) have not only kept silent films alive, but have created countless film history writers, teachers, and devoted audience members who have gladly followed in his footsteps. Thanks to Mr. Brownlow, my shelves are littered with the books of William K. Everson, Scott Eyman, Peter McGilligan, Barry Paris, and so many more. Thanks go to all the authors and historians, the film archives, the silent movie accompanists, and the film festival organizers that made it possible for me to view so many of the films of William Powell and Myrna Loy. Without these dedicated professionals and deeply dedicated fans, these films would have dissolved into the ether long, long ago.

Thanks to the Cinema and Television Arts Department at Columbia College Chicago: Karla Lee Fuller, Sandy Cuprisin, Lee Ferdinand, Dirk Matthews, Samantha Sanders, Clint Vaupel, Katie Kosinski, Francine Sanders, and Alaric Dirmeyer and so many others.

I spent much of the past four years writing this book from our temporary home in Palmer, Alaska, and a more beautiful place to retreat and focus on this project I could not possibly imagine. Thanks go out to everyone, especially Mary Ann, Jess, Ruth, and Justice at Fireside Books, the passionate weirdos at Bleeding Heart Brewery and, of course, the mountains.

Thanks especially to my wife, Jen, and our menagerie of goofballs. You make life pretty great.

BIBLIOGRAPHY

AFI Catalog of Feature Films: The First 100 Years 1893–1993 (n.d.). Accessed September 21, 2022, from https://catalog.afi.com/Film/6162-THE-LASTOFMRSCHEYNEY?sid=255bd4a2-f841-4fd5-9e7a-e4f62c826c9a&sr=11.7 30046&cp=1&pos=1.

Ager, C. (1933, February 14). "Going Places." *Variety*, p. 17.

Ager, C. (1934, June 12). "Going Places." *Variety*, p. 58.

American Academy of Dramatic Arts (n.d.). Accessed September 21, 2022, from www .aada.edu.

Ashley, L. (1921, November 7). "'Spanish Love' Is Attractive as Ever." *Washington Times*, p. 4.

Bureau, W. C. (1935, February 6). "Sutherland to Direct Ziegfeld." *Film Daily*, p. 2.

Canary Murder Case Production Files. (1928). Margaret Herrick Library, Beverly Hills, CA.

Canby, V. (1981, February 1). "How a 1936 Screwball Comedy Illuminates Movie History." *New York Times*, pp. 119, 122.

Chase, R. R. (1977). *Life Is a Banquet.* New York: Random House.

Cheatam, M. (1933, June). "Secrets of a Siren." *New Movie Magazine*, pp. 45, 77.

Chicago Daily Tribune. (1927, November 8). "And This Is Interesting and Quite Entertaining." p. 33.

Colman, R. (1929, September). "The Siren from Montana." *Photoplay*, pp. 63, 112.

Crowther, B. (1940, August 16). "The Screen." *New York Times*, p. 11.

Crowther, B. (1941, June 6). "The Screen in Review." *New York Times*, p. 24.

Crowther, B. (1945, January 26). "The Screen in Review." *New York Times*, p. 16.

Cruikshank, H. (1928, December). "State Street Sadie." *Motion Picture Magazine*, p. 68.

Cunningham, J. P. (1936, April 4). "What Exhibitors May Expect in New Season from 40 Companies." *Motion Picture Herald*, p. 20.

Daily Northwestern. (1914, January 20). "Amusements." p. 6.

Darnton, C. (1935, April). "The Man in the Mirror." *New Movie Magazine*, pp. 18, 50.

Exhibitors Daily Review and Motion Pictures Today. (1930, August 5). "Wm. Powell Returns Here from Europe." p. 1.

Exhibitors Daily Review and Motion Pictures Today. (1930, August 25). "Powell Shooting En Route West." p. 6.

Exhibitors Herald. (1925, December 25). "White Mice" (advertisement). p. 147.

Exhibitors Trade Review. (1925, August 1). "My Lady's Lips." p. 59.

Eyman, S. (1999). *Print the Legend: The Life and Times of John Ford*. New York: Simon & Schuster.

Fergus, N. (1925, May). "To the Rescue of the Villain." *Picture-Play Magazine*, p. 74.

Fidler, J. M. (1933, August). "A Secret Wedding for Myrna and Ramon?" *Motion Picture Magazine*, pp. 41, 76.

Film Daily. (1922, August 15). "Outcast."

Film Daily. (1922, December 10). "Performance of Elsie Ferguson the Real High Light of This." p. 3.

Film Daily. (1928, April 29). "William Powell Featured." p. 1.

Film Daily. (1929, April 28). "William Powell Elevated to Stardom by Paramount." p. 1.

Film Daily. (1930, September 2). "Paramount Has Assigned Juliette Compton." p. 7.

Film Daily. (1931, January 18). "Signing Stars Just Daily Routine, Says H. M. Warner, Denying 'War.'" p. 1.

Film Daily. (1932, April 24). "Lawyer Man." p. 4.

Film Daily. (1934, May 23). "William Powell, Myrna Loy in 'The Thin Man.'" p. 7.

Film Daily. (1938, March 15). "Metro Will Spend $35,000,000 on 52; 3 for Shearer; 3 More to Be in Color." p. 8.

Flint, P. B. (1984, March 6). "William Powell, Film Star, Dies at 91." *New York Times*, p. 11.

Friedman, H. B. (n.d.). Harry B. Friedman Papers at the Margaret Herrick Library, Beverly Hills, CA.

Gehring, W. D. (2003). *Carole Lombard: The Hoosier Tornado*. Indianapolis: Indiana Historical Society Press.

Goodrich, D. L. (2001). *The Real Nick and Nora: Frances Goodrich and Albert Hackett, Writers of Stage and Screen Classics*. Edwardsville and Carbondale: Southern Illinois University Press.

Gray, E. (1931, February). "Mystery of William Powell." *New Movie Magazine*.

Gray, G. (1931, October). "The New Mr. and Mrs." *Screenland*, pp. 27, 116.

Hall, G. (1931). Gladys Hall papers, 1918–1969, Margaret Herrick Library, Bevery Hills, CA.

Hall, M. (1924, October 14). "The Rich Poor Girl." *New York Times*, p. 21.

Hall, M. (1924, December 2). "A Florentine Story." *New York Times*, p. 13.

Hall, M. (1925, March 3). "Too Many Girls."*New York Times*, p. 20.

Hall, M. (1925, November 23). "The Hero Pays." *New York Times*, p. 25.

Hall, M. (1926, May 17). "Gilds Gray." *New York Times*, p. 19.

Hall, M. (1926, September 20). "The Bridge Builder." *New York Times*, p. 21.

Hall, M. (1926, June 4). "Whole Slaughter." *New York Times*, p. 21.

Hall, M. (1927, February 21). "The Banker's Letters." *New York Times*, p. 14.

Hall, M. (1928, November 17). "A Talking Melodrama." *New York Times*, p. 28.

Hall, M. (1932, August 19). "Maurice Chevalie and Jeanette MacDonald in a Charming Romantic Musical Fantasy." *New York Times*, p. 20.

Hall, M. (1932, October 15). "Another Murder Mystery." *New York Times*, p. 13.

Hall, M. (1934, May 5). "The Lawyer and the Gambler." *New York Times*, p. 22.

Hall, M. (1934, June 30). "A Nonchalant Criminologist." *New York Times*, p. 18.

Hammett, D. (n.d.). Thin Man Sequel, 8. Margaret Herrick Library, Beverly Hills, CA.

Hammett, D. (1989). *The Thin Man* (reprint edition). New York: Vintage Crime/Black Lizard.

Hammett, D. (2012). *Return of the Thin Man*, edited by R. L. Rivett. New York: The Mysterious Press.

Herman, J. (1995). *A Talent for Trouble: The Life of Hollywood's Most Acclaimed Director William Wyler*. New York: G. P. Putnam's Sons.

Hollywood Reporter. (1934, May 10). "'The Thin Man' Is Sure-Fire." p. 3.

House, M. (1931, April). "Not a Ladies' Man: Bill Powell Denies All!" *Screenland*, pp. 21, 119.

Internet Broadway Database. Accessed September 21, 2022, from www.ibdb.com.

Leider, E. W. (2011). *Myrna Loy: The Only Good Girl in Hollywood*. Los Angeles: University of California Press.

Los Angeles Times. (1963, May 1). "Actor William Powell Tells of his Victory Over Cancer." p. 3.

Loy, M., and J. Koltsilibas-Davis. (1988). *Myrna Loy: Being and Becoming*. New York: Donald I. Fine Inc.

Manners, D. (1931, December). "Can the Newlyweds of Hollywood Stay Married?" *Movie Classic*, pp. 22–23.

Margrave, S. (1934, June 25). "The Charm of William Powell and Myrna Loy." *Daily Mail*.

Marysville Appeal. (1926, August 13). "The 1926 Model in Vampires." p. 3.

McCarthy, T. (1997). *Howard Hawks: The Grey Fox of Hollywood*. New York: Grove Press.

Modern Screen. (1931, June). "Body and Soul." p. 90.

Modern Screen. (1932, November). "Love Me Tonight." p. 48.

Mook, S. (1937, July). "The Girl Hollywood Couldn't Beat." *Hollywood Magazine*, p. 25.

Motion Picture Daily. (1940, May 16). "Untitled." p. 10.

Motion Picture Herald. (1932, August 6). "The Ten Biggest Money Makers." pp. 10–11.

Motion Picture Herald. (1934, July 28). "Signed . . . MGM." p. 52.

Motion Picture Magazine. (1925, September). "Myrna Loy." p. 27.

Motion Picture Magazine. (1931, May). "Body and Soul." p. 61.

Motion Picture Magazine. (1931, November). "The Road to Singapore." p. 60.

Motion Picture News. (1930, August 23). "Lukas Replaces Powell." p. 26.

Moving Picture World. (1927, December 24). "The Girl from Chicago." p. 16.

New York Daily News. (1921, January 29). "Cheapest Man." p. 1.

New York Times. (1917, November 21). "Leo Ditrichstein a Hit in 'The King.'" p. 11.

New York Times. (1922, September 15). "A Dazzling Spectacle." p. 24.

New York Times. (1931, January 16). "War on Paramount by Warners Reported." p. 27.

New York Times. (1942, November 2). "Screen News Here and in Hollywood." p. 17.

Nugent, F. S. (1939, November 24). "The Screen in Review." *New York Times*, p. 29.

Oregon Daily Journal. (1914, September 7). "Manager Baker Presents Strong Aggregation at Opening Play."

Oregon Daily Journal. (1914, September 20). "In Stageland." p. 32.

Oregon Daily Journal. (1914, December 7). "Leading Man at Baker Theatre Has an Unusually Good Part." p. 8.

Oregon Daily Journal. (1915, January 4). "Play Is Intended to Teach Lesson to Prudish Parents, at Baker." p. 5.

Oregon Daily Journal. (1915, March 15). "Baker Players Put on 'Tess of Storm Country'; Splendid." p. 7.

Oregon Daily Journal. (1915, May 2). "Weddings." p. 46.

Paris, B. (2000). *Louise Brooks*. Minneapolis: University of Minnesota Press.

Photoplay. (1924, December). "Dangerous Money." p. 53.

Photoplay. (1926, December). "Across the Pacific." p. 55.

Photoplay. (1929, June). "The Squall." p. 56.

Photoplay. (1931, April). "Body and Soul." p. 51.

Photoplay. (1931, November). "Consolation Marriage." p. 51.

Photoplay. (1934, August). "The Thin Man." p. 49.

Picture Play. (1928, January). "Among Those Present." p. 71.

Pinchot, L. G. (1969). *The Movies, Mr. Griffith and Me*. Englewood Cliffs, NJ: Prentice-Hall.

Powell, W. (1948, July 31). "The Role I Liked Best . . ." *Saturday Evening Post*, p. 78.

Powell, W. (2018, November). "A William Powell 18-page Handwritten Letter to His Aunt, 1912." Accessed September 14, 2022, from https://www.bonhams.com/auction/24838/lot/243/a-william-powell-18-page-handwritten-letter-to-his-aunt-1912/.

Reid, L. (1926, June 19). "Why Girls Go Back Home." *Motion Picture News*, p. 2880.

Reid, L. (1926, October 16). "Across the Pacific." *Motion Picture News*, p. 1497.

Reid, M. (1929, June). "She Pays the Penalty." *Picture Play*, p. 43.

Riskin, V. (2019). *Fay Wray and Robert Riskin: A Hollywood Memoir.* New York: Pantheon Books.

Rode, A. K. (2017). *Michael Curtiz: A Life in Film.* Lexington: University Press of Kentucky.

Schatz, T. (1989). *The Genius of the System: Hollywood Filmmaking in the Studio Era.* New York: Pantheon Books.

Screenland. (1932, February). "Consolation Marriage." p. 85.

Selznick, D. O. (1972). *Memo from David O. Selznick.* New York: Viking Press.

Sennwald, A. (1934, November 10). "Myrna Loy and William Powell in 'Evelyn Prentice.'" *New York Times*, p. 19.

Sewell, C. (1924, December 13). "Romola." *Moving Picture World*, p. 625.

Spensley, D. (1926, August). "Bold but Not Brazen: A Good Bad Man, a Cheerful Villain, an Agreeable Friend—Bill Powell." *Photoplay*, p. 129.

Spensley, D. (1929, March). "Not Guilty: Bill Powell Declares He Is Not a Picture Stealer." *Photoplay*, p. 54.

Standish, J. (1931, September). "William Powell Weds Carole Lombard." *Movie Classic*, p. 37.

Stenn, D. (1993). *Bombshell: The Life and Death of Jean Harlow.* New York: Doubleday.

Stenn, D. (2000). *Clara Bow: Runnin' Wild.* New York: Cooper Square Press.

Stromberg, H. (1934, August 29). Memo: "Nick and Nora," Margaret Herrick Library, Beverly Hills, CA.

Tinee, M. (1940, September 1). "I Love You Again." *Chicago Sunday Tribune*, p. 5.

Variety. (1922, December 8). "Outcast." pp. 19–22.

Variety. (1932, May 10). "Agents Fear Ban Spread." p. 5.

Variety. (1933, May 9). "Powell's $40,000 Per Pic for WB Means a Shrinkage of 60 G's." p. 2.

Variety. (1934, May 8). "Manhattan Melodrama." p. 14.

Variety. (1934, June 5). "The Key." p. 12.

Variety. (1934, June 5). "Powell's Ziegfeld." p. 4.

Variety. (1938, October 26). "Inside Stuff—Pictures." p. 23.

Venice Vanguard Evening Herald. (1922, August 1). "Culver Girl Posed for Statue." p. 1.

Walsh, K. (2013, Spring). "Selling Masculinity at Warner Bros.: William Powell, A Case Study." *Spectator.*

Waterbury, R. (1940, March). "The Third Mrs. William Powell." *Photoplay*, pp. 18, 75.

Whitfield, E. (1997). *Pickford: The Woman Who Made Hollywood.* Lexington: University Press of Kentucky.

Wilk, R. (1934, December 27). "A 'Little' from Hollywood 'Lots.'" *Film Daily*, p. 7.

Wilk, R. (1934, November 5). "A Little from 'Lots.'" *Film Daily*, p. 12.

Wilk, R. (1935, February 25). "A Little from 'Lots.'" *Film Daily*, p. 4.

Wilk, R. (1935, October 31). "A 'Little' from Hollywood 'Lots.'" *Film Daily*, p. 14.

Wilk, R. (1935, November 19). "A 'Little' from Hollywood 'Lots.'" *Film Daily*, p. 12.

Wilk, R. (1937, October 13). "A 'Little' from Hollywood 'Lots.'" *Film Daily*, p. 10.

Woollcott, A. (1920, August 18). "The Play." *New York Times*, p. 6.

Woollcott, A. (1922, August 17). "Mr. Locke's Error." *New York Times*, p. 14.

INDEX

abortion, in *Men in White*, 119

Academy Awards: of *Libeled Lady*, 171; of *The Thin Man*, 139

Across the Pacific (film), 53

Adele Clark (fictional character, *Dangerous Money*), 38

Adolpho Spini (fictional character, *Romola*), 36

advancement, of skill of Powell, W., Sr., 107

advancing roles, of Loy, 80–81

affair, in *Arrowsmith*, 81

After the Thin Man (film), 76, 82, 161–65, *163*, 167

Ager, Cecelia, 91, 92–93, 119

Aggie Lynch (fictional character, *Within the Law*), 13

Agnes (fictional character, *Star of Midnight*), 147

Alan (fictional character, *Man-Proof*), 177

Alisande (fictional character, *A Connecticut Yankee*), 77

Alma (fictional character, *Street of Chance*), 65–66

Alma Harding (fictional character, *Too Hot to Handle*), 159–60

Al Stephenson (fictional character, *The Best Years of Our Lives*), 208

American Academy of Dramatic Arts, 11–12

American Red Cross, 196

Andres Escobar (fictional character, *The Bright Shawl*), 32

Andy Kerr (fictional character, *The Key*), 113, 114

Angels with Dirty Faces (film), 119–20

The Animal Kingdom (film), 89–90, 92, 93

Ann Barton (fictional character, *Test Pilot*), 158–59

Another Thin Man (film), 177, 180–84, *181*, 185–86, 203

Archibald Graham (fictional character, *The Blindness of Virtue*), 15–16

army comedies, 196–97

Arrowsmith (film), 80–81

Asta (dog in *The Thin Man*), 126, 135, 166, 199

Astor, Mary, 31–32

Aubrey (fictional character, *Consolation Marriage*), 80

August, Joseph H., 60–61

Auguste Topaze (fictional character, *Topaze*), 92

Aunt Katherine (fictional character, *After the Thin Man*), 165

Azuri (fictional character, *The Desert Song*), 57–58

Babe (fictional character, *Street of Chance*), 65–66

Baer, Max, 98, 99

balcony scene, in *Too Many Kisses*, 39

Baldassarre Calvo (fictional character, *Romola*), 36–37

banter, of Nick and Nora in *The Thin Man*, 126–27, 133–34

The Barbarian (film), 93–94

Bardo Bardi (fictional character, *Romola*), 36

the Baron (fictional character, *Jewel Robbery*), 106

The Baroness and the Butler (film), 176–77

Baroness de La Tour-La Tour (fictional character, *Topaze*), 92

Baroness Katrina (fictional character, *The Baroness and the Butler*), 176

Baroness Tina (fictional character, *Jewel Robbery*), 105–6, *105*

Baron Georg (fictional character, *The Baroness and the Butler*), 176

Baron Philippe de La Tour-La Tour (fictional character, *Topaze*), 92

Baron Stephan Wolensky (fictional character, *The Emperor's Candlesticks*), 173

Barrymore, John, 19–20, 27–28, 91–92

Barthelmess, Richard, 31, *32*, 34, 35–36

Barton, Ralph, 12

Beal, John, 173, 175–76

Beau Geste (fictional character, *Beau Geste*), 42

Beau Geste (film), 42

bedroom scene, in *The Thin Man*, 133–34

Belle Mercer (fictional character, *The Prizefighter and the Lady*), 98–99

The Benson Murder Case (film), 66

Berkeley, Busby, 24, 112

Best, Edna, 113–14

The Best Years of Our Lives (film), 3, 172, 203–4, 208

Bill (fictional character, *Lucky Night*), 177

Bill Chandler (fictional character, *Libeled Lady*), *169*, 169–71

Bill Dennis (fictional character, *Too Hot to Handle*), 159–60

The Birth of a Nation (film), 27

Blackie Gallagher (fictional character, *Manhattan Melodrama*), 119, 121, 132

Blackie Morgan. *See* Harold Jones

The Blindness of Virtue (play), 15–16

Bloch, Bertram, 106–7

blocking, for microphones, 45

Blondell, Joan, 103, 108

Bob (fictional character, *The Girl from Chicago*), 53

Bobby (fictional character, *Thirteen Women*), 85–86

Bob Harrison (fictional character, *Reckless*), 144–45

Bogart, Humphrey, 76

Boldini (fictional character, *Beau Geste*), 42

Boleslavsky, Richard, 118–19

Bow, Clara, 40–41, 47, 75

box office attractions, of MGM, 82

Brecher, Irving, 193–95

Breen, Joseph, 117, 169–70

The Bright Shawl (film), 31–33

Bringing Up Baby (film), 167

Brogan (fictional character, *The Thin Man Goes Home*), 201

Brook, Clive, 45, 68

Brown, Clarence, 154, 179

Brown, Joe E., 109
Buckner, Robert, 210
Burke, Billie, 150–52

Cagney, James, 104, 119–20
Calhern, Louis, 101
The Canary Murder Case (film), 46
Canby, Vincent, 171–72
cancer, of Powell, W., Sr., 177
"Can The Newlyweds of Hollywood Stay Married?" (Manners), 74–75
Cantor, Eddie, 41–42
Capra, Frank, 117–18, 147
Captain Bill Tennant (fictional character, *The Key*), 113, 114
Captain de Vaca (fictional character, *The Bright Shawl*), 33–34
Captain Jack Absolute (fictional character, *The Rivals*), 10
Captain Santacilla (fictional character, *The Bright Shawl*), 33
Carlo (fictional character, *My Man Godfrey*), 148–49
Carlo (fictional character, *Romola*), 36
Casablanca (film), 42
Catholic Legion of Decency, 117
Cecelia Henry (fictional character, *The Animal Kingdom*), 90
censorship, in *Men in White*, 118–19
Central High School, 10
Central Shakespeare Club, 10–11
change in roles, of Powell, W., Sr., 99–100
characterization: of Larry Wilson in *I Love You Again* of Powell, W., Sr., 189; of Margrit in *Double Wedding* by Loy, 175–76
character of Loy, in *Turn Back the Hours*, 56
character of Vance, softening of, 47–48, 111

Charlemagne de La Tour-La Tour (fictional character, *Topaze*), 92
Charles Abbott (fictional character, *The Bright Shawl*), 31–33
Charles Brandon (fictional character, *When Knighthood Was in Flower*), 28–30
Charles Stewart Parnell (in *Parnell*), 157
Charlie (fictional character, *The Last of Mrs. Cheney*), 172
Charlie Lodge (fictional character, *Double Wedding*), 175, 176
Cheaper by the Dozen (film), 215
chemistry between Powell, W., Sr. and Loy: in *Manhattan Melodrama*, 120–21; in *The Thin Man*, 133–34, 152, 166–67
Chevalier, Maurice, 83–84, *84*
Chicago Daily Tribune (newspaper), 53–54
childhood: of Loy, 20–21; of Powell, W., Sr., 10–11
"Chinese Fantasy" (musical number), 61
Chris Hunter (fictional character, *Too Hot to Handle*), 159–60
Chris Jorgenson (fictional character, *The Thin Man*), 138
Christmas party, in *The Thin Man*, 130–33
Claire (fictional character, *Shadow of the Thin Man*), 195
Clare (fictional character, *When Ladies Meet*), 96
Clarence Day (fictional character, *Life With Father*), 210–11
class difference, between romantic comedy protagonists, 168
class system: depression-era films on, 168; *My Man Godfrey* on, 148
Clay "Dal" Dalzell (fictional character, *Star of Midnight*), 146

Clifford Dudley (fictional character, *When Girls Go Back Home*), 51
Club Eileen, in *The Wet Parade*, 83
Clyde Winant (fictional character, *The Thin Man*), 122–23, 134–38
Coco (fictional character, *Topaze*), 92
"Code to Govern the Making of Motion Pictures" (industry document), 117
Colbert, Claudette, 118, 168
Colman, Ronald, 36, 37, 42, 63, 69; in *Arrowsmith*, 80–81
Colonel MacFay (fictional character, *Another Thin Man*), 182
comedy, in *I Love You Again*, 190
comic moments of Loy: in *The Thin Man*, 138; in *Turn Back the Hours*, 56
comic skills, of Powell, W., Sr., 171–72
comic timing, of Powell, W., Sr. and Loy, 134
Commandant (fictional character, *Beau Geste*), 42
Compton, Juliette, 69–70
A Connecticut Yankee (film), 76–77, 77
Connie Allenbury (fictional character, *Libeled Lady*), 169, 169–71
Consolation Marriage (film), 79–80
contract, of Loy, 50
Cooper, Gary, 20, 180
Cosmopolitan Pictures, 35
Costello, Lou, 196
Countess Olga Mironova (fictional character, *The Emperor's Candlesticks*), 173
Countess Valentine (fictional character, *Love Me Tonight*), 83–84
Count Sandor (fictional character, *The Baroness and the Butler*), 176
Crawford, Joan. *See* Le Sueur, Lucille
credit listing, of Powell, W., Sr., 100
The Crimson City (film), 56
Cromwell, John, 65, 69
Crowthers, Bosley, 190–91, 192, 202

Cuba, 31–33
Culver City, California, 3, 21, 82
Cumberbatch, Benedict, 27
Curtiz, Michael, 111, 113, 114

Daisy Sage (fictional character, *The Animal Kingdom*), 90–91
Dan (fictional character, *One Way Passage*), 107
dancing lessons, of Loy, 21
Dangerous Money (film), 38
Dan Hogan (fictional character, *Private Detective 62*), 111
Daniels, Bebe, 38, 46
Davies, Marion, 28–29, 29
Davis, Bette, 108, 112–13
Day, Clarence, Jr., 211
Day, Katherine, 209–10
Deborah Kane (fictional character, *Interference*), 44–45
declaratory technique, of acting, 5
defense lawyer (in *For the Defense*), 69
DeMille, Cecil B., 23, 38
detective story films, start of genre of, 48
Deucalion (fictional character, *Renegades*), 62
De Valle (fictional character, *Outcast*), 31
The Devil to Pay (film), 63
dialogue, of *The Thin Man*, 128
Diana (fictional character, *The Barbarian*), 93–95
Dieterle, William, 105, 108
dissatisfaction with roles, of Loy, 57
divorce: from Hornblow of Loy, 186; from Wilson of Powell, W., Sr., 73
Doc (fictional character, *I Love You Again*), 188, 189
Donald Free (fictional character, *Private Detective 62*), 111
Don Juan (fictional character, *Don Juan*), 52
Don Juan (film), 51–52

Don Julio (fictional character, *Too Many Kisses*), 39

Donna Mantell (fictional character, *Star of Midnight*), 145–47

Dora Blake (fictional character, *My Lady's Lips*), 41

Dorothy (fictional character, *The Devil to Pay*), 64

Dorothy Winant (fictional character, *The Thin Man*), 122–23, 125, 130–33, *131*, 134; in dinner party scene, 138

Double Wedding (film), 90, 168, 173–75, *174*, 198

Douglas, Melvyn, 180, 187, 198

Dr. Bruce Clayforth (fictional character, *The Thin Man Goes Home*), 202

Dressler, Marie, 82, 109

Dr. Fu Manchu (fictional character, *Paramount on Parade*), 68

Dr. Fu Manchu (fictional character, *The Mask of Fu Manchu*), 86–87

Dr. George Ferguson (fictional character, *Men in White*), 118

Dr. George March (fictional character, *The Road to Singapore*), 100–101

Dr. Gottlieb (fictional character, *Arrowsmith*), 81

drinking, in *The Thin Man*, 124–25, 199

Dr. Lawrence "Brad" Bradford (fictional character, *The Ex Mrs. Bradford*), 147

Dr. Martin Arrowsmith (fictional character, *Arrowsmith*), 81

duel, between de Vaca and Charles, 34

Duke d'Orleans (fictional character, *Under the Red Robe*), 35

Duke Francis (fictional character, *When Knighthood Was in Flower*), 29–30

Duke Sheldon (fictional character, *I Love You Again*), 189–90

Dunne, Irene, 79–80, 85–86, 197–98, 211

Earhart, Amelia, 160

early career, of Loy, 3

early talking roles, of Loy, 60

East Side, West Side (Reisenberg), 78

Eddie Beagle (fictional character, *Special Delivery*), 41–42

Edgar Draque (fictional character, *The Thin Man Goes Home*), 201–2

efficient studio systems, 129

Eileen (fictional character, *The Wet Parade*), 83

Elaine (fictional character, *Consolation Marriage*), 79–80

Eleanor (fictional character, *Manhattan Melodrama*), 120–21, 132

Eleanor (fictional character, *Renegades*), 62

Ellie Andrews (fictional character, *It Happened One Night*), 168

El Moro (fictional character, *The Squall*), 59

elopement with Lewis, D., of Powell, W., Sr., 186

Emma (fictional character, *Emma*), 82–83

Emma (film), 82–83

The Emperor's Candlesticks (film), 173

English Eddie (fictional character, *Within the Law*), 13

Ensign Phillip Drake (fictional character, *Turn Back the Hours*), 55–56

entertainment families, 10

equal relationship, of Nick and Nora in *The Thin Man*, 128

Escapade (film), 143; experience of Loy with, 144

Europe trip, of Powell, W., Sr., 69

Evelyn Prentice (fictional character, *Evelyn Prentice*), *140*, 140–42, 143

Evelyn Prentice (film), 139–40, *140*

Evelyn Prentice (Woodward), 139

Exhibitors Trade Review (magazine), 41

The Ex-Mrs. Bradford (film), 147
"exotic" type, typecasting of Loy as, 53, 87
exterior location shots, in *After the Thin Man*, 163–64

Fah Lo See (fictional character, *The Mask of Fu Manchu*), 85, 87
Fairbanks, Douglas, 23, 35
Fanchon and Marco (dance team), 23
fan magazines, on Powell, W., Sr., wedding with Lombard, 74–75
Farrell, Charles, 76, 109
Fashions of 1934 (film), 112, 113
Fast and Loose (film), 71
Fay, Frank, 61, 62
Fay Cheyney (fictional character, *The Last of Mrs. Cheney*), 172
film, inexperience of Kaufman with, 1
film actors, as second class, 4–5, 9
Film and Television Archive, of UCLA, 55–56
Film Daily (magazine), 129–30
filming, of *Interference*, 44–45
Fingers (fictional character, *After the Thin Man*), 163
Fitzmaurice, George, 64, 172
Fleming, Victor, 62, 158, 159
Flint, Peter, 217
Florence (fictional character, *Lonelyhearts*), 216
Florenz Ziegfeld, Jr. (in *The Great Ziegfeld*), 150–51, *151*, 152
Fodor, Ladislas, 106–7
Fonda, Henry, 213–14, *214*
Forbes Lombard (fictional character, *My Lady's Lips*), 40–41
Ford, John, 3, 60–61, 80–81, 213
Forman Wells (fictional character, *Sherlock Holmes*), 28
For the Defense (film), 69
Fowler, Gene, Jr., 1

Fox, William, 75–76
Fox Film Co., 50, 62, 64, 75; dropping of Loy by, 78; signing of Loy with, 76
Francis, Kay, 66, *67*, 69, 70, 104; in *Jewelry Robbery*, *105*, 106; in *One Way Passage*, 107; roles with Powell, W., Sr., of, 108
Fred Derry (fictional character, *The Best Years of Our Lives*), 208
Frederick (fictional character, *Emma*), 82
freedom, of directors at Fox, 76
friendship, of Powell, W. Sr., and Loy, 6

Gable, Clark, 50, 98, 109, 118, 121; in *Gone with the Wind*, 160; in *It Happened One Night*, 168; Loy and, 153–54; in *Manhattan Melodrama*, 122; marriage to Lombard of, 161; in *Parnell*, 156–57; in *Test Pilot*, 158–60; in *Wife vs. Secretary*, 154–55, *155*
Gaby (fictional character, *Paid to Love*), 43
gambler, in *Private Detective 62*, 111
Garbo, Greta, 54, 180
Gar Evans (fictional character, *High Pressure*), 102–3, 104
Garrett, Oliver H. P., 69
Garrick Theater, Wilmington, Delaware, 49
gathering of suspects, in detective stories, 137, *137*
Gaynor, Janet, 76, 109
General Electric Theater (TV series), 207
General Rojas (fictional character, *White Mice*), 40
Genghis Khan (in *The Mask of Fu Manchu*), 87
The Genius of the System (Schatz), 178
George Carey (alternate personality of Wilson, in *I Love You Again*), 188, 189–90

Gerald (fictional character, *The Barbarian*), 93, 95

Gertie (fictional character, *Penthouse*), 96–97

Gilbert, John, 14, 54

Gilder's Department Store (in *Within the Law*), 12–13

Ginsberg (fictional character, *High Pressure*), 102

Girardot, Etienne, 111

The Girl from Chicago (film), 53–54, 55

A Girl in Every Port (film), 56

The Girl Who Had Everything (film), 213

Gish, Dorothy, *33*, 36

Gish, Lillian, 35–36

Gladys (fictional character, *Libeled Lady*), *169*, 169–70

Glory for Me (Kantor), 208

Godfrey (fictional character, *My Man Godfrey*), 148

"Going Places" (Ager), 119

Goldwyn, Samuel, 63, 80–81, 208

Gone with the Wind (film), 154, 157, 160, 178, 185

Goodrich, Frances, 96, 97, 123, 127–28, 129–30; *After the Thin Man* and, 162–64; *Another Thin Man* and, 180–81; dialogue in *The Thin Man* of, 133, 137

Gordon A. McClellan (fictional character, *Skyline*), 79

Grand Duke Sergius Alexander (fictional character, *The Last Command*), 43–44

Grand Hotel (film), 78, 108

Grant, Cary, 123

The Grapes of Wrath (film), 3

Grauman's Egyptian Theatre, 23

the Great Depression, 65, 100, 109

The Great Divide (film), 61

Great Guns (film), 197

The Great Train Robbery (film), 5

The Great Ziegfeld (film), 144, 150–51, *151*, 191; reception of, 152

Green, Alfred E., 101

The Green Murder Case (film), 47

Griffith, D. W., 5, 26, *31*

Griffith, Ned, 89–90

Gunner Morse (fictional character, *Test Pilot*), 158–59

Hackett, Albert, 86, 97, 123, 127–28, 129–30; *After the Thin Man* and, 162–64; *Another Thin Man* and, 180–81; dialogue of *The Thin Man* of, 133, 137

half-talkies, 54–55

Hall, Gladys, 70

Hall, Mordaunt, 37, 38, 39, 45, 85; on *Thirteen Women*, 86

Ham and Eggs at the Front (film), 54

Hamilton, Cosmo, 15–16

Hammett, Dashiell, 112, 122, 129–30, 137, 139; *After the Thin Man* and, 161–62; sale of rights to Nick and Nora of, 180

Handsome Joe (fictional character, *The Girl from Chicago*), 53

Hank Martin (fictional character, *A Connecticut Yankee*), 77, *77*

Harding, Ann, 90, 96

Hard to Handle (film), 104

Hardy, Oliver, 196–97

Harlow, Jean, 75, 144–45, 154–56, *155*, 168; death of, 174; in *Libeled Lady*, *169*, 170

Harold Jones (fictional character, *Special Delivery*), 41–42

Harry (fictional character, *Too Hot to Handle*), 159–60

Harry Taylor (fictional character, *Man of the World*), 72

de Havilland, Olivia, 208

Hawks, Howard, 42–43, 56, 98, 148

Hearst, William Randolph, 28, 35–36

Helena, Montana, 20

Helene Fendley (fictional character, *Ladies' Man*), 72

Henry Graham (fictional character, *Transatlantic*), 78

Hergesheimer, Joseph, 31

hero roles, of Powell, W., Sr., 40

Hertz, David, 191

Hertz, John, Jr., 196, 198

Hertz, John Daniel, Sr., 198

Heywood, Elizabeth "Lizzie," 11–12

High Pressure (film), 102–3, *103*, 104, 115, 134

His Girl Friday (film), 145, 167, 187

Hollander Juwelier (in *Jewel Robbery*), 106

Homer Parrish (fictional character, *The Best Years of Our Lives*), 208

Hopkins, Miriam, 151–52

Hornblow, Arthur, Jr., 63, 80–81, 90, 161

Horton, Edward Everett, 14

Howard, William K., 77–78, 141, 145

Howard Drake (fictional character, *Test Pilot*), 158

Howe, James Wong, 78, 119, 125–26, 134, 136–37; skill of, 178

How to Marry a Millionaire (film), 213

Hugh Dawltrey (fictional character, *The Road to Singapore*), 100–102

hysterectomy, of Johnson, 20–21

I Am a Fugitive from a Chain Gang (film), 104

Illington, Margaret, 12

I Love You Again (film), 187–88, *188*, 191–92

IMP. *See* Independent Motion Pictures

Independent Motion Pictures (IMP), 5

Inez (fictional character, *White Mice*), 40

Inspiration Pictures, 31, 36

Interference (film), 44–45, 103, 216–17

Irene (fictional character, *Man of the World*), 72

Irene Adler (fictional character, *Double Wedding*), 175

Irene Bullock (fictional character, *My Man Godfrey*), 148–50, *149*

Irma (fictional character, *The Squall*), 59

Isabelle (fictional character, *Emma*), 82–83

Isobel (fictional character, *Love Crazy*), 191

It Happened One Night (film), 117–18, 153, 167, 168

It's a Wonderful Life (film), 204

Jackson Durant (fictional character, *Penthouse*), 96–97

Jamie Darricott (fictional character, *Ladies' Man*), 72, 73

Jamil (fictional character, *The Barbarian*), 93, 95

The Jazz Singer (film), 44

J. B. Allenbury (fictional character, *Libeled Lady*), 169, 170–71

J. D. Hanley (fictional character, *How to Marry a Millionaire*), 213

Jewel Robbery (film), *104*, 104–7, *115*, 134

Jim Lane (fictional character, *Test Pilot*), 158–59

Jimmie (fictional character, *When Ladies Meet*), 96

Jim Montgomery (fictional character, *Shadow of the Law*), 68

Jimmy (fictional character, *Jimmy the Gent*), 112–13

Jimmy the Gent (film), 112

Jim Wade (fictional character, *Manhattan Melodrama*), 119, 120–21

Joan (fictional character, *One Way Passage*), 107

Johann Porok (fictional character, *The Baroness and the Butler*), 176

John Breen (fictional character, *Skyline*), 79

John Prentice (fictional character, *Evelyn Prentice*), 140–41, *141*
Josef Lajos (fictional character, *The Squall*), 59–60
Joyce, Frank Coleman, 109
The Judge of Zalamea (play), 17

Kara (The Firefly) (fictional character, *The Truth About Youth*), 62–63
Karloff, Boris, 86–87
Katie O'Shea (in *Parnell*), 157
Kaufman, George S., 1, 3–4
Kay (fictional character, *I Love You Again*), 188, 189–90, 192
Kay (fictional character, *Transatlantic*), 78
Kay Elliot (fictional character, *The Naughty Flirt*), 75
The Kennel Murder Case (film), 111–12
The Key (film), 113–15
King, Henry, 33, 36, 37–38
King Leopold III (fictional character, *Paid to Love*), 42–43
King Louis XII (fictional character, *When Knighthood Was in Flower*), 28–30
Kurnitz, Harry, 187, 193–95

La Cava, Gregory, 148–50
La Clavel (fictional character, *The Bright Shawl*), 33
Ladies' Man (film), 69, 70, 72–73
Lady Edwina Esketh (fictional character, *Noah's Ark*), 179
The Lady of the Lamp (play), 19
Laemmle, Carl, Jr., 150–51
La Jolla, California, 20
Lambs Club, 19–20
Larry Wilson (fictional character, *I Love You Again*), 188–90, 192
The Last Command (film), 43–44
The Last of Mrs. Cheyney (film), 157, 172–73

Laura (fictional character, *Thirteen Women*), 85–86
Laura Hudson (fictional character, *Men in White*), 118
Laurel, Stan, 196–97
Lavinia (fictional character, *Life With Father*), 210
Lawrence Kennard (fictional character, *Evelyn Prentice*), 140–41
Lawyer Man (film), 108–9
lead role, of Loy, 53–54
Lederer, Charles, 187, 191
Leo Andreyev (fictional character, *The Last Command*), 43–44
LeRoy, Mervyn, 102, 103–4, 111
Le Sueur, Lucille (Joan Crawford), 24, 98, 144, 156, 172
Lewis, Diana (Mousie), 1–2, 185–86, 212, 217
Libeled Lady (film), 144, 145, 167, 168, *169*; Canby on, 171–72; *Double Wedding* compared with, 175–76; structure of, 169–70
Lieutenant Abrams (fictional character, *Shadow of the Thin Man*), 194–95
Lieutenant Guild (fictional character, *The Thin Man*), 134–35
lifetime achievement Oscar, of Loy, 216
Life with Father (film), 189, 204, 209–11
Linda (fictional character, *The Naughty Flirt*), 75
Linda (fictional character, *Wife vs. Secretary*), 154–56, *155*
Link (fictional character, *Shadow of the Thin Man*), 195
list of roles, of Powell, W., Sr., 14–15
Little Caesar (film), 42, 104
loan-outs, of Loy, 93
Lola (fictional character, *My Lady's Lips*), 40–41
Lombard, Carole, 71, 72, 73–74, 148–50, *149*

Lonelyhearts (film), 215–16

Lonsdale, Frederick, 63, 64, 69, 70, 172

Lorenzo de Medici (as portrayed in *Romola*), 36

"Love Came Last," (*General Electric Theater* episode), 207

Love Crazy (film), 191–92

Love Me Tonight (film), 83–84, *84*, 134

love scene, in *A Connecticut Yankee*, 77

Loy, Myrna, *2*, *22*, *52*, *58*, *77*; in *After the Thin Man*, *163*; in *The Animal Kingdom*, *91*; in *The Barbarian*, *94*; in *Double Wedding*, *174*; in *I Love You Again*, *188*; in *Libeled Lady*, *169*; in *Love Me Tonight*, *84*; in *Manhattan Melodrama*, *120*; in *Shadow of the Thin Man*, *193*; in *Song of the Thin Man*, *205*; in *The Thin Man*, *127*; in *The Thin Man Goes Home*, *201*; in *Wife vs. Secretary*, *155*. See also specific topics

Lubitsch, Ernst, 49, 51, 71, 104, 106

Lucky Night (film), 177–78

Lucrezia Borgia (fictional character, *Don Juan*), 52

Lulu (fictional character, *Pandora's Box*), 47

Lydia Languish (fictional character, *The Rivals*), 10

Lynn (fictional character, *Fashions of 1934*), 112

MacCaulay (fictional character, *The Thin Man*), 129, 134, 137, 138

Madge (fictional character, *Special Delivery*), 41

Maia (fictional character, *Don Juan*), 52

Major Rama Safti (fictional character, *Noah's Ark*), 179

Major Sculley (fictional character, *Shadow of the Thin Man*), 195–96

The Maltese Falcon (film), 123

Malvolio (fictional character, *Twelfth Night*), 10–11

Manhattan Melodrama (film), 113, 119, 120, 120–22, 130; Gable and, 153; Powell, W., Sr., and Loy in, 142; withholding of information in, 132

Manners, Dorothy, 74–75

Man of the World (film), 71–72

Man-Proof (film), 177–78

Manuella (fictional character, *The Great Divide*), 61

The Man Who Knew Too Much (film), 114

The Marabout (fictional character, *Renegades*), 62

Margit (fictional character, *Double Wedding*), 175–76

Maria del Carmen (fictional character, *Spanish Love*), 18

Maria Lajos (fictional character, *The Squall*), 59–60

Marie (fictional character, *When Girls Go Back Home*), 51

Marie Antoinette (film), 179

marriage: with Hornblow of Loy, 161; with Lombard of Powell, W., Sr., 74–75

martini, in *The Thin Man*, 125

Mary (fictional character, *Consolation Marriage*), 79–80

Mary (fictional character, *Man of the World*), 72

Mary (fictional character, *The Devil to Pay*), 63

Mary Carlton (fictional character, *The Girl from Chicago*), 53–54

Mary Howard (fictional character, *When Ladies Meet*), 96

Mary Smith. *See* Agnes (*Star of Midnight*)

Mary Tudor (fictional character, *When Knighthood Was in Flower*), 28–29

Mary Turner (fictional character, *Within the Law*), 12–13

Maskerade (film), 143

The Mask of Fu Manchu (film), 85, 86–87, 97

Maurice Coutelin (fictional character, *Love Me Tonight*), 84, *84*

May (fictional character, *Thirteen Women*), 85

Mayer, Louis B., 143, 178, 194

McHugh, Frank, 103, *103*, 107–8, 112, 189

Men in White (film), 118, 139–40

Metro-Goldwyn-Mayer (MGM), 2–3, 24, 66, 81–82, 98; decline of, 178, 206; *The Great Ziegfeld* sale to, 150–51; Howard, W., and, 141; inaugural contract of Loy, 143; Loy and, 198; *The Thin Man* and, 129, 161–62, 167; working conditions at, 153–54

Michael Trevor (fictional character, *Man of the World*), 71–72

Mike Donahey (fictional character, *High Pressure*), 102

Milly (fictional character, *The Best Years of Our Lives*), 208, 209

Mimi (fictional character, *The Thin Man*), 130

Mimi Montagne (fictional character, *Penthouse*), 96–97

Mimi Swift (fictional character, *Man-Proof*), 177

minstrel show, 9

Mister Roberts (film), 207, 213–15

Mitchell, Margaret, 160, 185

modeling work, of Williams, M., 23

Modern Screen (magazine), 76, 86

Momma (fictional character, *The Senator is Indiscreet*), 4

Mona Leslie (fictional character, *Reckless*), 144, 145

Monte (fictional character, *Across the Pacific*), 53

motion picture, emergence of, 9

Motion Picture Herald (magazine), 86, 109

Motion Picture Magazine (magazine), 55, 95, 101–2

Motion Picture News (magazine), 51, 53, 69

Motion Picture Producers and Distributors of America (MPPDA), 117

motorized camera, 45

Mousie. *See* Lewis, Diana

Movie Classic (magazine), 74–75

Moving Picture World (magazine), 37

MPPDA. *See* Motion Picture Producers and Distributors of America

Mr. Blandings Builds His Dream House (film), 215

Mr. Hollander (fictional character, *Jewel Robbery*), 106

Mrs. Cooper (fictional character, *Love Crazy*), 191

Mr. Simmons (fictional characters, *Too Many Kisses*), 39

Mrs. Jorgenson (fictional character, *The Thin Man*), 135

Mrs. Lanyan (fictional character, *Arrowsmith*), 81

Mutiny on the Bounty (film), 153

My Lady's Lips (film), 40

My Man Godfrey (film), 148–49, *149*, 167, 171; reception of, 150

Myrna Loy: Being and Becoming (autobiography), 216

My Sister Eileen (film), 145

mystery, in *The Thin Man*, 130–31, 133

Nancy Harrison (fictional character, *Evelyn Prentice*), 140–41

Narcissa (fictional character, *The Bright Shawl*), 34

Natalie Dobrova (fictional character, *The Last Command*), 43–44

Natural Davis (fictional character, *Street of Chance*), 65–66

The Naughty Flirt (film), 75

Ned Riley (fictional character, *Reckless*), 145

New Morals (film), 69–70

New Morals for Old (film), 83

New Movie Magazine (magazine), 93

"new" roles, of Loy, 93

new surname choice, of Loy, 50

New Year's Eve, in *After the Thin Man*, 163–64

New York District Attorney Markham (fictional character, *The Canary Murder Case*), 46

New York Times (newspaper), 17, 30, 37, 39, 45; on *Love Me Tonight*, 85; on *Thirteen Women*, 86

"Nick and Nora" glasses, 125

Nick Charles (fictional character, *The Thin Man*), 7, 101, 112, 122–24, *127*; in *After the Thin Man*, 162–65, *163*; in *Another Thin Man*, 182; detecting skills of, 134–35; Dorothy Winant and, 131, *131*; Powell, W., Sr., on roles after, 146; relationship with Nora of, 128–39, 165–66; in *Shadow of the Thin Man*, 193–96; in *The Thin Man Goes Home*, 199–203; underworld connections of, 168, 194

Nick Jr. (fictional character, *Another Thin Man*), 181–83, 194

Night Flight (film), 97

Noah's Ark (film), 179

Nora Charles (fictional character, *The Thin Man*), 7, 97, 122, 123–26, *127*; in *After the Thin Man*, 162–65, *164*; in *Another Thin Man*, 182; attempt of Russell to copy, 146; banter of, 135; Dorothy Winant and, 131–32, *132*; love for Nick of, 135–39; pregnancy of, 166; relationship with Nick of, 128, 131–32; in *Shadow of the Thin Man*, 193–96; in *The Thin Man Goes Home*, 199–203; wealth of family of, 165

Norah (fictional character, *The Key*), 113, 114

Norma Page (fictional character, *Ladies' Man*), 72

Novarro, Ramon, 93–94; relationship of Loy with, 95

Nubi (fictional character, *The Squall*), 58–60, 85

Nunheim (fictional character, *The Thin Man*), 135

O'Brien, Pat, 119–20

Office of War Information and its Bureau of Motion Pictures, 197

Oland, Warner, 68, 86

Olga (fictional character, *Lawyer Man*), 108

One Way Passage (film), 107–8, 114, 134

Oppenheimer, George, 170, 187

Oregon Daily Tribune (newspaper), 14–16

Orientalism, 87

Orphans of the Storm (film), 35–36

O'Shea, Katie, 156

O'Sullivan, Maureen, 123

other woman roles of Loy, 78–81

Outcast (film), 31

Paid to Love (film), 42–43

Pallette, Eugene, 47–48, 68, 111

Pandora's Box (film), 47

Paramount Films, 38, 45–47, 65–66, 70–71, 83; Powell, W., Sr., and, 102

Paramount on Parade (film), 67–68

parents of Nick Charles, in *The Thin Man Goes Home*, 199–200

Parker, Albert, 19–20, 26

Parnell (film), 156–57, 172, 173

party scene, in *The Great Divide*, 61

Paul (fictional character, *Shadow of the Thin Man*), 195

Paula (fictional character, *The Ex-Mrs. Bradford*), 147

Paula Lambert (fictional character, *Skyline*), 79

Paul Lajos (fictional character, *The Squall*), 59–60

PCA. *See* Production Code Administration

Peador Conlan (fictional character, *The Key*), 113, 114

Peggy (fictional character, *The Best Years of Our Lives*), 209

Pendleton, Nat, 135, *151*, 152

Penthouse (film), 96–97

perfect wife roles, of Loy, 99, 156, 208–9

Peter (fictional character, *The Squall*), 59–60

Peter Roberts (fictional character, *Paid to Love*), 43

Peter Warne (fictional character, *It Happened One Night*), 168

Phil Church (fictional character, *Another Thin Man*), 182, 183

Philippa March (fictional character, *The Road to Singapore*), 100–101

Phillip Voaze (fictional character, *Interference*), 44

Philo Vance (fictional character, Vance films), 46–48, 66, 68, 111–12

Photoplay (magazine), 6, 10, 35, 53, 57–58; on *Body and Soul*, 76; on *Consolation Marriage*, 80; on Powell, W., Sr., and Lewis, D., 186; on *The Squall*, 60

Phyl (fictional character, *New Morals for Old*), 83

Phyllis Ericson (fictional character, *The Truth About Youth*), 63

Picture Play (magazine), 54, 57, 59

picture stealing reputation, of Powell, W., Sr., 35

Pidgeon, Walter, 55–56, 159

pilot, in *Night Flight*, 97

politics, involvement of Loy in, 187

Pom Pom (fictional character, *Body and Soul*), 76

Poulsen, William A., *181*

Powell, Horatio Warren, 10

Powell, William, 2, 29, 32, 67, *103*; in *After the Thin Man*, *163*; in *Another Thin Man*, *181*; in *Double Wedding*, *174*; in *I Love You Again*, *188*; in *Jewel Robbery*, *105*; in *Libeled Lady*, *169*; in *Manhattan Melodrama*, *120*; in *Mister Roberts*, *214*; in *My Man Godfrey*, *149*; in *Shadow of the Thin Man*, *193*; in *Song of the Thin Man*, *205*; in *The Thin Man*, *127*; in *The Thin Man Goes Home*, *201*. *See also specific topics*

Powell, William, Jr., 73, 217

pressure for blockbusters, of studios, 129

Pretty Ladies (film), 24

previous comic roles, of Powell, W., Sr., 134

Primo Carnera (fictional character, *The Prizefighter and the Lady*), 99

Prince Arnolfo da Pescia (fictional character, *Dangerous Money*), 38

Prince Erich (fictional character, *Paid to Love*), 43

Princess Jeannette (fictional character, *Love Me Tonight*), 84, *84*

prior comic roles, of Loy, 134

Private Detective 62 (film), 111

The Prizefighter and the Lady (film), 98

Production Code Administration (PCA), 117, 144, 157

Professor Moriarty (fictional character, *Sherlock Holmes*), 28

public service work, of Loy, 215

Queen Morgan le Fay (fictional character, *A Connecticut Yankee*), 77, *77*

Rachel (fictional character, *Ladies' Man*), 72

Rainer, Luise, 143–44, 152, 173

The Rains Came (film), 179–80

Ralph (fictional character, *New Morals for Old*), 83

Rambova, Natacha, 24–25

Rancho Santa Anita, Arcadia, California, 3

Randolf, Anders, 34–35

Reckless (film), 144–45

Redbook (magazine), 129, 130

Red Dust (film), 118, 144, 154

The Red Pony (film), 215

Red Shadow (fictional character, *The Desert Song*), 57–58

Reid, Laurence, 51, 53

relationship of Nick and Nora, in *The Thin Man*, 128–29

Rendezvous (film), 145–46

Rene (fictional character, *The Road to Singapore*), 101

Renegades (film), 62

respectability, of friends of Nora Charles in *After the Thin Man*, 164

retirement, of Powell, W., Sr., 207

reveal scene, in *The Thin Man*, 137, 137–38

Rhett Butler (fictional character, *Gone with the Wind*), 154, 157

Richard Dane (The Imp) (fictional character, *The Truth About Youth*), 63

Richard Gaylord, Jr. (fictional character, *Too Many Kisses*), 39

Richard Gilder (fictional character, *Within the Law*), 13

Richard Snow (fictional character, *Manhattan Melodrama*), 121

Riffs (in *The Desert Song*), 57

Rin Tin Tin (dog), 49, 61

The Rivals (play), 10

RKO Pictures, 89–90, 98

The Road to Singapore (film), 100–101

Robber (fictional character, *Jewel Robbery*), 105, 106

Robert Landis (fictional character, *After the Thin Man*), 165

Roberts, Stephen, 146, 147

Robertson, John S., 31, 32

Robinson, Edward G., 31–32, 104, 108–9

Roche, Arthur Somers, 96, 146

Roddy Forrester (fictional character, *White Mice*), 40

Roger Chilcote Jr. (fictional character, *The Wet Parade*), 83

Rogers, Ginger, 146–47

Rogers, Will, 76–77, 77, 153

Rogers Woodruff (fictional character, *When Ladies Meet*), 96

Rogue of the Rio Grande (film), 85

role: in *A Connecticut Yankee* of Loy, 76–77; in *The Devil to Pay* of Loy, 63–64; with Gable of Loy, 118; as heavy of Powell, W., Sr., 33–35, 38, 42; as Maia of Loy, 52; in *The Mask of Fu Manchu* of Loy, 87; as Nora Charles of Loy, 126–27; as Nubi of Loy, 60; in *One Way Passage* of Powell, W., Sr., 107

Roma (fictional character, *Across the Pacific*), 53

romantic comedies, complications in, 167–68

Romola (fictional character, *Romola*), 36

Romola (film), 36

Ronnie (fictional character, *Emma*), 82

Rooney, Mickey, 168, 186

Russell, Rosalind, 145, 187

Ruth Gordon (fictional character, *The Great Divide*), 61

Sally Short (fictional character, *When Girls Go Back Home*), 51

Sandor the Strong man (in *The Great Ziegfeld*), 152

Sargeant, Howland H., 215

Schatze Page (fictional character, *How to Marry a Millionaire*), 213

Schenck, Joseph, 13, 75, 109

Scott Seddon (fictional character, *My Lady's Lips*), 40–41

screen acting, craft of, 5, 42

Screenland (magazine), 73, 74, 80

screen team, Powell, W., Sr., and Loy as, 121–22

screen test, of Williams, M., 24

screwball comedy, 118

script approval, of Powell, W., Sr., 109

self-censorship, 117

Selma (fictional character, *After the Thin Man*), 165

Selznick, David O., 66, 70, 87, 89–90, 91; *Gone with the Wind* and, 178; *Manhattan Melodrama* and, 113; MGM and, 113; *Night Flight* and, 97–98; style of, 119

Selznick, Myron, 70, 71, 108, 110, 111

Senator Melvin G. Ashton (fictional character, *The Senator Was Indiscreet*), 1–2

The Senator Was Indiscreet (film), 1, 3–4

Sergeant Heath (fictional character, *Paramount on Parade*), 47–48

Sergeant Heath (fictional character, Vance Films), 47–48, 111

Shadow of the Law (film), 68

The Shadow of the Thin Man (film), 193–96, 197, 203

Sheik films, 94

"She Pays the Penalty" (Reid, M.), 57

Sheridan, Richard Brinsley, 10

Sherlock Holmes (film), 19–20

Sherlock Holmes (film) (Parker), 27

Sherlock Holmes (in *Paramount on Parade*), 68

Sherlock Holmes (play), 16

Sherman Antitrust Act, Supreme Court on, 211–12

Sherwood Nash (fictional character, *Fashions of 1934*), 112

Show of Shows (film), 61

silent-film producers, 10, 12

Skyline (film), 78–79

Smitty (fictional character, *Another Thin Man*), 182

Snap (fictional character, *Fashions of 1934*), 112

Soak the Rich (film), 152

Society of Pythagoras (in *Romola*), 36–37

Song of the Thin Man (film), 203–6

So This Is Paris (film), 51

Spanish Love (play), 18–19

speaking film career, of Powell, W., Sr., 47–48, 66

Special Delivery (film), 41

Spensley, Dorothy, 6

Spring Cleaning (play), 69

The Squall (film), 58–61, *59*, 85

Star of Midnight (film), 146–47

start of professional career, of Powell, W., Sr., 12–14

State Street Sadie (film), 55

Stella (fictional character, *Shadow of the Thin Man*), 194

Stephen Ghent (fictional character, *The Great Divide*), 61

von Sternberg, Josef, 43, 44, 98

Steve (fictional character, *One Way Passage*), 107

Steve Ireland (fictional character, *Love Crazy*), 191–92

Steve Morgan (fictional character, *The Prizefighter and the Lady*), 98–99

Steven Baird (fictional character, *Ready Money*), 15

Steve Porter (fictional character, *Consolation Marriage*), 79–80

Stewart, James, 82, 166, 212

Stinky Davis (fictional character, *The Thin Man Goes Home*), 200

Street of Chance (film), 65, *67*, 68

strike, of Loy, 143, 152

Stromberg, Hunt, 96, 97, 154, 162; departure from MGM of, 196; Nick and Nora and, 183–84; Powell, W., Sr., and, 180, 181

structure of *The Great Ziegfeld*, lack of, 152

Studio Park, St. Petersburg, Florida, 40

Such a Little Queen (play), 14

Sunrise (film), 205

Susan (fictional character, *Turn Back the Hours*), 58

Susan Ireland (fictional character, *Love Crazy*), 191–92

Swami Yogadachi (fictional character, *Thirteen Women*), 85

talking pictures: advancement of, 65; introduction of, 44; Warner Bros. and, 54

Tarzan the Ape Man (film), 96

Taylor, Robert, 177–78

Taylor, Sam, 78–79

Temple, Shirley, 153

The Ten Commandments (film), 23

Tessa (fictional character, *Romola*), 36

Tess of the Storm Country (play), 16

Test Pilot (film), 158–60

Thalberg, Irving, 81, 93, 178

The Thief of Bagdad (film), 23

The Thin Man (film), 4, 6, 97, 113, 119, 123–38; banter in, 126–27, *127*; casting of, 121; reception of, 139, 144; screen time of murder suspect in, 147; *Star of Midnight* compared with, 146; story of, 122

The Thin Man Comes Home (film), 197–99

Thin Man series, problems with continuing, 196–97

The Third Degree (film), 53

Third Finger Left Hand (film), 187

Thirteen Women (film), 85

Tim Sullivan (fictional character, *Dangerous Money*), 38

Tin Gods (film), 41

title credit, of Loy, 118–19

Tito (fictional character, *Romola*), 36–37

Tiza Torreon (fictional character, *Turn Back the Hours*), 55–56

Tol'able David (film), 31, 33

Tom Collier (fictional character, *The Animal Kingdom*), 90–91

Tommy (fictional character, *The Thin Man*), 125, 138

Tom Ransome (fictional character, *Noah's Ark*), 179

Tom Siddall (fictional character, *Penthouse*), 96–97

Too Hot to Handle (film), 159, 160

Too Many Cooks and Seven Keys to Baldpate (play), 16

Too Many Kisses (film), 38–39

Topaze (film), 91–92, 93

top-billing, of Powell, W., Sr., 65

top money-making stars, list of, 109

Torrance, Ernest, *33*, 69

Tracy, Spencer, 153, 158, 168–69, *169*

tragic hero roles, of Powell, W., Sr., 69

Transatlantic (film), 77–78, 141

Transatlantic, S.S. (ship), 78

The Treasure of Lost Canyon (film), 212–13

Trouble in Paradise (film), 71

trust, between Nick and Nora in *The Thin Man*, 132–33

The Truth About Youth (film), 62–63, 80

Turn Back the Hours (film), 55–56

Tuttle, Frank, 38, 47

Twelfth Night (Shakespeare), 10–11

Twentieth Century (film), 71, 148
20th Century Pictures, 75
Twenty-First Amendment, 124
typecasting, of Powell, W., Sr., and Loy, 5–6

UCLA Film and Television Archive, 40–41
Uncle Dani (fictional character, *The Squall*), 59
Under the Red Robe (film), 35
Under the Texas Moon (film), 62
United States, as new country, 9
Universal Pictures, 150, 157
Ursula (fictional character, *Thirteen Women*), 85–86

Valentino, Rudolph, 24, 25, 94
vamp, of Warner Bros., 50–51
Van Dine, S. S., 46, 119
Van Dyke, W. S. "Woody," 96, 97, 98, 121, 125; *After the Thin Man* and, 162; *Another Thin Man* and, 181–82; death of, 198; MGM pictures of, 130
Van "V. S." Stanhope (fictional character, *Wife vs. Secretary*), 154, *155*, 156
Variety (magazine), 91, 109, 114, 119, 150; on Powell, W., Sr., and Loy, 180
vaudeville, 9–10, 12
Venice High School, 21, 23
Venice Vanguard Evening Herald (newspaper), 23
villain roles, of Powell, W., Sr., 31–35, 38, 42
Vincente Escobar (fictional character, *The Bright Shawl*), 32
Vitagraph studio, 49
Vitaphone Corporation, 51–52
voice, of Powell, W., Sr., 45

Waldo Beaver (fictional character, *Double Wedding*), 175
Wallis, Hal B., 49, 110–11

Wallis, Minna, 49–50, 63, 78, 81
war, in *The Thin Man Goes Home*, 199–200
war effort, Loy and, 196
Warner, Harry M., 71, 109
Warner, Jack, 49–50, 209–10
Warner, Sam, 51–52
Warner Bros., 49–54, 62, 70–71, 73, 99–101; Powell, W., Sr., and, 108–9
Warren Haggerty (fictional character, *Libeled Lady*), 169, *169*, 171
The Warrens of Virginia (play), 10
Watkins, Maurine Dallas, 170, 187
Waxman, Henry, 23–24, 25
The Way of All Flesh (film), 44
Western Electric, 51
The Wet Parade (film), 83
What Price Beauty? (film), 25
What Price Glory? (film), 54
When a Man Loves (film), 53
When Knighthood Was in Flower (film), 28–30, 34
When Ladies Meet (film), 96
Whipsaw (film), 152–53, 168
White Mice (film), 40
White Mice Club (in *White Mice*), 40
Whitey (fictional character, *Shadow of the Thin Man*), 195
Whitey (fictional character, *Wife vs. Secretary*), 154–56, *155*
Why Girls Go Back Home (film), 51
wife of Pilot, in *Night Flight*, 97–98
Wife vs. Secretary (film), 153–55, *155*; reception of, 156
William Gordon (fictional character, *Rendezvous*), 146
William Hale (fictional character, *The Devil to Pay*), 63
Williams, David Franklin, 20–21
Williams, Myrna. *See* Loy, Myrna
Willie Ryan (fictional character, *The Prizefighter and the Lady*), 98, 99
Wilson, Eileen, 13, 16, 19, 73

Winebreiner, Harry Fielding, 21, 23
Within the Law (play), 12–14
witness (fictional character, *Shadow of the Law*), 68
The Wizard of Oz (film), 178
The Woman in Room 13 (film), 81
The Woman Who Laughed (play), 30
Women Who Play (film), 70
The Wonderful Wizard of Oz (film), 38
Woollcott, Alexander, 18–19, 30–31
working conditions, of film industry, 56–57

Wright, Willard Huntington. *See* Van Dine, S. S.
Wyler, William, 3, 172, 208–9

Young, Loretta, 62–63
Yvonne (fictional character, *Too Many Kisses*), 39

Zanuck, Darryl F., 49, 53, 75, 100, 103; departure from Warner Bros. of, 109; *The Rains Came* and, 179; style of, 104, 111
Ziegfeld, Florenz, Jr., 150